Evo's Bolivia

Evo's Bolivia

Continuity and Change

LINDA C. FARTHING AND BENJAMIN H. KOHL

University of Texas Press ⟷ *Austin*

Requests for permission to reproduce material from this work should be sent to:
  Permissions
  University of Texas Press
  P.O. Box 7819
  Austin, TX 78713–7819
  http://utpress.utexas.edu/index.php/rp-form

♾ The paper used in this book meets the minimum requirements of ANSI/NISO
Z39.48–1992 R1997 Permanence of Paper.

Library of Congress Cataloging-in-Publication Data
Farthing, Linda C.
    Evo's Bolivia : continuity and change / by Linda C. Farthing and Benjamin H.
Kohl. — First edition.
        pages cm
    Includes bibliographical references and index.
    ISBN 978-0-292-75727-1 (cl. : alk. paper) —
    ISBN 978-0-292-75868-1 (pbk. : alk. paper)
1. Bolivia—Politics and government—2006-   2. Bolivia—Economic policy.
3. Bolivia—Social policy.   4. Morales Ayma, Evo, 1959-   I. Kohl, Benjamin H.
II. Title.
F3327.F37   2014
984.05′42—dc23
                                                                            2013033155

doi:10.7560/757271

This book is dedicated to the memory of my much-beloved partner of over thirty years, Ben Kohl 1954–2013. ¡Benjamín Kohl, presente! It is also dedicated to the memory of Domitila Barrios de Chungara 1937–2012 and the millions of people around the world who, like her, struggle for more just societies and understand that change is too important to be left in the hands of even enlightened leaders.

Contents

Preface

In December 2005, when Evo Morales was elected president of Bolivia, we got caught up in the excitement that swept the small Andean country where we have spent ten of the last thirty years. Since then, we have talked with dozens if not hundreds of people, from street sellers to government ministers, and spent hours with friends, colleagues, and acquaintances, asking about their reactions to the new government and its policies. What had changed? What had this turn in the country's often turbulent history accomplished? From many businesspeople and middle-class intellectuals, the answer was often a resounding "Nothing!" followed by a polemical, frequently factually inaccurate diatribe against Morales and his government. How could this be, we asked? The economy was booming, there was visibly more money around than during the previous thirty years, and signs of material changes—from new schools to roads—were everywhere.

This book is an effort to respond to these questions, which are urgent ones for Bolivians and Bolivia and those committed to progressive social change anywhere. For though Bolivia is small and economically, spatially, and politically marginal, a tide pool in the sea of the global economy, we are convinced something important is going on that provides insight into critical regional and global processes.

In this book, we not only consider issues from the reorganization of the state to the drug trade, we also locate the Bolivian experience within the context of similar profound changes under way in the region. Our goal is to ground the work in our own commitment to social and economic justice within a vision of respect for the natural environment, while recognizing the pragmatics of the global economy at the beginning of the twenty-first century. Given the scope of the topic, we decided to focus on how the left has done by its own measure and according to its own values.

We set out to write a book accessible to a broad audience, although it draws from academic scholarship within and on the region. It includes lots of conversations and anecdotes and is punctuated with boxes culled from interviews—short accounts that provide the words of the actors themselves. We have attempted to balance these quotes and interviews by region, class, ethnicity, gender, and sexual identity.

We touch briefly on many topics to provide a coherent overview, which, of course, results in a superficial treatment of complex themes. Given the general lack of knowledge about Bolivia beyond its borders, however, we decided to provide enough context to make the country legible. We have used many English-language sources, as we want English speakers to be able to easily access additional information on topics that interest them. We have also drawn extensively from the academic literature for those looking for more in-depth perspectives.

Acknowledgments

We recognize our considerable debt to Bolivians and Latin Americans whose work we have drawn on, and whose writing rarely, if ever, appears in English. These include writers and researchers such as Xavier Albó, Rossana Barragán, Fernando Calderón, Fernando Mayorga, Manuel de la Fuente, Pablo Mamani, Gustavo Rodríguez, Raúl Zibechi, Raúl Prada, Luis Tapia, Pascale Absi, Pablo Stefanoni, Raquel Gutiérrez, Magdalena Cajías, Silvia Rivera Cusicanqui, Claudia Peña Claros, Ximena Soruco Sologuren, Rafael Puente, Hervé do Alto, Horst Grebe, Carlos Torranza, Esteban Ticona, Adalberto Kopp, Carlos Hugo Molina, María Teresa Zegada, Roberto Fernández Terán, Pablo Rossell Arce, Rosario León, Pablo Regalsky, Roberto Laserna, Pedro Portugal Mollinedo, Álvaro García Linera, Maristella Svampa, Ramón Rocha Monroy, José Antonio Quiroga, Silvia Escóbar de Pabón, Pilar Mendieta, Jorge Komadina, Zulema Lehm, Juan Antonio Morales, Carlos Mamani Condori, Esteban Ticona, Roberto Choque, Juan Antonio Quiroga, and Maria Eugenia Choque. Other friends, with whom we have spent hours talking, may not be cited much here, but they are critical to how we came to understand the processes we observed. We have also drawn significantly on the work produced by the Bolivian Documentation and Research Center CEDIB, the Center for Investigation and Documentation for the Development of the Beni CIDDEBENI, the Center for Legal Studies and Social Research CEJIS, Fundación Tierra, the now-closed Center for Documentation and Research CEDOIN, Somos Sur, and the Center for Studies of the Economic and Social Reality CERES. Research Institutions including the Bolivian Program for Strategic Research PIEB and the Center for Labor Development and Agrarian Studies CEDLA and magazines such as *T'inkazos*, *Cuarto Intermedio*, *Pukara*, *Pulso*, *Le Monde Diploma-*

tique Bolivia, and *Nueva Sociedad* have all provided important sources for this book.

We owe thanks to the excellent solidarity and research work conducted by the English-language groups that have emerged over the years since the humble beginnings of the Bolivia Bulletin at CEDOIN during the 1980s: the Andean Information Network AIN, which Linda was involved in from the start, Bolivia Solidarity Network, Boliviamundo, Bolivia Rising, Upside Down World, the Bolivia Information Forum BIF, the Democracy Center, and the Bolivia Solidarity Action Network.

We want to particularly acknowledge the people who generously helped us in conducting interviews: Jessica Robinson from the Andean Information Network, Freddy Condo of the Unity Pact, Felix Muruchi, Anne Catherine Bajard, and Brian Johnson, who tried unsuccessfully to get an interview with the elusive Vice Minister for Traditional Medicine. We owe a special thanks to Sara Shields for organizing bits of logistics when we weren't in Bolivia. Niki Fabricant provided helpful contacts in Santa Cruz. Thanks, too, to our transcribers, Daniela Prieto and Estela Machaca. Thanks to Marcelo Apaza, who rescued a troubled computer at a critical moment.

A vital contribution was made by those who kindly read the manuscript or parts of it: Nancy Postero and Bret Gustafson, who made excellent suggestions in their careful and thorough reviews; AIN's Kathryn Ledebur, who commented on the coca and land chapters; Karen Marie Lennon and Brian B. Johnson, who reviewed education and health sections respectively; Mark Anner, who sent comments on labor; Jason Tockman, who commented on indigenous autonomy; and our friend Craig Michaels, who gave us the perspective of a general reader. We also owe a special thanks to Nancy Warrington for going the extra mile in the final review of the manuscript. Ben would like to thank Temple University and the Department of Geography and Urban Studies for supporting his work with a sabbatical that came at the right time.

Of course, a long list of people helped in one way or another: Juan Arbona, Denise Arnold, Abdul Aspiazu, David Aruquipa, Vicky Aillón, Tony Bebbington, Richard Beckett, Alberto Borda, Cristina Bubba, Julio Calla, Nano Calla, Andrew Canessa, Ann Chaplin, Albertina Castro, Tomás David Colque, Lee Cridland, Sonya Dávila, Juan de Dios Yatipa, Manuel de la Fuente, Damian and Santusa Flores, Diego Giacoman, Ibeth Garabito, Pete Good, Phillip Green, Soledad Gutiérrez, Sergio Hinajosa, Rocio Jiménez, Sonja Killoran McKibben, Jorge Komadina, Chris Krueger, María Lagos, Kath Ledebur, Estela Machaca, Wilmer

Machaca, Fernando Mayorga, Carmen Medeiros, Javier Medina, Pedro Montes Blanco, Joe Loney, Khantuti Muruchi Escobar, Felix Muruchi, Julieta Paredes, Pati Parra, Pepe Pereira, Claudia Peña, Eli Peredo, Tom Perreault, José Antonio Quiroga, Susanna Rance, Godofredo Reinicke, Carlos Revilla, Silvia Rivera, Juanita Roca, Rafo and Nene Rojas, Ton Salman, Alix Shand, Jim Shultz, Alison Spedding, Nico Tassi, Juan Tellez, Jaime Villela, and Marina Vargas. As always we couldn't have done it without the support and companionship of Reyna Ayala, who is always there with a thermos of coca tea and a broad smile when we step off the plane in El Alto. We owe a debt to them all for sharing their insights and experience with us, although we alone are responsible for the errors that the text may contain.

List of Abbreviations

ADN Democratic Nationalist Action; Acción Democrática Nacionalista
AIN Andean Information Network
ALBA Bolivarian Alliance for the Peoples of Our America; Alianza Bolivariana para los Pueblos de Nuestra América
ANAPQUI National Association of Quinoa Producers; Asociación Nacional de Productores de Quinoa
APG Guaraní People's Assembly; Asamblea del Pueblo Guaraní
APTDEA Andean Pact for Trade and Drug Enforcement Agreement
BG British Gas
BIF Bolivia Information Forum
BOA Bolivian Aviation; Boliviana de Aviación
BP British Petroleum
CEBIAE Bolivian Center for Educational Research and Action; Centro Boliviano de Investigación y Acción Educativas
CEDIB Bolivian Documentation and Research Center; Centro de Documentación e Investigación Boliviana
CEDLA Center for Labor Development and Agrarian Studies; Centro de Estudios para el Desarrollo Laboral y Agrario
CEDOIN Center for Documentation and Research; Centro de Documentación e Investigación
CEJIS Center for Legal Studies and Social Research; Centro de Estudios Jurídicos e Investigación Social

CEPO First Nations Educational Councils; Consejos Educativos de Pueblos Originarios

CERES Center for Studies of the Economic and Social Reality; Centro de Estudios de la Realidad Económica y Social

CIDDEBENI Center for Investigation and Documentation for the Development of the Beni; Centro de Investigación y Documentación para el Desarrollo del Beni

CIDOB Confederation of Indigenous Peoples of Bolivia; Confederación de Pueblos Indígenas de Bolivia

CLAD Latin American Center for Administration and Development; Centro Latinoamericano de Administración para el Desarrollo

CNRDG National Coordinator for the Recovery and Defense of Gas; Coordinadora Nacional de la Recuperación y Defensa del Gas

COB Bolivian Workers' Central; Central Obrera Boliviana

COMIBOL Bolivian Mining Corporation; Corporación Minera de Bolivia

CONAMAQ National Council of Ayllus and Markas of Qullasuyu; Consejo Nacional de Ayllus y Markas del Qullasuyu

CONDEPA Patriotic Conscience; Conciencia de Patria

CSCIB Confederation of Unions of Intercultural Communities of Bolivia; Confederación Sindical de Comunidades Interculturales de Bolivia

CSUTCB Unified Confederation of Campesino Unions of Bolivia; Confederación Sindical Única de Trabajadores Campesinos de Bolivia

CTA Argentina Workers' Central; Central de Trabajadores de Argentina

CUT Unified Workers' Central; Central Única dos Trabalhadores [Brazil]

DEA Drug Enforcement Agency

DS Presidential Decree; Decreto Supremo

EPSAS Public Social Business for Water and Sanitation; Empresa Pública Social de Agua y Saneamiento

EU European Union

FARC Revolutionary Armed Forces of Colombia; Fuerzas Armadas Revolucionarias de Colombia

FDI Foreign Direct Investment

FEJUVE Federation of Neighborhood Associations; Federación de Juntas Vecinales

FELCN Special Forces in the Fight against Drug Trafficking; Fuerza Especial de la Lucha contra el Narcotráfico

FENCOMIN National Federation of Mining Cooperatives of Bolivia; Federación Nacional de Cooperativas Mineras de Bolivia

FONADAL National Alternative Development Fund; Fondo Nacional de Desarrollo Alternativo

FSTMB Federation of Bolivian Miners' Unions; Federación Sindical de Trabajadores Mineros de Bolivia

GDP Gross Domestic Product

GMO genetically modified organism

GOB Government of Bolivia; Gobierno de Bolivia

IADB Inter-American Development Bank

ICSID International Center for the Settlement of Investment Disputes

IDH Direct Hydrocarbons Tax; Impuesto Directo a los Hidrocarburos

IMF International Monetary Fund

INRA National Agrarian Reform Institute; Instituto Nacional de Reforma Agraria

ISI import substitution industrialization

LGBT lesbian, gay, bisexual, and transgender

LIDEMA League for the Defense of the Environment; Liga de Defensa del Medio Ambiente

LMAD Law on Autonomies and Decentralization; Ley Marco de Autonomías y Descentralización

LPP Law of Popular Participation; Ley de Participación Popular

MAS Movement towards Socialism; Movimiento al Socialismo

MDRI Multilateral Debt Relief Initiative

MEFP Ministry of Economy and Public Finance; Ministerio de Economía y Finanzas Públicas

MIR Revolutionary Left Movement; Movimiento de la Izquierda Revolucionaria

MNR National Revolutionary Movement; Movimiento Nacionalista Revolucionario

MSM Movement without Fear; Movimiento Sin Miedo
MST Landless Movement; Movimiento Sin Tierra [Bolivia]
MST Movement of Landless Workers; Movimento dos Trabalhadores Sem Terra [Brazil]
MUSOL Solidarity with Women; Solidaridad con la Mujer
NDP National Development Plan
NEP New Economic Policy
NGO nongovernmental organization
OAS Organization of American States
OEP Plurinational Electoral Office; Órgano Electoral Plurinacional
OSPE-B Social Observatory of Educational Policies of Bolivia; Observatorio Social de Políticas Educativas de Bolivia
PACS Support Program for Social Control of Coca Leaf Production; Programa de Apoyo al Control Social de la Producción de Hoja de Coca
PAHO Pan American Health Organization
PIEB Bolivian Program for Strategic Research; Programa de Investigación Estratégica en Bolivia
SAFCI Intercultural Community Family Health; Salud Familiar Comunitaria Intercultural
SEDEM Development Service for Public Productive Enterprises; Servicio de Desarrollo de las Empresas Públicas Productivas
TCOs First Nations or "Original" Community Territories; Tierras Comunitarias de Origen
TI Transparency International
TIOC Territory of Indigenous First Nations Campesino Community; Territorio Indígena Originario Campesino
TIPNIS Isiboro Sécure National Park and Indigenous Territory; Territorio Indígena y Parque Nacional Isiboro Sécure
UCS Civic Unity and Solidarity; Unidad Cívica Solidaridad
UDAPE Unit for Analysis of Social and Economic Policies; Unidad de Análisis de Políticas Sociales y Económicas
UMOPAR Mobile Rural Patrol Unit; Unidad Móvil de Patrullaje Rural
UN United Nations
UNASUR Union of South American Nations
UNCTAD United Nations Conference on Trade and Development

UNDP United Nations Development Program
UNIBOL Bolivian Indigenous University; Universidad Indígena de Bolivia
UNICEF United Nations Children's Fund
UNODC United Nations Office on Drugs and Crime
UNT National Union of Workers; Unión Nacional de Trabajadores [Mexico]
USAID U.S. Agency for International Development
USDA U.S. Department of Agriculture
WHO World Health Organization
WWF World Wildlife Fund
YPFB Bolivian State Oilfields Company; Yacimientos Petrolíferos Fiscales Bolivianos

Evo's Bolivia

CHAPTER I

Why Bolivia? Why Now?

Evo Morales's spectacular rise to the Bolivian presidency captured world imagination. A socialist, anti-imperialist, and indigenous president was a novelty, as were many of his campaign promises, such as international legalization of the much-maligned coca leaf and an ambitious plan to decolonize society. Before he was sworn in, Evo, as he is popularly known, set off on a whirlwind tour of Europe, China, and South Africa, pointedly ignoring the United States. Dressed in a boldly striped sweater, which turned the international leadership dress code of dark suits on its head, Evo made it clear that he had no intention of abandoning his union and indigenous roots (although he has since made concessions in dress, trading his controversial sweater for an elegant alpaca jacket decorated with Andean textiles).

As the most famous Bolivian ever, Morales elicited starkly different responses. The Americas' approximately forty million indigenous peoples, and particularly those in Bolivia, were ecstatic.[1] For the first time since the Spanish Conquest five hundred years ago, Bolivia's indigenous majority were led by one of their own. Morales embodied a "process of change," as his program is called, that broke with almost five hundred years of a distinctly Andean form of apartheid. Expectations were high that the country's abundant natural resources would be channeled to developing local industries. The poor, who typically see themselves as beggars seated on a throne of gold, believed that their time had come at last.

Supporters of collapsed traditional political parties, including the 5 percent of property owners who, sixty years after the first agrarian reform, still concentrated 70 percent of arable land,[2] were less sanguine. Some forecast economic disaster if resources were nationalized; others believed that another agrarian restructuring would mean state seizure of land, including rental properties and second homes. Wealthy parents worried that educational reform could force their children's private schools to close, and the Roman Catholic Church was anxious about threats to its state-sanctioned privileges. Smaller, extreme right-wing groups predicted race war and uploaded websites on how to prepare for the coming holocaust.

Internationally, Morales and his project of change were likewise demonized by the right and celebrated by the left. U.S. officials accused Hugo Chávez and Fidel Castro of taking advantage of Evo to create a "populist Marxist-socialist" regime in the heart of South America, as Bolivia became Latin America's sixth country to elect a self-described left-wing president.[3] Morales retorted by denouncing George W. Bush as a terrorist. Europeans were generally intrigued, although the Spanish worried that the new government might expropriate the holdings of their hydrocarbon giant, Repsol, even though these considerations got less press coverage than Evo's sweater. Activists committed to causes ranging from indigenous rights to environmental protection heralded the election as a sign that a more just and equitable world is not only possible but under construction in the Andes.[4]

Bolivia joins an unprecedented process unfolding in Latin America.[5] By the 1990s, armed struggle had largely been renounced, and with the end of persecution from military regimes and a return to electoral democracy, many left-wing groups became convinced that a focus on the ballot box was the preferred path to progressive social change.[6] At the same time, pressure from women, as well as ethnic and sexual minorities, pushed a new generation of leftists to graft broader rights onto the roots of Marxist class-oriented analysis.[7]

Tying together strands from trade unions, peasant organizations, indigenous communities, feminist groups, religious institutions, radical nationalist militaries, and former left-wing guerillas, these newly constituted left configurations gradually gained national power at the turn of the twenty-first century. Significant ideological and material constraints provoked by the 1989 collapse of the Soviet bloc and the ascent of global neoliberalism meant that the ambitious plans of these new governments ran headlong into considerable obstacles. Not only was the existing socialist model being profoundly questioned, but elites and transnational firms had been empowered by twenty years of neoliberal policies that improved the mobility of capital and reduced state capacity.[8] At the same time, the leftists in power found themselves with unparalleled room for action thanks to discredited oppositions, supportive peers, an easing of

U.S. hegemony, and a spike in commodity prices.[9] Bolivia, a country of superlatives in areas ranging from its environmental and resource wealth to its social movements, provides a particularly dramatic case to assess what has been achieved, what difficulties persist, and what the transformations mean for the region's future.

Some conservative political scientists and economists, drawing from the thesis of Venezuelan politician Teodoro Petkoff, divide the new regimes into a "good" and "bad" left, while progressive and leftist observers often reverse the labels.[10] In the often polemical debate, conservatives tend to extol the so-called social democratic regimes (characterized by Brazil, Chile until 2010, and sometimes Argentina) as opposed to the pejoratively denominated "populist" regimes (exemplified by Venezuela, Ecuador, and Bolivia). We concur with Bolivia's vice president, Álvaro García Linera, that the differences in both style and substance more reflect political processes internal to each country than abstract ideological differences, a contention seconded by political analyst Julia Buxton in relation to Venezuela.[11]

It proves more illustrative to place regimes along a continuum, as political theorist Benjamin Arditi proposes, rather than in opposing camps.[12] And it is important to remember that other factors are at play in determining their orientation. Weak party structures in Venezuela, Bolivia, and Ecuador have propelled all three countries down a more radical path, notes political scientist Gustavo Flores-Macías.[13] We would add that the differences also echo economic realities: Venezuela, Bolivia, and Ecuador are all more dependent on resource extraction than Brazil, Chile, and Argentina. Extractive economies—those with large-scale natural resource operations geared to export with little or no domestic processing capacity—typically have fragile institutions and parties, as well as proclivities toward populist leadership.[14]

PRESIDENT EVO MORALES[15]

What we want is equality and justice; to repair the damage of five hundred years of colonization. We want to change the western economic rules that cause so much damage to Mother Earth and the planet, because they allow plunder and create hunger and misery.

During the colonial period, we indigenous people were literally considered savages and treated like animals. Those policies of extermination continued during the Republic, and my mother used to tell me that because she was an Indian, she did not have the right to come into the city. During the neoliberal period that did so much damage to my country, discrimination and marginalization continued, and they persist even now. But let me be very clear: we are not looking for revenge against anyone.

Resistance to western domination has grown. Indigenous peoples realize that we don't just need to liberate ourselves, but that we must nationalize our natural resources. I believe in the power of social movements, and especially in the indigenous movement, to bring about peaceful change. We are not in a time of confrontation. We are not in a time of war. We must have a democratic revolution.

We are not asking for help or for solidarity as if we were beggars, but that you put your hands on your hearts and see how you can help defend life, how to save humanity, and protect the planet. And if we want to save Mother Earth, we have the obligation to think about the ecological debt the northern countries owe the south.

What I ask of rich countries is that you renounce your luxuries. Stop turning our lands into garbage dumps. You can't destroy all humanity to satisfy your greed. And to people who have a lot of money, I say that if they do not pay attention to what is happening to Mother Earth and its environment, all their money will not save them.

We are in the process of moving Bolivia forward. We want this millennium to be the millennium of life. The great advantage that we indigenous peoples have is that ours is a culture of life, not a culture of death.

Seven years on, Morales and his Movement toward Socialism—MAS[16]—are often larger than life, and Evo's theatrics regularly capture international press attention better than those of most backwater presidents. On International Workers' Day in 2006, Morales was photographed atop a tank as he "nationalized" natural gas reserves. A year later, he created a buzz when he announced his country "wants partners not masters" and passed control of all mineral rights to the state.[17] Evo grabbed headlines again when he expelled the U.S. ambassador in 2008 for allegedly fomenting a right-wing revolt. His call for aggressive approaches to climate change thrust him into the spotlight once more, and after the failure to make meaningful progress at the 2009 Copenhagen talks, Bolivia hosted the "World People's Conference on Climate Change and the Rights of Mother Earth" the following June. In 2012, Evo was pushed into the international news again when protests erupted both for and against his government's proposed construction of a road through the tropics, highlighting the environmental costs of the current development model on the one hand and the sometimes sharply divergent interests of different indigenous groups on the other. And when Evo proclaimed the U.S. Agency for International Development (USAID) no longer welcome in 2013, accusing it of meddling in internal affairs, Bolivia became the ninth country worldwide to expel the agency. Two months later, Evo recaptured world attention when European countries refused his plane passage on return from meetings in Russia, ostensibly because U.S. whistleblower Edward Snowden might be on board. Several Latin American countries bristled at the European intervention and denounced the United States as behind the plane's delayed trip.

Why has this small landlocked country provoked such interest? Certainly not because of its size: its population of just over ten million is barely half that of Mexico City or Seoul. Rather, since the Cochabamba Water War in 2000, Bolivia has embodied the hopes of anti-globalization movements and those who reject the neoliberal notion that, in the words of former British prime minister Margaret Thatcher, "there is no alternative" to unrestrained markets. Morales's government—and rather than attribute changes to Evo the individual, as political observers so often do, we recognize his rise to power as the front man for a diverse national movement—vowed in 2006 to eliminate the type of economics that privileges growth, regardless of environmental and social costs. The new model pursues a "pluralistic" economy so that people can "live well" in harmony with nature. This requires not only "reinvention" of the state but also, even more fundamentally, a program of decolonization—throwing off the social, ideological, and cultural shackles fashioned when the Spaniards first devastated Andean societies and successively reshaped them under colonial, republican, and nationalist rule. Thus the small nation serves as a living workshop for those who believe that another world is possible.

Bolivia is also critical for those who share Thatcher's worldview and seek a more seamless integration of its massive resources into global markets. This is not an offhand concern: the country possesses the second-largest natural gas reserves in South America, one of the world's leading iron-ore deposits, two of its biggest silver mines, as well as half the known global deposits of lithium with the potential to manufacture the batteries necessary to replace the gas guzzlers of today with the electric vehicles of tomorrow. It encompasses the third most sizable share of the Amazon Basin, currently suffering the region's most rapid deforestation, and is considered essential by some as a global carbon sink, and by others as one of the world's critical biodiversity hotspots, a place where jaguars, river dolphins, and some fourteen hundred bird species may be under threat but still survive.[18]

Shades of Gray in a Black-and-White World

When we first lived in Bolivia, the country was known for its high number of coups (reported at 157 between 1825 and 1982),[19] as a contender for the highest rate of inflation (estimated at up to 25,000 percent), as the reputed hideout of Butch Cassidy and the Sundance Kid, and, forty years later, home to the "Butcher of Lyon," Nazi Klaus Barbie. Like much of Latin America at the time, the military hadn't completely retreated to the barracks: in 1984, generals placed newspaper ads calling on their colleagues to "recognize their duty to restore order" to a country that, two years after its return to civilian rule, was plagued by constant strikes and an economic meltdown.

We had a house behind the university in central La Paz during the late 1980s, and the annual budget appropriation played a crucial role in the rhythm of urban life. Almost every midday for a couple of weeks, student demonstrators blocked the main road that connected the city center with wealthy neighborhoods farther south. After a forty-five-minute flurry of protesters flinging rocks and riot police firing teargas, everyone would head off for lunch—the main meal of the day and the most important social time for families. We scurried along the edge of the confrontation, taking our kids, then two and four, home from daycare, only bothering to detour when the gas was intolerably strong.

Underlying the frequent political and economic upheaval was a daily life deeply embedded in a shared sense of family and community. We came to appreciate that Bolivian culture—actually a diversity of cultures—was neither simply urban nor rural, indigenous nor western, but a synergistic blend that, for us, coming from more homogeneous North America, was intriguing. We had plunged into a world that had rules—lots of them—but they weren't really meant to be followed. Like two one-way streets that meet head-on, it was often impossible to legally navigate passage. We found ourselves in a world composed not of black and white, but black, white, and gray, where the gray is more than simply the melding of the parts.

One day a plumber arrived to repair a leaky tap. He went into the bathroom, banged around for twenty minutes, and then emerged.

"It's fixed," he announced.

We paid him the equivalent of US$3 he asked for and inquired, "Does it still leak?"

The plumber shot a quizzical, what-type-of-question-is-that? look and responded, "Yes, a little."

"Then it's not fixed."

"It is. I put in a piece of string, as the washer was worn out. It's okay now."

"But it still leaks."

"Yes, but only a little."

For most northerners, a tap either leaks or it doesn't. In the Andes, this third state is common. Silvia Rivera Cusicanqui describes it as the Aymara concept of *ch'ixi*, which recognizes that something can be simultaneously white and not white and black and not black. She uses the example of a fabric woven with black and white threads that we may simplistically observe as gray, but in fact it responds to the logic of a third state: it both is and is not black and white and not gray either.[20]

We are reminded of this concept as we come across the reactions that Morales and the process of change evoke. To date, most of what we have read contemplates recent events in a polarized light that prevents a well-considered analysis and is rarely grounded within the broader transformations sweeping the region. In particular, stories in the international press have little to do with what we have seen on the ground every day.

With this book, we aim to introduce an analysis that is neither white nor black, aimed especially at those who know little about Bolivia. We consider the macro-structural factors—history, geography, population, economy, and relations with the rest of world—that restrict what a government can achieve in any context. In a small, historically unstable country with an impoverished majority, both the limitations and the aspirations of the Morales administration are greater than average. On the one hand, part of the ability to revolutionize the country, paradoxically, springs from the fact that ineffectual states lack the strong bureaucratic institutions that can prove so resistant to change. On the other, the absence of governmental capacity curbs the ability to implement new programs. This reality simultaneously enables and constrains transformation. Our portrayal also takes agency into account—the micro, contingent processes of individual actors and their organizations—as well as how leaders like Evo and the governments they form influence society even though much of daily life occurs outside the state's reach.

Many people tend to have faith (or fear) that individual leaders, whether Barack Obama in the United States or Evo Morales in Bolivia, will single-handedly revolutionize society. Yet these leaders rose to power not simply as individuals but as actors embedded in local historical, social, and political processes. As an ex-Jesuit and former vice minister of the interior in Evo's government, Rafael Puente, puts it, "Make no mistake. It's not a government or an individual that transforms a country, but the people organized into movements that accomplish change."[21] To tell Bolivia's current story, then, we must begin with the powerful movements that propelled Evo's meteoric rise to the presidency and underpin the present left turn, arguably more compellingly than in any other country in the region.[22] While often called "new" social movements, they are more accurately the latest expression of a centuries-long struggle for economic and social justice.

Social Movements and the "Process of Change"

The militant movements that placed Evo Morales in power had just thrown two presidents out of office, first in 2003 and again in 2005. This considerable feat was far from unique in the region: Argentina's *piquetero* movement ousted three governments in 2001, and social movements brought down three Ecuadorean administrations between 1997 and 2005.[23]

Social movement demands framed around the 2003 "October Agenda" constituted key items of Morales's electoral campaign: nationalization of gas, an assembly to rewrite the constitution, and an end to impunity for those who had unleashed lethal state forces against unarmed civilian protesters. The intense pressure to honor these commitments and the constraints they generated shaped the new MAS government from its earliest days.[24] Leaders such as Rubén Paz of the El Alto Federation Neighborhood Association (FEJUVE[25]) express it in no uncertain terms, "We are the ones driving the process of change, so the government has an obligation to fulfill our demands."[26]

Bolivia's social movements are among the world's most militant, with a tradition of fierce resistance dating from the Spanish invasion. In a place where the indigenous majority did not win the vote until the national revolution in 1952, where before 1982 coups were the norm and voter manipulation and blatant fraud were common, political struggle is still more often resolved in the streets than at the ballot box.

From 1952 until the 1980s, battles to restore democracy and for economic justice were primarily spearheaded by the trade union confederation, the Bolivian Workers' Central (COB),[27] which embraced everyone from street vendors to health care workers and was headed by the powerful left-wing Federation of Bolivian Miners' Unions (FSTMB).[28] After neoliberal policies adopted in 1985 gutted the union through massive mine closures, this dependence became a liability.[29] By the end of the

1990s, new movement configurations stepped into the vacuum the COB's decline had created, increasingly framing their demands around identity and territory.

This mirrors an indigenous resurgence that has flourished from Mexico to Chile. In Bolivia's highlands in the early 1970s, a small group of Aymara intellectuals, inspired by writer Fausto Reinaga, coalesced into two factions. One concentrated on resisting racism (*indigenistas*), while the other merged indigenous identity with class consciousness (*kataristas*). Their influence swelled throughout a decade of military dictatorship, especially following the 1974 army massacre of over one hundred Cochabamba valley campesinos.[30] By 1979, the first independent national campesino union, Unified Confederation of Campesino Unions of Bolivia (CSUTCB),[31] was affiliated with the COB. It soon flexed its political muscle by mounting a road blockade that ground the country to a halt, presaging future strategies in staging rural protests. The CSUTCB then went on to play a critical role in the 1982 restoration of democracy after eighteen years of almost uninterrupted military dictatorship.

In 1980, an affiliated women's organization coalesced in highland Oruro and La Paz. Given indigenous women's extremely low educational levels, the Bartolinas, as they became known,[32] provided vital support and education to their grassroots membership. By Morales's 2005 election twenty-five years later, not only had they emerged as the country's largest women's organization, but they had matured significantly, articulating a voice increasingly independent from their male counterparts in the CSUTCB.

In the broad eastern tropical plains that make up two-thirds of the territory but contain only one-third of its inhabitants, opposition is constituted very differently. In no small measure because the 1953 agrarian reform was never applied, lowland indigenous groups and highland immigrants have been subjugated by powerful local oligarchies that control vast agricultural estates of soy, cattle, cotton, and sugar. The late 1990s discovery of substantial natural gas reserves has only intensified the regional elite's economic clout.

As lowland indigenous groups were never aggressively courted by leftwing parties and movements, they coalesced organizationally twenty years later than the highlands, more often basing their claims on indigenous rather than class-oriented identities.[33] They totalled around 470,000 people and included over thirty different cultures at the time of the 2001 census. In the early 1980s, they overcame a myriad of obstacles to form the Confederation of Indigenous Peoples of Bolivia (CIDOB),[34] which first launched lowland demands onto the national stage with the renowned 1990 March for Dignity and Territory on La Paz.

Highland and valley peoples who migrated to the lowlands formed what is now called the Confederation of Unions of Intercultural Communities of Bolivia (CSCIB,[35] or "Interculturales") in 1971, with an affiliated women's confederation emerging some forty years later. The CSCIB totals over a million members scattered throughout the country, but despite their high numbers, they have never played a critical role in national leadership. Another important eastern coalition consolidated in the late 1990s, when the campesino-indigenous Eastern block was pulled together from three indigenous groups, joined by campesino unions, the landless, and agricultural laborers.[36]

During the 1990s, opposition was spearheaded by coca-growing indigenous farmers (*cocaleros*) living in the Chapare, the common name for the lowland tropics east of Cochabamba, who were organized into six powerful federations under Evo Morales. Their activism was propelled by the human rights violations and harassment inflicted by the U.S.-financed "War on Drugs." By the mid-1990s, an uneasy balance prevailed in the Chapare, with the government trying to appease the United States while not destroying a vital income source. This shifted abruptly when Hugo Banzer was elected president in 1997 at the head of a shaky multiparty coalition referred to as a "pacted democracy" that was more interested in rent-seeking and personal gain than in promoting a coherent program.[37] Anxious to please the U.S. embassy, Banzer deployed the military to forcibly rip out the sturdy coca bushes.[38] Just as happened with the miners before them, as the coca growers scrambled for survival, others, principally from the rural and urban altiplano,[39] stepped into the political void.

At the same time, a 1994 decentralization law (Law of Popular Participation) opened formal political space to grassroots opposition groups for the first time, and coca growers in particular took advantage of it to elect local mayors, gaining valuable public administration experience.[40] Decentralization, part of the neoliberal reform package, was widespread throughout the region, providing important opportunities for the left to gain experience in municipal public office in places such as Mexico City, Bogotá, Montevideo, Buenos Aires, and hundreds of cities in Brazil.[41]

As the recalibration of indigenous identity intensified throughout the 1990s, new life was injected into communities in the southern altiplano that maintain a much-transformed version of the pre-Hispanic *ayllu*[42] structure. In 1997, these coalesced into the National Council of Ayllus and Markas of Qullasuyu (CONAMAQ), which perceives the CSUTCB campesino union structure as alien to indigenous culture.[43] CONAMAQ strongly criticized leftist political party influence within the CSUTCB, although by November 2004 they had joined them and other indigenous movements in a historic Unity Pact.[44] Farther north, Felipe Quispe, a flamboyant Aymara leader who was jailed as a revolutionary in the 1990s, was elected in 1998 to head the CSUTCB as representative of an indigenous political movement that went on to play a critical role during the 2000 to 2005 protest cycle.

The Cochabamba Water War in 2000, led by a broad-based coalition known as the Coordinadora, provided the new constellation of forces with its first major victory, as campesinos and Chapare coca growers successfully rallied with city residents to reverse the privatization of Cochabamba's water company. The center of opposition then shifted to the sprawling low-income, mostly Aymara city of El Alto, perched above the capital city of La Paz, which had swollen to about 650,000 people by 2001.[45] Unemployed miners had flocked there en masse, keeping much of their union organizational matrix alive, which gradually broadened to encompass their Aymara neighbors who had migrated from the countryside.[46] Neighborhood organizations (FEJUVE) mushroomed from 166 in 1989 to almost 550 by 2006 and fused the political strategies of class-based ex-miners and indigenous territorial claims with long-standing urban political party patronage practices. Only slightly less important were the Federation of School Organizations and the Parents' Federation,[47] which surfaced as important sites for women's political participation.[48]

The result was a militant coalition in which the labor movement played an important role but was no longer in charge, and that had the capacity to mobilize thousands and in some cases hundreds of thousands of people. The movements organized not only to press the municipal government to install basic services but also to advance a broader political agenda. Shouting "El Alto on its feet, never on its knees," these grassroots militants are a force to be reckoned with: more than once, Alteños have pushed aside their leadership to block the roads to La Paz, lying in the deep basin below.[49]

Like Latin America's other territorially based movements, the new configurations were often lauded as more horizontal and inclusive than the COB labor confederation. As political scientist Susan Spronk points out, while the social base for participation may have expanded, these alliances soon ran into the same political infighting and inflexible hierarchical structures as the COB.[50]

In the 2002 elections, Morales came in a startling second, with 22 percent of the vote, only 1.5 percent behind Gonzalo Sánchez de Lozada (known as Goni), a principal architect of neoliberalism in the 1980s and president from 1993 to 1997, who was elected president once again. Not only did Evo's success represent a repudiation of neoliberal policies and traditional parties, but explicitly indigenous candidates demonstrated a credibility they had never attained before.[51] Led by El Alto, in 2003, a broad national coalition was forged despite significant leadership conflicts, different organizational styles, and a laundry list of disparate demands. Their proximate target was a proposed natural gas pipeline through Chile, championed by Goni.

The conflict was fueled by the inordinate symbolic potency of natural resources in the public imaginary, a trait common in resource-rich countries of the global south. This discourse merges nationalist and anti-imperialist ideologies with resource-based demands, built on a deep collective memory of historic looting by outsiders.[52] Prevalent across the political spectrum, resource nationalism has been the most successful narrative in mobilizing the population for over sixty years and has often created wildly unrealistic expectations of what state control of resources might do.[53]

The proposed pipeline sought to ship gas to Mexico and the western United States. A National Coordinator for the Recovery and Defense of Gas (CNRDG), modeled on the Cochabamba Water War's Coordinating Committee, assembled to "recuperate gas for Bolivians."[54] Twenty-one organizations and many individuals joined, including Filemón Escobar, senator-elect of the MAS, and Evo Morales. The unlikely coalition included military generals, local anti-globalization activists, neighborhood organizations, octogenarian pensioners, veterans of the 1930s Chaco War with Paraguay, union representatives, highland campesinos, and coca growers.

Chile was the best option, given the shorter route and higher local demand than in Peru. When the government chose this alternative, opposition quickly unified, in no small measure because of long-standing resentment over Bolivia's loss of seacoast to Chile during the 1879 War of the Pacific. That memory's potency is reinforced annually on the Day of the Sea as soldiers parade in nineteenth-century uniforms, reminding the public that "It is the duty of all Bolivians to claim the right to the sea," a slogan that for years was seen painted above the doors to customs facilities and even on the spine of the La Paz phonebook.

By early September 2003, the CNRDG was calling for nationwide protests, but Goni's ouster was ultimately triggered by an event that had little to do with natural gas. Aymara leader Felipe Quispe called for a road-block to demand the release of Edwin Huampo, a campesino jailed for the alleged murder of two cattle rustlers. The blockade trapped about two hundred foreign tourists in Sorata, four hours northeast of La Paz. The military broke through the makeshift stone barriers to evacuate busloads of tourists, and in the melee, three civilians and two soldiers were killed.[55] The deaths united rural and urban Aymara, as people poured into the streets clamoring for Goni's resignation. "The spirit was incredible: tens of thousands of people full of the feeling that we could change our country," recalls El Alto activist Felix Muruchi. "Many shouted 'It's now or never' . . . The air was filled with energy, passion, political commitment and determination . . . Even though I was well into my fifties, I never felt tired or worn out through the long days of protest."[56]

MARCELINA MENDOZA MAMANI, VENDOR, ALTO LIMA, EL ALTO[57]

Those days in October 2003 were really amazing because of the sense we had of fighting and working together to prevent the government from once again selling our natural resources to foreigners with no benefit to the country or to poor people like us. But the rebellion was also terrifying because you just didn't know if you were going to make it alive through each day. We constructed barricades throughout my neighborhood to keep the military out. Everyone helped each other. People in El Alto are tough—neither tanks nor machine guns could stop us even though we were only armed with sticks and knives. And most of us are just ordinary people like me and my family—I sell food in an El Alto market, and my husband works in construction whenever he can. We don't make much, but both our children are still in school and don't have to go out to work.

About fifteen of our neighbors were killed in 2003. They were mostly young men who were heading into La Paz to their jobs. They had to walk because there were no buses, and [they] found themselves in street battles. I remember when we carried them all to the cemetery and the coffins were lined up in a row. It was terrible. And so hard for those families who lost someone. We went house to house asking for people to help out the families. Some people gave us some change, others provided more, and one family donated Bs. $100 [about US$15]. We put it all together and then divided it among the families. It wasn't much, but it showed our solidarity with our dead.

The massive mobilizations proved that despite the COB's demise and failure to effectively rearticulate an agenda, social movements could mold a national coalition that creatively blended indigenous, nationalist, and working-class identities and demands.[58] They repeated their triumph less than two years later, obliging Goni's replacement, President Carlos Mesa, to resign as 500,000 people marched from El Alto to La Paz and another 500,000 flocked to demonstrations nationwide that mounted over 110 roadblocks at their peak.[59]

Mesa's resignation on June 6, 2005, elevated Supreme Court Chief Justice Eduardo Rodríguez Veltzé to an interim presidency. He was charged with holding national elections by December. After a spirited campaign, Evo won an astounding first-round victory with 54 percent of the vote, almost twice that of the closest contender. It was the first time a candidate had achieved an absolute majority since the country's 1982 return to civilian rule.

The MAS's successful channeling of these social movements draws heavily on the enduring indigenous recollection of five hundred years of colonization, anchored from the mid-1980s in the popular defense of the embattled coca leaf.[60] The fact that widely divergent indigenous groups share cultural emblems does not, however, mean they always agree on a broader agenda. Indigenous cultures are far from unitary, and differences within and across social groups have contributed to diverse synergies between protest discourses built around class and ethnicity in different parts of the country.

Lowland peoples' anxiety that they will be swallowed by much bigger Andean organizations has repeatedly proven a hurdle to building a united national front. Many highland groups have historically regarded the eastern lowlands as "empty," inhabited by "savages," and colonization schemes to relieve rural altiplano population pressure have repeatedly bred conflicts—and continue to do so—over land and resources. Despite these differences, the unity they achieved in the early 2000s facilitated the MAS's national electoral victories, making the dramatic climb of Evo Morales from the coca fields to the presidential palace possible.

Assuming Leadership

The MAS remained virtually indistinguishable from the coca growers unions that gave it birth until the early 2000s. It had built its legitimacy from an explicit self-identification as the "political instrument" (rather than party) of the unions and their allies, as political parties were derided as not much more than tools for distributing spoils among competing elites.[61] While the MAS has gradually come to employ similar tactics, its major rupture with past practices remains unprecedented.[62]

Remarkably, given the upsurge in urban population, the MAS had its beginnings in the countryside.[63] It originated as a new type of political movement: one that masterfully borrowed from both indigenous traditions and labor struggles, and that could take advantage of the new political space at the municipal levels thanks to 1990s neoliberal electoral restructuring. Its members quickly learned the benefits of combining marches and blockades with ballot box strategies to expand their command of national political space.[64]

The MAS is more reminiscent of the old COB labor organization than a political party, where conflicts were kept internal so as to present a united front. But its practice of incorporating disparate grassroots organizations under a single tent, as well as the opening of its voter rolls in 2002 to middle-class leftists and other local political leaders, has left it poorly consolidated, resulting in often contradictory policies and limited capacity.[65] As Rafael Puente describes it, "The MAS is not a party, it's like jelly—there's no structure, no debate."[66] However, as historian Laura Gotkowitz suggests, what it lacks in institutional structure, it makes up for with an impressive strategic flexibility.[67]

The MAS's three ideological tendencies—indigenist, Marxist, and popular nationalist—compete and overlap, creating a hybrid organization.[68] It has variously been described as a political movement (rather than a social movement coalition or an ideologically determined leftist political party);[69] a populist, neopopulist, or national populist party;[70] or a plebeian nationalist movement.[71]

FILEMÓN ESCOBAR, MINING LEADER AND MAS FOUNDER[72]

I was involved from the beginning in constructing the MAS and educating its members in Aymara-Quechua-Guaraní philosophy. United by the symbolism of the coca leaf, in less than twelve years, we put the political instrument of social movements, with Evo at its head, in charge of the government. We proclaimed to the world the continued strength, not just of Andean-Amazonian culture but of the viability of its civilization.

A strong indigenist current in the MAS claims that the time has come to throw the minority whites out and make this a country only for indigenous peoples. This merges with the traditional left-wing parties that the MAS has recruited into its inner circle, many of whom want to overthrow the white oligarchy. This road will only lead us to violent confrontation, which would be political suicide for the MAS and disastrous for the whole country because this process we are living is more important than even the 1952 revolution. All my years in the mining union and the left have taught me that the road of violence will not take us where we want to go. The left has the idea that the revolution can only happen through constructing political parties because unions only focus on their own interests, making them incapable of broader political consciousness. I disagree: the union in Bolivia is not a union in the western sense. In the coca-growing Chapare, unions incorporated ex-miners, who in turn came from the *ayllus* in the north of Potosí. What is an *ayllu*? It's a small state. In the Chapare, the *ayllu* and the western union structure fused together, which facilitated us building an organization capable of taking power.

We are neither a plurinational nor a multicultural country; we have two civilizations: one indigenous and the other western. While western society privileges individual rights, capitalist accumulation, and representative democracy, indigenous society prioritizes the communal. We need to balance these two worldviews, which we can do within the indigenous concept that opposites are complementary. This involves recognizing our western orientation at the same time as strengthening communal production and distribution systems such as the *ayllu*, encouraging reciprocity, and consolidating community justice systems. What we need is a federal system, just like indigenous rebel Zárate Willke proposed over one hundred years ago.

At the heart of Morales's unambiguous electoral victories in 2005 and 2009, which mirror the widespread success the region's leftist presidents have had in securing consecutive terms, is how deftly the MAS engages long-standing social movement claims. "This process is driven by the social movements. The state is the instrument," Vice President García Linera emphasized in 2007.[73] This commitment to "rule by obeying"[74] has frequently blurred roles and responsibilities, hampering government response to punishing skirmishes with the right wing, as well as to ever-narrower social movement agendas.[75]

Morales's strong leadership has been the glue that binds the divergent strands together, with decision making concentrated in a National Directorate composed of a small group of Evo's most trusted advisers. Even when the MAS government is harshly criticized, personal loyalty to Evo runs deep. His agility in power struggles throughout his political career[76] reflects his roots in this populist political style, versions of which have always shaped Latin America's history. Charismatic populist leaders like Morales tend to prioritize a direct relationship between leaders and people and deftly draw on notions of a sovereign oppressed group with a constituted shared identity.[77]

While Venezuela's late Hugo Chávez and Evo are frequently disparaged for relying on populism, the style is perhaps the region's first "homegrown regime model."[78] Political scientist Juan Pablo Luna argues that the *populist* is too often confused with the *popular*, and agrees with journalist Michael Reid that this approach to leadership can be interpreted as a creative response to inequality and conservative dominance, particularly in settings where political parties are unreliable and representation is low.[79] Underlying this debate is the normative position taken by some European and U.S. scholars who claim an unassailable superiority for representative democracy over a more direct and participatory version, even while recognizing liberal democracy's limits in bringing about rapid change or creating space for substantive participation.[80] Political scientist Francisco Panizza argues that positing such a dichotomy is superfluous, suggesting that complementary forms of political representation exist in every context and are expressed through a mix of involvement in political parties, social organizations, and the type of personal relationship between leaders and their supporters.[81] Benjamin Arditi concurs, arguing that populism is neither intrinsically democratic nor anti-democratic; it is a fundamental element of all democracy, potentially increasing participation even while threatening to mutate into authoritarianism.[82]

When the MAS spread into cities after 2000, it lacked the participatory structures that had kept it accountable, even if poorly constructed, in rural areas. Particularly in El Alto, the MAS replaced two 1990s patronage-based parties, CONDEPA (Patriotic Conscience) and UCS (Civic Unity and Solidarity),[83] when their larger-than-life leaders died unexpectedly in the late 1990s. The MAS steadily absorbed their hierarchical structures into its still coalescing political movement. But rapid expansion also proved an Achilles heel, stunting the ability to organize from the grass roots up and overcome the politics of rent-seeking that have plagued the country since its founding.[84] The MAS resembles a smorgasbord, with considerable roots in rural social movements and growing influence from urban indigenous traders and vendors. These owners of small and medium-sized businesses—both rural and urban—tend to favor public investment that directly benefits their own immediate economic interests.[85]

Just as in South Africa when apartheid collapsed, the expectations in Bolivia in 2006 for the MAS political project were immense across left-wing and marginalized populations. Indigenous leaders spoke of a *pachakut'i*—a revolution that turns the world on its head—while intellectuals such as Fernando Calderón[86] proposed nothing less than combining indigenous cultural recognition with equitable economic development by creating a new institutional order. Others have been just as ambitious, heralding an accelerated decolonization that questions the fundamental assumptions underlying modernity and western democracy in the search for a completely new relationship between the individual, society, and government.[87]

FELIX MURUCHI POMA, EX-MINER, LAWYER, AND COMMUNITY LEADER[88]

I remember January 21, 2006, so well—it was the day Evo Morales, an indigenous person like me from the altiplano, received the *bastón de mando*,[89] the symbol of indigenous authority. The joy I felt was reinforced by the wonderful music played by groups scattered about Tiwanaku, the center of an empire that lasted fifteen hundred years. All around me I saw people dressed in indigenous clothes: men in red ponchos and *chullos*, the characteristic Andean hats with flaps over the ears, and women in traditional wide skirts and bowler hats.

The thunder of drums and fireworks filled the air along with a powerful feeling of brother- and sisterhood that spread like wildfire: coca, bread, bananas, and tea were freely shared. Many people had traveled through the night along bumpy dirt roads in buses or open trucks, but their hunger and exhaustion were forgotten in the excitement of the moment. The hope was palpable that an indigenous leader— one of our own—as president would improve the lives of our people far more than the *criollos*, descendants of the Spanish conquerors, had ever done. Moved by that hope, we danced to the panpipe music that echoed throughout the valley.

Amid the revelry, suddenly the loud boom of the horns called *pututus* boomed, instantly focusing everyone's attention. The transfer of authority was about to begin. The cry "*Jallalla* Evo" (Long live Evo!) bounced off the hills surrounding the meadow. Evo gradually approached the stage at the Door of the Sun. While I was quite far away, between the loudspeakers and the radios around me we listened in a hushed silence to the symbolic transmission of office. A momentous change for us all that was over in a flash. All around me people cried and embraced as we shared the dream that Evo's taking office had given life to.

When I was born some sixty years earlier, indigenous people lacked almost all rights. Our decades of struggle brought us to this day: for the first time, we truly felt represented when Evo Morales became President of the Republic.

Despite the lofty aspirations, Morales had to quickly produce results to satisfy his supporters, who have repeatedly proven their willingness to deploy the politics of the streets regardless of who occupies state office.

The challenges were formidable. The country is almost entirely reliant on revenues from natural gas to cover public expenses, replicating historic patterns of dependence on foreign capital. Pressures to expand resource extraction to drive economic growth and improve living standards were relentless, at the same time as Evo quickly became celebrated internationally for his pro-indigenous, pro-environment discourse. The new government had to balance eliminating the surplus coca that finds its way into cocaine production with demands from Evo's union to permit more leaf cultivation. And perhaps the most daunting of all: incoming public employees, whose experience mostly came from community organizations or small-scale nongovernmental organizations (NGOs), needed to acquire basic governing skills.

From 2006 to 2010, the MAS successfully consolidated power and popular support despite often virulent attacks from the right wing and the media, in a chronically unstable political culture characterized by abrupt power transfers and authoritarian leadership.[90] How well has it done after eight years in fulfilling its agenda? No matter where you live, Bolivia's latest chapter is instructive for identifying the challenges inherent in the progressive dream of achieving greater social, economic, and political justice while respecting our natural environment.

CHAPTER 2

Land of Unintended Consequences

Bolivia is renowned for extremes: in its history, landscape, and natural resources. One of the most culturally, physically, and ecologically diverse places on the planet, the country encompasses two Andean mountain ranges with the cold altiplano, the dry inter-Andean plateau over 11,500 feet above sea level, between them. Eastward the landscape drops steeply through temperate valleys some 8,000 feet high, before plunging into vast Amazonian rain forests that give way to grassy wetlands to the north and the semidesert Chaco in the south. Covering an area about the size of Texas and France combined (or of Ontario), it is split into nine departments (the equivalent of states or provinces), with Peru, Brazil, Paraguay, Argentina, and Chile as its neighbors.

The environment is marked by superlatives: the world's highest navigable lake (Titicaca, straddling the border with Peru); the largest salt flat (southwestern Salar de Uyuni); and the second-largest wetlands (the Pantanal). The landscape is spectacular: magnificent snow-covered mountains surround wind-battered plateaus and tranquil deep blue lakes; precipitous valleys plunge into dense jungles or unfold into open savanna and wetlands. This fractured terrain yields an astonishingly diverse plant and animal life, much of it within tropical forests, which account for 17 percent of the national territory.[1]

Bolivia boasts one of South America's lowest population densities. Roughly 65 percent of Bolivians describe themselves as indigenous, a percentage higher than any other country in the Americas, although this identity is a fluid, social, rather than racial, category expressed in widely divergent forms. In some remote areas, indigenous people still discard their traditional clothing for visits to market towns because they feel they will be treated better if they appear less "Indian." Despite such ex-

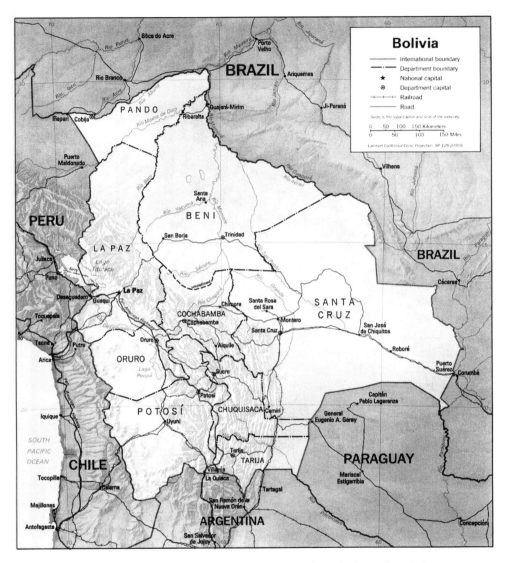

Map of Bolivia. Source: U.S. Central Intelligence Agency, from the Perry-Castañeda Library Map Collection, University of Texas, www.lib.utexas.edu/maps/

plicit racism, the percentage of people claiming indigenous heritage has steadily grown over the past twenty years.[2]

Most indigenous people are Aymara or Quechua speakers from various groups who have settled in communities for thousands of years throughout the densely populated western altiplano and high valleys. Over the last two generations, this population has migrated in massive waves to the cities, and about 62 percent of urban dwellers claim indigenous identity, although this had dropped by the 2012 census.

Those commonly known as "the Quechua" encompass a conglomeration of different ethnicities merged in the fourteenth century by the Inka Empire. Highland Aymara speakers demonstrated some success in resisting the Inka and the Spaniards after them, successfully retaining their own language and many of their cultural practices.[3]

The largest eastern groups are the Chiquitanos (also known as the Chiquitos) and the Guaraní, roughly 195,000 and 130,000 people respectively.[4] The Chiquitanía, as Chiquitano lands are called, is a seasonally dry tropical deciduous forest, northeast of the city of Santa Cruz. The Chiquitanos are a conglomeration of several groups forged into a single ethnicity when they were both herded and lured into settled communities by the Jesuits from the late seventeenth to the mid-eighteenth century.[5] Later they suffered debt peonage and forced labor during the nineteenth- and early twentieth-century Amazon rubber boom and the 1940s and early 1950s railroad construction that linked Santa Cruz eastward to the Brazilian border.[6]

The Guaraní, who live farther south in drier scrub woodlands, are the northern branch of the much larger Paraguayan group. They were not fully conquered until 1892 and, ever since, have been continuously dispossessed of their ancestral territories while frequently compelled to labor on huge estates.[7] Thirty-four smaller groups, each with a distinct culture and language, among them Guarayos, Ayoreos, Chimanes, Trinitarios, Ese Eja, and Moxeños, total another 150,000 people. Their pre-Hispanic seminomadic communities have been devastated by disease, herded into Jesuit missions, lured into debt peonage, and repeatedly deprived of their territory.[8]

About 25 percent of Bolivians call themselves mestizos, strictly speaking those of mixed European and indigenous heritage, but often urbanized indigenous people who no longer observe rural customs. Though less than 10 percent of the population, the criollos, who claim European heritage, are the most powerful economically and, until recently, politically.

Two-thirds of the population now lives in cities. Average life expectancy is sixty-eight years, and, paralleling other lower-income countries, just over a third of the population is under fifteen years old. The gender wage gap—what women earn compared to men—at 68 percent is about average for the region.[9] In 2005 when Evo was elected, the country had one of the most unequal income distributions in the world's most unequal region. The wealthiest 10 percent earned over ninety times more than the poorest 10 percent. Sixty percent of the population lived below the poverty line, 37 percent suffered extreme poverty, and rural poverty was almost twice that of urban areas.[10]

Andean Indigenous Cultures

Archaeologists calculate that humans settled the Andean region about 20,000 years ago, and they situate the region among the six principal sites in the world where sophisticated human cultures evolved. In what is now Bolivia, the Tiwanaku civilization flourished on the shores of Lake Titicaca between 300 CE and 1000 CE.[11] Complex hydrological systems aided agricultural expansion across the dry altiplano, although Tiwanaku collapsed during a seventy-year drought in the eleventh century. The culture's fragmented remains split into twelve Aymara-speaking kingdoms that stretched from central Peru to northern Argentina.[12]

In the fifteenth century, a hundred years before the 1532 Spanish invasion, the Inkas from highland Cuzco spread rapidly throughout the region, dominating through a skillful combination of conquest and negotiation. At its height, their empire stretched along the spine of the Andes from southern Colombia to northern Chile, with a total population estimated between six and twelve million.[13] By relocating entire communities, the Inka effectively obligated people to adopt their language (Quechua), religion, and culture, while ensuring loyalty through guaranteeing freedom from military conquest as well as food security, no small feat in the inhospitable highlands.

Populations were organized into *ayllus*—a nested kinship system that still shapes local governance, despite significant mutations since the Spanish Conquest.[14] Integrated agricultural production and exchange between villages operated through extended family networks scattered across different ecological zones. The steep geography lent itself to ecological niches where human activity was determined by altitude or rainfall. Areas above 14,000 feet, too cold (or dry) for most agriculture, were (and continue to be) dedicated to growing quinoa or raising llamas for use as pack animals and for their meat. Bolivia still has the world's largest number of llamas and their smaller cousins, alpacas, whose high-quality wool is prized in knit goods. Land between 10,000 and 13,000 feet that is protected from frost or with water access is apt for cultivation, most importantly of potatoes, with over seventy varieties, from bright purple to golden brown, found throughout local markets. Farther down the mountain slopes, crops such as corn and broad beans gradually give way to semitropical and then tropical products like coca, bananas, and yucca.

The saying "Reciprocity begins with a gift" reflects widespread Andean practices of complementarity with their roots in a perceived balance between male and female.[15] In many rural communities, people still collaborate through family labor exchanges such as *ayni* and *mink'a*, forms of collective community work.[16] Leadership is considered a duty, with tasks rotating yearly as people assume positions with increasing responsibility and higher costs as they mature. While the *jilakata*—the maximum local authority—is always a man, his female partner, the *mamatalla*, replaces him when he is away or ill.[17] As the collective still often wields greater weight than the individual, status is often measured by contributions to group well-being rather than by individual wealth or other achievements.[18]

Despite considerable regional variations, indigenous cosmovision often mingles animism with an abiding respect for nature. In the high Andes, the sun, the moon, the highest mountains, water, and natural phenomena such as lightning and thunder are venerated. Viracocha is considered the creator, while the earth mother, the Pachamama (*pacha* = earth, *mama* = mother), is the personification of fertility and growth, a living being. Unlike for western cultures, space and time are simultaneous realities expressed in the same word: *pacha*. Indigenous peoples generally revere ancestors, as the dead either actively ensure the well-being of the living or, if not treated with proper respect, can provoke all sorts of difficulties. Frequent fiestas have their roots in lengthy religious and social celebrations that mark the changing seasonal and agricultural cycles. Symbolism and rituals are captured in haunting and emotive music, refined ceramics, and some of the world's finest textiles in the highlands, while wood carvings and delicate fiber weavings flourish in the lowlands.

While highland and valley indigenous cultures share characteristics, they are far from homogeneous, but rather include ideas, processes, and relationships that vary both across and within regions, genders, genera-tions, and historical moments.[19] Anthropologist Andrew Canessa con-tends we can best understand indigeneity as a reflection of an often site-specific historical consciousness informed by a sense of injustice.[20]

Five Centuries of Globalization: From the Conquest to the Twenty-First Century

Ever since the Spanish invasion, the country's enormous natural resource wealth has profited global, rather than local, interests. Consecutive re-source booms fueled by silver, quinine, rubber, tin, and, more recently, coca and hydrocarbons, have spawned a deeply entrenched extractive economy.

While legend shrouds the details of silver's discovery at what quickly became known as Cerro Rico (Rich Hill) in the southern altiplano, one thing is certain: the Spanish explorers who laid claim to it in 1545 thrust Bolivia onto the world stage. For the next century, Potosí's mines ac-counted for half of the world's silver and gold, as volumes of ore began to pour across the Atlantic on a scale never seen before in global trade.[21] By the seventeenth century, Potosí had become a world-class city, rival-ing London and Paris in size and crammed with fortune seekers from all over Europe.

The insatiable hunger for silver took an enormous human toll, with estimates ranging from one to four million indigenous miners dying from accidents, exhaustion, or black lung. For almost one hundred years, Potosí's mines yielded more than half of the world's silver and gold, allow-ing Spain's aristocracy to live in enormous luxury.[22] The Spanish expres-sion "It's worth a Potosí" remains synonymous with "It's worth a fortune," which is more than a little ironic, given that the region remains among Bolivia's poorest. Potosí's mint manufactured the world's first global cur-rency, the famed pieces of eight, which were traded from China to Scot-land. The Spanish Crown's enormous debt drove Potosí's silver north-ward, where it served as a significant input in financing northern Europe's industrial revolution.

The conquest and exposure to European diseases cost Native Ameri-cans more than the mines did. Over 75 percent—by some estimates as high as 90 percent—of the indigenous population died within forty years of contact.[23] In the east, the decimation was delayed, as indigenous lands were largely untouched until the nineteenth century. Local populations, however, continued to diminish throughout the twentieth century, and fifteen of these groups are currently considered at risk of extinction.[24]

Resistance to external domination has been constant: The Aymara alone spearheaded highland uprisings in 1769, 1771, 1781, and 1821 during the colonial period. In the lowlands, the Guaraní's fierce autonomy kept both the Inka and the Spaniards at bay for hundreds of years. Bolivia's 1825 independence from Spain failed to improve indigenous peoples' lot as mining and landowning elites effectively steered the country's governments to serve their own interests. Aymara speakers continued rebelling, most notably in 1899 and 1921. They, along with Quechua speakers, played a critical role in the 1952 revolution and, with active participation from lowland groups, in the social unrest of the early 2000s.

Rebellion is not limited to the indigenous majority, however, for elites have also continuously jostled for position and power. The country has the dubious distinction of having one of the highest number of coups d'état in the world, and its rulers are not known for their civility or timidity. The infamous General Mariano Melgarejo, who ruled in the late nineteenth century, took such offense to a British ambassador who refused to attend a reception honoring Melagarejo's mistress that he tied the hapless man backward on a mule and trotted him around La Paz's central square. When Queen Victoria heard of this insult, she declared with the full force of her imperial authority that "Bolivia no longer exists" and had the country scratched off the map.

The diverse regions have persistently chafed under centralized government control. When the country was created as a buffer state between more powerful Peru and Argentina, its founders had little grasp of the problems that lay ahead for the poorly consolidated nation. Like other countries patched together from former colonies, Bolivia has struggled to forge internal cohesion and a national identity. Whenever the mining economy flagged, central rule weakened, which set off power struggles as regions clamored for greater autonomy. The vast and long-isolated department of Santa Cruz, which was not connected to the rest of the country by paved road until 1954, has acted as the locus of these demands since the late nineteenth century, rising up against central authority in 1876, 1891, and 1957.[25]

Silver dominated the economy until the late nineteenth century when enormous tin deposits were discovered south of La Paz. Within twenty years, Bolivia's tin mines produced over 30 percent of world supply, and, in South America's poorest country, three "Tin Barons" created by the newfound wealth, Simón Iturri Patiño, Carlos Víctor Aramayo, and Mauricio Hochschild, were among the continent's richest men. For forty years, they largely controlled successive governments. Popular legend has it that Simón I. Patiño, the most famous of the three, stumbled across a very rich vein of tin, later called "La Salvadora" (The Savior), and made a pact with the devil to exploit it.

The nationalist revolution in 1952—Latin America's second chronologically after Mexico's—unleashed profound transformations in a semi-feudal society. The government of the Tin Barons was deposed by a coalition forged from the tiny middle class, pressured by the mining labor movement and indigenous peasants. The revolution won the vote for indigenous people and nonliterate women, nationalized the mines, and reallocated large highland and valley estates (haciendas) to the indigenous serfs who toiled there, although it was unable to extend the measure to the eastern lowlands.[26]

The middle-class-dominated National Revolutionary Movement (MNR)[27] government was generally moderate, seeking modernization and creating a national identity by renaming "Indians" *campesinos*—literally, "people who live in the countryside"—in an effort to overcome indigenous "backwardness" and create a mestizo, or mixed-race, nation. It practiced import substitution industrialization (ISI), prevalent in Latin America until the 1980s, which shielded local industries while extending government control over the economy. Although the revolution freed the rural poor from the worst excesses of the haciendas, the criollo minority preserved most of their wealth and political power. Campesino unions were encouraged after the 1952 revolution, but until the end of the 1970s, these were largely manipulated by whatever government was in office. Whether rural or urban, indigenous people remained second-class citizens.

The labor movement set up the COB, which not only cogoverned during the 1950s but was critical in pushing the new government to launch its most radical reforms.[28] Shaped by various strains of Marxist ideology, the COB headed the struggle for social and economic justice for the next forty years. Despite the MNR's best efforts, they were never able to turn the COB into a corporatist union confederation, as other national popular parties in more industrialized parts of Latin America managed to do, notably in Mexico, Brazil, Argentina, and Venezuela.[29]

In 1964, the army seized power, plunging the country into eighteen years of almost uninterrupted dictatorships. The COB fought relentlessly to restore democracy despite sustained and often brutal repression.[30] The first military regime promised campesino unions that the gains made in the 1952 revolution would not be reversed, forging a pact that was vital to the armed forces' ability to retain power. Campesinos, with memories of bonded labor on haciendas still fresh in their minds, perceived that they had little option other than to accept military rule.

By the late 1970s, the private sector had come to consider military dictatorships as antithetical to a stable business climate and joined popular movements to pressure for a return to democracy. A fragile center-left coalition recovered civilian government in 1982, on the heels of five years of almost uninterrupted military coups and elections that rotated through five different presidencies. Facing economic catastrophe that was due as much to the 1970s global debt crisis as to military mismanagement and corruption, and squabbling within its center-left coalition, the new government collapsed when inflation soared out of control. Elections were called, and in 1985, conservatives were voted into power. Within weeks of assuming office, under the aegis of the International Monetary Fund (IMF) and the World Bank, the MNR's president, Víctor Paz Estenssoro, embraced one of the world's earliest and most severe neoliberal structural adjustment programs. The New Economic Policy (NEP) slashed public spending, fired tens of thousands of workers, floated the currency, and cut tariffs and trade restrictions.[31] Inflation, estimated at 25,000 percent, fell close to zero almost immediately, and Bolivia was lauded as a neoliberal triumph.[32] Structural adjustment rested on a foundation of international aid, which skyrocketed to three times the world average; the informal sector's capacity to absorb labor; the boom in coca (and cocaine) production; and the almost unfettered flow of contraband.

The COB met its match when the global price of tin, which had sustained the small export economy for most of the twentieth century, plunged.[33] State mines, registering huge operating losses, were shuttered, and 23,000 of a total of 30,000 miners—the heart of the COB—were fired. This evisceration of Bolivia's labor movement is comparable to what happened after the 1984–1985 unsuccessful strike against pit closures under Britain's Margaret Thatcher. Unlike what happened in Latin America's more industrialized countries, the neoliberal attack on labor didn't lead to the emergence of new union confederations, such as the Unified Workers' Central (CUT) in Brazil and the National Union of Workers (UNT) in Mexico, but instead steadily drained the COB's vitality.[34]

Over 50,000 jobs in the public and private sectors had disappeared by 1988. Thousands migrated to the cities, many men working as day laborers or in other parts of the informal economy, which generates 75 percent of all new jobs, a trend considerably more extreme than in the rest of Latin America.[35] Women often joined the "contraband of the ants," trekking across borders to purchase small quantities of goods and returning to sell them on city streets.[36] Other unemployed workers flocked to the Chapare, where the thriving coca fields permitted survival. This swing from a partially unionized to a largely informal workforce undermined working-class identity and solidarity, cultivating the individualism that characterizes neoliberalism.

The annihilation of the miners' union fostered the rise of "cooperative" mining, organized into the National Federation of Mining Cooperatives (FENCOMIN)[37] that by 2013 had mushroomed to 80,000 members. Similar to the informal mining that is widespread throughout Latin America, cooperatives operate with little regard for safety, working conditions, or the environment. Most typically, they are family-owned businesses with a high degree of community and self-exploitation, although control is increasingly concentrated into the hands of a few who subcontract day laborers.[38] Bolivia's first Hummers appeared on the narrow streets of impoverished Potosí driven by wealthy cooperative miners. More guilds than unions, these cooperatives operate under the logic that individual production and protecting access to mineral resources are more vital than collective union demands for better wages, health care, and working conditions.

Decentralization in 1994 channeled 20 percent of the national budget to over 311 (339 by 2013) newly created municipalities, about three-quarters with populations under 50,000. For the first time, small cities and rural communities were able to elect municipal governments with budgets, although they amounted to less than US$25 a person.[39] Thanks to new local oversight mechanisms, political participation expanded, in the process strengthening indigenous identity because political parties had historically largely ignored rural areas.

Despite ambitions of crafting a modern state, neoliberalism ultimately failed to reduce endemic poverty, furnish indigenous peoples with basic rights, or satisfy regional demands for local control.[40] By the end of the 1990s, as financial crisis shook Latin America, growth had stagnated, and the worsening economic climate drove renewed protest. When the 2000 Cochabamba Water War reversed the World Bank–promoted privatization of a public water company, Bolivia morphed again from neoliberal poster child to a leading light of the anti-globalization movement.[41] Emboldened by this achievement, protest engulfed the country and culminated in the Gas Wars of 2003 and 2005 that sent two presidents packing and proved that people in a small, poor country could successfully challenge powerful companies, governments, and institutions.

The Country the MAS Inherited

When Evo Morales was sworn in, Bolivia was in the midst of what has become the longest period of democratic rule in its turbulent history. However, it was still overly centralized and poorly integrated, had been debilitated by twenty years of neoliberalism, and was reeling from years of social unrest. The economy had grown haltingly since the beginning of the 1990s, even though reserves of natural gas, silver, gold, and zinc were immense. Seventy percent of the population worked in informal jobs, and many young people fled the country in search of a better life. Buenos Aires housed over a million of them, with tens of thousands more in Europe, Brazil, Chile, and the United States.

Just like the rest of the global south, Bolivia has undergone an abrupt transition over the past fifty years from a rural to an urban society. The largest city is now Santa Cruz, ignored during the colonial period because it lacked the mineral riches the highlands possess. It has exploded from its sleepy colonial core of 40,000 people in 1950 into a sprawling metropolis of over 1.8 million, one of the world's fastest-growing cities. The "March to the East" after the 1952 revolution connected Santa Cruz to the rest of the country and targeted national and international investment there, particularly in export agriculture and hydrocarbons. As the region's political and economic influence grew, so did its frustration with traditional Andean political and economic domination.[42]

Economic growth in Santa Cruz has been strong since the early 1990s, thanks to booming agribusiness and natural gas production. The department, which in the 2012 census edged out La Paz for the first time as the country's most populous, also boasts the most diversified income and largest volume of exports, allowing for relatively high standards of living. On the ground, this translates into a small number of luxurious neighborhoods surrounded by a sea of misery, as urban poverty rates reach 50 percent. In some rural provinces, poverty soars as high as 80–90 percent.[43]

Early municipal plans envisioned a series of expanding concentric rings but failed to take into account accelerating highland migration. The push of economic crisis, droughts, and structural adjustment mixed with the pull of regional growth to draw huge numbers of working-class and indigenous migrants, principally from impoverished areas in Cochabamba,

Chuquisaca (Sucre), and Potosí but also from Santa Cruz's own indigenous populations, including Guaranís, Chiquitanos, and Ayoreos. With little formal or well-paid employment, these migrants have reshaped the city by crowding into marginal far-flung neighborhoods without basic services and prone to flooding.

La Paz, the seat of national government, sits in a sharply eroded basin 1,000 feet below El Alto—literally "the heights." Together they form a fragmented metropolis of 1.8 million people that has been aptly described as an indigenous urban center overlooking a colonial city, with El Alto serving as the hinge linking La Paz to the altiplano hinterland.[44] La Paz–El Alto has grown exponentially since 1950 when the entire urban area registered 320,000 people, only 11,000 of them in El Alto. Neoliberal economic policies drove many peasants, unable to compete with the ensuing flood of agricultural imports, to cities, including El Alto, where they were joined by thousands of fired miners. Open unemployment is higher than in other urban areas. By 2010, El Alto outstripped La Paz in size, with 60 percent of its population under twenty-five and 74 percent self-identified as Aymara.[45]

Perched on the unstable, scoured cliffs surrounding La Paz are precarious houses known to collapse during annual summer mudslides and flooding. This contrasts with the valleys to the south of its historic center, which are filled with middle- and upper-class subdivisions where spacious, modern homes sit behind fortified walls, surrounded by trees, open streets, and paved roads. Service workers from the surrounding hills and El Alto appear first to build the houses of the rich and then to clean and repair them, allowing a relatively few privileged families to enjoy the lifestyle common to elite enclaves throughout the developing world.

While La Paz's built environment reflects decades of public investment, El Alto's sparse physical infrastructure proclaims a city that outgrew its municipal government's limited resources and abilities. Roads are largely cobblestone or dirt, buildings stand in varying degrees of completion, and open sewers still flow through some neighborhoods. When Evo Morales was elected, 54 percent of El Alto residents relied on outdoor plumbing for their access to water.

Even though El Alto has about 15 percent more people, La Paz raises roughly five times more tax revenue per capita. The culture of rent-seeking that has been far more prevalent in El Alto than in La Paz in recent decades exacerbates this problem, reducing the purchasing power of public funds. More than ten mayors were removed from office in both cities between 1994 and 2004, most on corruption charges.[46]

El Alto is the hemisphere's most indigenous, most radical, and, ironically, most neoliberal city. Although it has mobilized to shut off access to La Paz twice for extended periods since 2000, its streets are choked with the informal markets prevalent in cities of the developing world. In municipal elections, El Alto's voters fluctuate between rightist and leftist parties, generally favoring the populist candidate who offers the most in the way of public works and assistance.

A generation ago, Cochabamba was the largest municipality after La Paz. While it may have dropped in rank, the temperate "garden city" has swollen to 630,000 people, with about 1,000,000 in its metropolitan area.[47] Cochabamba's fertile valley has been inhabited for thousands of years, and soon after the Spanish founded it in 1542, it became the country's granary, supplying much of the food for Potosí's mines. Its current economy relies on goods and services, with a small industrial sector, and since the 1980s has been shaped by the ebb and flow of the coca/cocaine economy in the nearby Chapare. As in all of Bolivia's cities, explosive growth has overcome sporadic efforts at modernist planning as impoverished rural migrants have rushed in, creating a chaotic urban landscape. The resulting communities are regarded by municipal authorities as illegal.[48] Together, Santa Cruz, Cochabamba, and La Paz–El Alto form the "central axis" of the country, dislodging Sucre, the judicial capital, and Potosí, which were the major cities as long as silver dominated the economy.

Farther south, Tarija, whose fertile western valleys have suffered a terrible toll from deforestation, hosts the country's largest natural gas fields. The department's success at capturing revenues from gas means that in 2013 it has the highest per capita income and most rapid economic growth nationally. Although the money mostly flows through rather than stopping, the city of Tarija is transforming rapidly through a construction boom and a wave of migration.

Trinidad, capital of the northeastern department of Beni, remains largely isolated from national life, although the Morales government hopes to create a new development pole there through massive public investment and road construction. Like many other Latin American urban areas, all of these cities were founded during the Spanish colony and are characterized by a central historic core surrounded by impoverished neighborhoods and unequal distribution of basic public services.

In the countryside, poverty was endemic when Evo came to power. This often drove campesinos to work the harvests on massive estates in Santa Cruz, or to Argentina or Chile in search of cash to complement their meager incomes. Traditionally, mostly the men left, leaving women

Table 2.1. Economic and Social Indicators for Bolivia

	2000	2005	2012
Life expectancy (age in years)	63	65	67
Total population living in poverty (%)	68	60	50
Rural population living in poverty (%)	87	80	75
Infant mortality (per 1,000 live births)	61	53	41
Education (number of years of schooling attained by those over fifteen)	7	8	9
Adult literacy rate (%) over the age of fifteen	86	87	95
Males:	93		
Females:	81		
Gross Domestic Product per capita (current US$)	$1,011	$1,044	$2,232
Real GDP growth (%)	2.5	4.1	5
Gini co-efficient of income inequality	63	58	56 (2008)
Human Development Index	612	649	675
Access to improved sanitation (%)		33	34

Sources: CIA 2011; United Nations 2012; World Bank 2013.

behind in charge of crops, animals, and children. Since 2000, escalating numbers of women, both urban and rural, have joined the migratory cycle, with large numbers traveling to Argentina and Spain as domestic workers.

Twenty years of neoliberal policies resulted in a real national per capita income growth of less than 2 percent, compared with 60 percent between 1960 and 1980. The economic stagnation worsened inequality, and as demands increased with the 1990s growth in formal political participation, the situation became increasingly unstable. When the MAS entered office, they faced ensuring that natural gas income continued to flow to multinational corporations while attending to nationalization demands from the newly empowered majority.[49] More than one progressive administration in countries far better consolidated and with more economic muscle than Bolivia has buckled under the pressure from international and national capital. Nelson Mandela's administration in South Africa is a case in point. And in Brazil, global money market managers heaved a collective sigh of relief when Lula committed to holding foreign reserves beyond the minimum required by the IMF.

Considering the dismal panorama it usually faces, Bolivia had some

advantages when Evo entered office. Natural gas revenues spiked before Evo's election, due to a controversial 2005 hydrocarbons law that
boosted royalties and taxes. In 2002, the government ran a public-sector
budget deficit of 8.8 percent of Gross Domestic Product (GDP), which
had dropped to 3.5 percent in 2005 as improved hydrocarbons revenues
started to flow.[50]

The MAS assumed power with considerable political leeway as well.
The three major parties that had rotated office in coalition governments
from 1985 to 2005 were in tatters.[51] A new social democratic party, the
Movimiento Sin Miedo (MSM; Movement without Fear), maintained regional stature through the popular mayor of La Paz, Juan del Granado,
who not only gave priority to the city's poor but served two terms without
being accused of corruption. An ally, albeit a critical one, until April 2010,
the MSM split with the MAS over what it perceived as the government's
sectarian and anti-democratic turn.

When the Morales administration moved into their new offices in January 2006, they faced five formidable challenges. First, they had to navigate around influential transnational actors, from the World Bank and
the IMF to the United States. Second, domestically, they faced the task
of diffusing opposition from powerful traditional political and economic
interests, including the Senate, judiciary, military, and regional elites, and
an urgency to address persistent demands for greater regional autonomy.
Third, the majority of those in public service owed their allegiance to
well-established patronage systems linked to previous clientelist parties
and business sectors. Fourth, the MAS could only count on a small pool of
trained professionals, and while committed to expanding indigenous and
women's representation, they found themselves confronted by supporters
convinced that access to government posts was part of their spoils of victory, irrespective of skills, training, or aptitude. Finally, the MAS had to
juggle maintaining support from its poor and indigenous supporters who
had enormous expectations of immediate and thorough change.

CHAPTER 3

Capturing or Captured by Power?

Our country has been transformed since we wrote a new constitution. Before, our wiphala[1] *was just a piece of cloth, but now it is a symbol of indigenous participation in national political life. Our communities are visible now in ways they have never been before. Regardless of whom the president is, the process of change we have started can't be stopped.*

ENRIQUE FLORES, MAYOR OF PUNA, POTOSÍ, APRIL 14, 2012

January 21, 2006, marked a watershed for indigenous rights in the Americas. Two hundred thousand people celebrated as Aymara priests named Evo Morales *apu mallku*, "maximum leader," at Tiwanaku, home to one of the Americas' most important pre-Hispanic cultures. The next day, tens of thousands jammed La Paz streets waving the multicolored indigenous *wiphala* alongside the red, yellow, and green Bolivian flag to witness Morales being sworn in at the presidential palace. The dancing, singing, and cheering throughout the fields and streets made visible the hope Evo's victory brought to the poor and marginalized.

The mandate was clear, but the trials ahead undeniable. The right was not ready to give up power, and the left was pushing for more radical change than the MAS could implement democratically, as it came to power with only twelve of twenty-seven seats in the Senate. In addition, sitting judges were mostly appointed by Goni and his MNR party.[2] Morales was clearly going to find it easier to resort to Presidential Decrees than to legislative action.[3] In this chapter we look at how Evo's government handled these challenges during two terms in office, given its meager administrative capacity, the negligible institutional structure it inherited, and the often insistent demands from every quarter.

One of Morales's earliest moves, which bolstered his already widespread popularity, was to cut his presidential salary 57 percent to US$1,875 a month, urging Congress to do the same with the argument that the additional funds would subsidize much-needed doctors and teachers.[4] While such high-profile moves played well with a public fed up with self-serving officials, they did little to protect the new government from habitual protest, although until 2011, the MAS could count on the broad base of social movements that made up the 2004 Unity Pact to back them up.

Not only did strikes and marches continue—such as the confrontation in March 2006 with former employees of the state airline that threw Cochabamba into turmoil—but a tragic misstep in October 2006 made a serious dent in public confidence. For two days, the treeless hillsides of the tin-mining town of Huanuni, home to countless struggles for miners' rights, bore witness to a fratricidal clash as so-called cooperative miners fought with unionized workers at a state-run mine.[5] When a stick of dynamite hit an explosives shop, the chain reaction blew up thirty-nine other buildings, many of them homes. Women raced to the main plaza, frantically waving improvised white flags and screaming "Enough, we want peace."[6] After the clouds of ammunition dust had settled, seventeen Huanuni miners were dead, over fifty were wounded, and the government was scrambling to explain why it hadn't intervened earlier. The warning signs were all there: the two groups' disagreements had reached a fever pitch months earlier, with repeated protests blockading main roads.

In one of the new government's first tough decisions, four thousand cooperative miners were absorbed into the unionized workforce of the Bolivian mining corporation (COMIBOL).[7] While this wasn't the outcome the cooperatives asked for, seven years later the decision appears to have been the right one, as former enemies now work side by side underground, paying homage to the god of the mine, the Tío, and watching each other's backs to survive another day of the never-ending night underground.[8]

In the politically charged El Alto, one of the government's first priorities was to break the contract with the French company Suez, the unpopular managers of both La Paz's and El Alto's privatized water supply, a move that repeated the early 2006 Buenos Aires takeover of the same company.[9] To please supporters, Morales appointed neighborhood association leader Abel Mamani, a key figure in the El Alto dispute, to the post of minister of public works. As he had no prior administrative experience, the public water company Mamani established, EPSAS,[10] proved less than successful in improving services, with multiple complaints of water shortages, accounting errors, and tariff increases. To make matters worse,

Mamani was forced out of office in a 2008 scandal. By 2013, EPSAS was functioning so poorly that its license was revoked and a new public water company was created.[11]

SILVIA RIVERA CUSICANQUI, SOCIOLOGIST AND ACTIVIST[12]

Just having Evo elected president allowed indigenous people to see themselves mirrored proudly every day. This has had an immeasurable impact on self-esteem, as it allows many people who previously were ashamed to be Indians to lift their heads for the first time. And for many acculturated Indians, Evo's election has inspired them to recover their heritage. This is an important ideological and cultural symbolic decolonization that without a doubt will have important future effects, particularly for children.

Nonetheless, the MAS inherited a series of paradoxes. One is the absolute attraction and fascination that power holds for middle-class intellectuals and mestizos, many of whom have historically carried out ideological pirouettes of all kinds in order to have it. While everyone from previous governments is discredited, certain mestizo sectors retain considerable influence through NGOs and universities. The MAS has tended to recruit these people for the state apparatus, and in the process has progressively lost its indigenous profile.

In addition, the MAS faced a structural inertia within the colonial and neo-colonial state. For example, the United States has superimposed its imperatives by investing a great deal in developing state management capacity, not only in the ministries involved in coca, but also in a good part of the Justice Ministry. Considerable penetration has also occurred through the USDA Foreign Agricultural Service's P.L. 480 food donation financing. This created a structural dependency on U.S. mandates. The MAS commitment to recovering Bolivia's sovereignty has had to deal not only with this colonial state structure but also with an entrenched unionized government bureaucracy that is difficult to dislodge.

Another challenge is the system of job spoils, which degrades citizenship through providing benefits to party loyalists and fostering clientelist relationships. This predominantly masculine inheritance facilitates the subordination of peasant and indigenous citizens and persists despite there being an indigenous president. This is the dead weight the MAS inherited in terms of political culture, and it reflects patriarchal authoritarianism, vertical subordination, and a lack of transparency. So there has been a dynamic of continuity with past neoliberal governments, along with efforts to bring change.

To date there has been no reconceptualization of citizenship that prioritizes the collective rather than the individual. However, the formal recognition of traditional forms of organization can prove beneficial for indigenous peoples. Most attention so far has been focused on how to incorporate community justice and turn jurisdiction over to indigenous communities. But in places where indigenous articulation is more precarious, such as urban areas, this model is less viable.

Pressure from the Left: The October Agenda

At a December 2011 meeting to formulate an agenda for the remainder of his second term, President Morales was triumphant: "We have completed the October Agenda with gas nationalization, a new constitution, and our efforts to bring Goni and his ministers to trial." His statement caused an uproar among independent social movement leaders. "Important advances have been made," retorted Roberto de la Cruz, one of the 2003 Gas War organizers, "but the October Agenda is still very much alive, and until it is fulfilled, nothing will replace it."[13]

More than in any other Latin American country with a progressive government, placating the social movements he considers himself part of is critical to Morales's hold on office. Just one hundred days after his inauguration, surrounded by soldiers and banners proclaiming "Property of all Bolivians," Evo chose the massive Margarita gas field in the southeastern Chaco to publicize a hydrocarbons nationalization decree. Thousands gathered in La Paz for International Workers' Day on May 1 roared their approval, and the government worked the "first nationalization of the twenty-first century" for all the political mileage possible.[14] "The sacking of our natural resources by international petroleum companies is over," Evo proclaimed jubilantly.[15] His approval rating shot up to 81 percent overnight.[16]

Morales was drawing on a widely held Latin American conviction that nationalization of natural resources is critical to public dignity and the answer to many economic ills. This tradition is particularly strong in resource-rich Bolivia, which was the region's first country to nationalize oil and gas when it seized Standard Oil in 1937. (Mexico quickly followed suit in 1938.) Evo's 2006 move was echoed by other leftist governments: Venezuela expropriated Exxon-Mobil and Conoco-Phillips holdings in 2007, Ecuador tightened rules for foreign energy firms in 2012, and Argentina nationalized the Spanish firm Repsol in the same year.

Despite the posturing, in fact the May Day decree was far from nationalization in the classic sense. No assets were expropriated and no companies expelled. Instead, Morales forced private firms to either negotiate new contracts or abandon the country. Royalties jumped to 50 percent, one of the region's highest, and combined with other corporate income taxes, the total government take shot up to about 70 percent of production, with hydrocarbons financing most government initiatives, much as oil income does in Venezuela.

Suddenly the Bolivian State Oilfields Company, YPFB,[17] found itself immersed in all stages of production and commercialization. This was no small challenge, as the 1990s privatization had whittled down the enterprise that once accounted for almost half of state revenues to about two hundred people.[18] Turmoil in 2003 combined with inadequate pipeline capacity had dampened private investment, and by 2006, Bolivia was scrambling, as it had to almost double daily production and expand pipelines to honor gas commitments to Brazil and Argentina.[19]

Vociferous protest to Morales's pronouncement from multinational corporations and northern governments, backed by international media, was swift. Both Brazil's public-private partnership, Petrobras, and Repsol threatened to suspend future investments. Brazilian president Lula da Silva intervened, and by February 2007, Petrobras had reluctantly conceded to higher gas charges. Months later, it announced US$900 million in new investments. Repsol capitulated as well and, two years later, relinquished majority ownership in its subsidiary Andina to YPFB. All in all, about twenty-five foreign firms were affected, including BP and BG from the United Kingdom, ExxonMobil from the United States, and Total from France. Almost half negotiated new agreements, although, like Repsol, they were cautious about expanding investments.[20]

Many social movements were furious that the state did not expropriate the private holdings, without giving much thought to how to finance development of gas reserves. Rufo Calle, of the CSUTCB, was blunt, "There's never been any nationalization of hydrocarbons; there's only been a new agreement with the multinational corporations."[21]

Political and social upheaval often heralds new constitutions, which are rewritten on average worldwide every nineteen years. The 1982 Canadian Charter of Rights and Freedoms has replaced the U.S. Constitution as the preferred prototype, as the latter has come to be seen as insufficiently expansive and too absolute.[22]

Bolivia is no different from countries as diverse as Egypt, Venezuela, Nepal, and Ecuador, which have all recently organized constituent assemblies. In Ecuador and Bolivia, the process of crafting a new constitution differs significantly from similar efforts in Peru and Colombia, as working-class, women's, poor, and minority participation has been prioritized, in essence seeking a revolution through a constitutional rather than armed struggle.[23]

Bolivia has been better at writing constitutions—seventeen at last count plus five constitutional reforms since 1826—than living by them.[24] Nineteenth-century General Melgarejo made clear what most rulers thought: at a lavish La Paz banquet, he stuffed the 1861 Constitution in one pocket and its 1868 replacement in the other, leaving little doubt that he ruled according to his whims alone.[25]

The most recent effort has its origins in demands formulated during the 1990 March for Dignity and Territory by lowland indigenous peoples. Other movements quickly took up the call.[26] A neoliberal constitutional reform in 1994 attempted to dilute these claims when it decreed significant formal gains for indigenous peoples through a "postmodern, multicultural and pluriethnic"[27] state with a market-directed economy. In practice, however, little changed.[28]

The March 2006 congressional consensus to convene the Constituent Assembly specified that electoral slates would alternate women and men, a measure that was effective in ensuring more female participation. However, ethnic minorities lost their call for representation by social sector rather than geography, and the MAS failed to achieve delegate allocation based on their favored winner-take-all formula. Once the votes were tallied, MAS had 134 of 255 seats, short of the two-thirds necessary to control the convention.[29]

The Constituent Assembly that convened in Sucre in August 2006 was the most representative body Bolivians had ever seen. For the first time, women in *polleras*, traditional broad pleated skirts,[30] and long braids sat as equals beside white men in business suits, and an indigenous woman, Silvia Lazarte, was elected Assembly President. "The Constituent Assembly is the most exciting and most important thing I have ever been involved in," says longtime Chiquitano-Guaraní organizer Marisol Solano.[31] The proceeding was boisterous and unruly: seven months were spent wrangling about voting procedures, but finally the Assembly drafted a broad and ambitious document that encompassed articles from forbidding water privatization to prohibiting foreign military bases.

In contrast to the U.S. Constitution, which was written in secret, Bolivia's effort more closely resembled Brazil's 1988 process, which entailed widespread participation by neighborhood organizations.[32] Public meetings took place in every department, and twenty-one committees convened to formulate the text. "The size of the Assembly was unwieldy—

at some points there were as many as fifteen hundred people involved," explains Raúl Prada Alcoreza, an Assembly representative and university professor, "and the right wing did everything possible to prevent any real reinvention of the country."[33] Conservative delegates insisted on two-thirds approval for each article, stalling proceedings until March 2007.[34]

Some months into the convention, a highly divisive crisis erupted. Drawing on a deep-seated conviction that the 1899 transfer of the capital to La Paz had slowed Sucre's economic growth, a conservative delegate demanded reconsideration of the decision. The appeal was embraced by a hastily formed right-wing Inter-Institutional Committee in Sucre that found in it a useful device to block the proceedings.[35]

Violent protests ground the Assembly to a halt for over a month. "Sucre turned into a battleground," remembers Raúl Prada, who was assaulted by a mob.[36] By late November 2007, three people were dead and two hundred had been wounded. Fears for Assembly representatives' safety precipitated a move to a nearby military facility. Then the conservative opposition, led by the party Podemos, announced a boycott and stormed out. When a draft was approved in highland Oruro without their participation, another round of clashes resulted in three more deaths and the right denouncing the proposed constitution as illegal and invalid.[37] The subsequent reconciliation in Congress triggered further and substantial compromises, weakening land redistribution, environmental controls, and indigenous rights.[38] "The constitution is simply not the groundbreaking and foundational document the Assembly wrote at considerable personal sacrifice," regrets sociologist Óscar Vega.[39]

The entire procedure was so fraught that it eroded MAS authority and menaced political stability. Nonetheless, when the document was finally put to a national vote in January 2009, 61 percent approved it.[40] The remarkable text, with close parallels to the new constitutions adopted by Venezuela in 1999 and Ecuador in 2008, describes Bolivia as a plurinational state with substantive degrees of indigenous autonomy and an indigenous quota in legislative bodies.[41] However, as anthropologist Robert Albro notes, the final document has a homogenizing impact, as it explicitly favors rural Aymara communitarian values more than those of other ethnic groups and urban indigenous people.[42]

Collective and state rights are privileged over those of private capital, indigenous land rights are more substantial than in Ecuador's 2008 Constitution,[43] and national investors are favored over international financiers in a mixed public-private economy.[44] Coca is protected as part of the country's cultural patrimony, judicial pluralism is guaranteed, and equal rights are assured for all religious faiths. Access to water and sewage systems are deemed a human right, and land redistribution is mandatory.[45] Two powerful institutions saw their privileges curtailed: the Roman Catholic Church lost its special status, and members of Congress forfeited immunity from criminal prosecution.[46]

Bolivia is now plurinational, not simply in terms of cultural diversity but also in its acceptance of varying values, cultural organizational forms, and worldviews. Depicting indigenous groups as separate nations within the broader state, each with substantive rights to consultation, autonomy, and self-determination, turns the idea of the nation on its head, upsetting long-standing notions of race, identity, and territory.[47]

With 411 articles, the new constitution's spirit is exemplified by two of them. Article 102 states that "the cosmovisions, myths, oral history, dances, cultural practices, knowledge, and traditional technologies are patrimony of the nations and communities of indigenous, original agricultural peoples, and form part of the expression and identity of the State." Article 306 articulates that the government "has the well-being of all human beings as its primary value, and will ensure equitable redistribution of wealth through social policies, health, education, and culture. The economic model . . . is designed to improve the quality of life, and 'living well' of all Bolivians."[48]

Social control is mentioned eighteen times within articles that allow oversight of government spending and policy, as well as public contracts with private companies.[49] Building on the 1994 Law of Popular Participation's (LPP) Oversight Committees,[50] social control is centered on a largely essentialized understanding of indigenous community structures mingled with a socialist discourse that derives from largely unsuccessful 1950s attempts by the COB to introduce cogovernment and worker control.[51] The Law of Participation and Social Control, which spelled out in detail how citizen oversight is to be applied, passed in 2013.[52] With a particular emphasis on battling rent-seeking by public officials, the concept has made an appearance in areas as diverse as ensuring health program quality and limiting coca cultivation.

Much of the constitution reads like a laundry list rather than a unified document, and it lacks a clear path to move from rhetoric to practice. On the one hand, it promises protection for the environment, and on the other, prioritizes the long-standing dream of industrializing natural resources. It establishes overlapping departmental, municipal, provincial, and indigenous autonomies, creating confusion, for it fails to define the powers of each level of government and specify in what matters each takes precedence.[53]

Just as in Venezuela's and Ecuador's constitutional assemblies, accusations flew by both the right and the left that Evo and the MAS appropriated the Assembly for their own ends. "We had the MAS trying to dictate what we did," complained Raúl Prada. "They were afraid of a real participatory process outside their control."[54] In Ecuador, indigenous movements, upset that Correa's calling of a constituent assembly hijacked what was historically part of their agenda, reluctantly supported the new constitution's approval, as it brought substantial, although incomplete, improvements in their rights.[55] Liberal critics have raised concerns that all three constitutions privilege direct over representative democracy, concentrate power in the executive, and undercut customary checks and balances, reflecting the long-standing tensions between liberal constitutionalism and popular democracy.[56] Chiquitano leader José Bailaba identifies a different problem: "The MAS's greatest accomplishment was the constitution," he says. "Its greatest failure has been its inability to carry it out."[57]

The most emotionally charged aspects of the October Agenda are the demands for an end to impunity and a call for extradition of Gonzalo Sánchez de Lozada (Goni), one of Bolivia's richest men, and nine of his government ministers for human rights violations during the 2003 Gas War. Their decision to unleash troops on unarmed protesters led to the deaths of 68 people and the wounding of about 470. So potent are the demands to hold him accountable that Evo joked to Assistant Secretary of State for Western Hemisphere Affairs Thomas Shannon in August 2008, "If you send back Goni, you will be made mayor of El Alto."[58]

Today Goni lives in a wealthy suburb just outside Washington, DC, and others of his ex-ministers live in Miami, Spain, and Peru. Bolivia, which signed an extradition treaty in 1995 largely so the United States could pursue drug traffickers, has repeatedly petitioned U.S. authorities to return Goni and two of his former ministers to face charges. The U.S. government rebuffed these requests on September 6, 2012, arguing that the extradition treaty contains a clause barring expulsion on "political" grounds. They maintain that Bolivia's petitions lack evidence that Goni in fact ordered the murder of civilians.[59]

VICKY AILLÓN PREPARED THE INITIAL CASE FOR BOLIVIA.[60]

I spent two weeks in El Alto during the October 2003 uprising, and what I saw affected me deeply. Fighting for Goni's extradition was one of the most important things I have ever done. But the U.S. government, through the Department of State and the Embassy, blocked us at every turn by insisting on approved translators, who turned out to be completely incompetent, and on minuscule details of formatting and presentation. When we finally got the documents accepted, we discovered just how powerful Goni is. Because he is closely connected to high levels of the Democratic Party and the Obama administration, chances were slim that we could ever succeed.

At the same time, in Sucre, the case against Goni and his ministers, and some members of the military, crept along, finally reaching a unanimous verdict in August 2011 that saw two ex-ministers and five military commanders imprisoned.[61] With tears in his eyes, the head of the families' association, Patricio Quispe, was tempered in his comments, "It was not what we asked for, but we think it is an important step. We have fulfilled our responsibilities to our dead family members, and the sentence sets an example, so that no government will ever again feel it has the right to murder its own citizens."[62]

In the United States, a team including lawyers from Harvard Law School, Stanford's International Human Rights and Conflict Resolution Center, the Center for Constitutional Rights, and private firms won an important ruling in 2009 from the U.S. District Court in Southern Florida that the victims of October 2003 have a viable civil claim. "It's a powerful example of how international law is making it harder to escape accountability simply by fleeing to another country," said Stanford's James Cavallaro.[63] The victory was only temporary however: in May 2011, the ruling was reversed on appeal. But the lawyers have not given up and, in 2013, submitted a new civil suit.

The Right Rebels: The Threat from the East

It took little time for the right wing centered in the eastern city of Santa Cruz to regroup around long-standing demands for regional autonomy. Bolivia's central, unitary state structure has always hampered effective government.[64] Echoing previous violent struggles that swung late

nineteenth-century political power from the Sucre-based silver ruling class to the tin elite in La Paz, as its economic star rose, Santa Cruz insisted on greater influence and independence.

With a stranglehold over local politics, media, and business, and never able or apparently interested in effectively articulating a national project, Santa Cruz's oligarchy claims to represent the entire *media luna* (half-moon, because of its crescent shape), as Santa Cruz, Beni, Tarija, and Pando, the four lowland departments that curve northwest around the Andes, are known.[65] While these four departments' criticism of ineffective and unresponsive national governments serves to divert attention from inequalities closer to home, the regional passion for autonomy has also led some *media luna* residents to no longer see themselves as Bolivians but rather as *cambas* (lowlanders) or Cruceños (from Santa Cruz).[66]

Similar to right-wing discourse throughout Latin America and elsewhere,[67] Santa Cruz's elite storyline is that light-skinned easterners are economically more dynamic than residents of the more indigenous highlands. Racial superiority is nowhere more spectacularly performed than by the "Magnificent Ones, "las Magníficas," long-legged beauty queens of European origin. The most infamous, the 2004 Miss Bolivia, Gabriela Ovieda, blurted out at a Miss Universe contest, "Unfortunately, people who don't know Bolivia think that we are all just . . . poor, very short Indian people."[68]

With Evo's election, Bolivian elites abruptly found themselves cut off from the access to government and military they usually enjoyed.[69] In coup-prone Bolivia, as in the rest of Latin America, democratically elected governments ignore the military at their peril. The threat is far from idle: in Venezuela, opponents of democratically elected Hugo Chávez engineered a short-lived military coup d'état in 2002. Military right-wingers also toppled democratically elected left-leaning Manuel Zelaya in Honduras in 2009 and Paraguay's Fernando Lugo in 2012. In Bolivia, the armed forces pledged their support to Morales early on, their fiercely nationalistic bent assuaged by Evo's commitment to nationalize natural gas. Evo boldly pressed his advantage to bring about the greatest changes in the military since the 1952 revolution, although his government has avoided bringing cases against the military for human rights abuses committed during the dictatorships between 1964 and 1982.[70] He effectively cut out the old command and authorized indigenous officer training for the first time.[71] This overhaul intensified in 2011 when he appointed a young lawyer, Cecilia Chacón, minister of defense. Chacón recalls:

The president wanted to send a clear signal that the armed forces world-view that focused on quarrels with neighbors and repression of its own people had to change. We agreed that a new antiracist and antisexist military doctrine must prioritize food security, facilitate access to health, and prepare for emergencies. Our conscripts should be granted the opportunity to extend their education, as well as build awareness of the rights and responsibilities of citizenship.[72]

Unable to count on the military, Santa Cruz's right wing instead turned to the type of paramilitary backup that Latin American elites have long relied on. "They used fear to motivate people, saying that Evo Morales would destroy our way of life, that there would be no private companies, and everything would be run by the state with racial violence toward whites," recalls sociologist and Minister of Autonomy Claudia Peña.[73]

The new Andean-oriented government had little grasp of what drives the east. Peña notes, "Particularly at the beginning, Evo's government was ignorant about the power behind Santa Cruz and how the dominant classes maintain their position. They just didn't understand how strong the regionalist discourse resonates with everyone—rich and poor alike."[74] Attributing autonomy demands solely to elites misread the region's significant working-class and indigenous population, who not only backed the MAS but also value greater autonomy.

The 2005 elections were the first for direct selection of prefects,[75] the top departmental official, roughly equivalent to a state governor or provincial premier. Conservatives claimed victory in the eastern departments, as well as Cochabamba and La Paz. With no guidelines in place to regulate their relationship to the central government, the new prefects consistently acted as independent agents, and the tripling of departmental revenues from skyrocketing gas income after 2005 served to further embolden them.[76]

The separatist rallying cry alarmed gas-dependent Brazil and Argentina, but it proved more bluff than real threat.[77] Rather, the eastern elites embraced tactics reminiscent of Chilean upper-class efforts to destabilize democratically elected socialist Salvador Allende in the early 1970s: large-scale farmers refused to ship agricultural produce west to Andean cities, instead channeling them to the black market.[78] "Morales is trying to turn us into Cuba," María Julia Gutiérrez, president of the conservative women's branch of the Pro–Santa Cruz Civic Committee, asserted, "and we know how people live in Cuba, the misery they suffer. He is trying to impose a communism driven by that man from Venezuela, Mr. Hugo Chávez."[79]

The government agreed to an autonomy referendum in July 2006. Predictably, all four eastern departments voted overwhelmingly in favor, while the western departments came out almost as strongly against. In December 2007, an estimated one million people—one in ten Bolivians—rallied for autonomy in downtown Santa Cruz. By May, locally organized referendums won there as well as in Tarija, Beni, and Pando, despite high abstention, a National Electoral Court ruling forbidding the vote, and general international disapproval. Offers to mediate by the Organization of American States (OAS) were dismissed by the right wing.[80] In an attempt to turn the demands to their advantage, the Morales government pushed for extending autonomy to poorer outlying regions within departments, which unsettled landowning elites accustomed to almost feudal control.

Suddenly, deeply entrenched racism erupted to the surface. Control over indigenous people had never before included mob attacks. That changed in 2007 on a dry, sunny January day as middle- and upper-class Cochabambinos[81] wielding baseball bats and golf clubs fought coca growers and peasants armed with sticks and machetes. The MAS had convoked Chapare coca farmers to occupy central Cochabamba to pressure for the resignation of right-wing prefect Manfred Reyes, who was mounting an increasingly belligerent challenge to the government. Reyes responded by urging his supporters out into the street to "protect" the city against an Indian takeover.[82]

"My younger brother started spewing all this racist nonsense I had never heard from him before about how he had to defend the city," explained one resident.[83] Three people died in a confrontation that profoundly shook the country. "The wounds are open . . . and it will be a long time before they heal," said another Cochabambino.[84] The MAS's failure to intervene and the common perception that the government had mishandled the situation did little to inspire confidence.

Racist-inspired misinformation spread like wildfire among the minority white population long fearful that someday Indians would murder them in their sleep. Graffiti such as "Evo = ignorant Indian" was scrawled across walls in wealthier neighborhoods. "Evo shouldn't be president because he's coarse and uneducated," declared Julio, a light-skinned Santa Cruz taxi driver, in a thinly disguised allusion to Evo's indigenous heritage.[85]

Then in May 2008, Sucre students and townspeople demanding their city's restoration as the country's capital began hurling rocks to protest Evo's presence in the city. Protesters grabbed about eighteen indigenous Morales supporters, punching, kicking, and hurling racial insults. The men were stripped to the waist, forced to kneel, and verbally abused. In César Brie's powerful video that documents the attacks, what is striking is that the aggressors appear to be the same racial phenotype as those they are attacking—but differently dressed and better fed.[86]

At the rebellion's height in mid-2008, Branko Gora Marinkovic, son of Croatian immigrants, a cattle rancher and cooking oil magnate who controlled 88,000 acres of land, headed the Pro–Santa Cruz Civic Committee.[87] "Branko is a visionary leader standing up to the dictatorship of the altiplano," declared Juan del Mar Paz, a member of the paramilitary group the Santa Cruz Youth Union.[88] As anthropologist Bret Gustafson notes, the Marinkovics accumulate and display their wealth Cruceño style: acquiring land during military regimes, growing businesses thanks to government credits and subsidies, marrying former beauty queens, and sending their children to U.S. universities. Though the regionalist discourse is constructed around carefully crafted notions of local uniqueness, in reality Santa Cruz is closely linked with circuits of global capital.[89]

As rumors of arms caches created even more apprehension, right-wing mobs in central Santa Cruz attacked people who looked indigenous. "They don't dare come here because we will defend our neighborhood with sticks and stones," said Margarita Salinas of Plan 3000, a sprawling low-income neighborhood largely populated by indigenous highland migrants.[90]

To break the growing impasse, the MAS administration took a significant political risk, agreeing to a referendum in August 2008 to determine public approval for the president, the vice president, and departmental prefects. The opposition-controlled Senate endorsed the proposal without much thought, which divided the right, as prefects elected by slim margins were petrified that the vote could force them from office. When Evo and Álvaro won a resounding 67 percent victory, a jubilant La Paz crowd filled the main square, waving the national flag alongside the *wiphala*. Lawyer René Vásquez was exuberant, "Evo is making changes, changes that no one made before."[91] Unsurprisingly, Evo lost the vote in the eastern departments, and several right-wing prefects were reaffirmed by margins as high as or even higher than Morales's. His victory speech was reconciliatory, "The vote was to unite the country. We respect the legitimacy of the ratified prefects. I call on them to work together."[92]

The right wing remained defiant. Santa Cruz prefect Rubén Costas quickly organized a civic strike to demand that the Direct Hydrocarbons Tax (IDH), slated to fund a small universal old-age payment, be transferred to the regions, a claim taken up by Tarija.[93] "We won't give in. The government must return the IDH and accept our autonomy. Nor will we allow the imposition of a racist and communist constitution," threatened Tarija civic committee president Reynaldo Bayard.[94]

Right-wing mobs sacked and burned government buildings, attacking indigenous people and left-leaning nongovernmental organizations along the way.[95] On September 10, 2008, they attempted to invade Plan 3000, where they met fierce local resistance. "The Youth Union came to intimidate, humiliate, and beat humble people. We had reached our limit, and we stopped them," declared a local activist.[96] Just before the strike, U.S. Ambassador Philip Goldberg met with Prefect Costas, who subsequently ordered an "official" takeover of national government offices in the region.[97] When it was revealed that USAID's Office of Transition Initiatives had funded opposition departmental governments to the tune of $4.5 million, both the MAS administration and much of the public were incensed.[98]

Goldberg was expelled on September 10, 2008, for having "conspired against democracy and Bolivia."[99] U.S. reprisal was swift: Ambassador Gustavo Guzmán was ejected from Bolivia's grand but tumbledown embassy on Washington's Embassy Row. President Hugo Chávez recalled his own ambassador, expelling U.S. Ambassador Patrick Duddy and telling him to "go to hell one hundred times."[100]

A day after Goldberg left, the tide turned in the MAS's favor. Another racist attack, this time in remote northern Pando, was captured on video, horrifying most Bolivians. The footage showed hundreds of peasants, largely highland immigrants, confronting roadblocks on their way to a department-wide assembly. During their struggle to push through, two people were killed. Armed locals awaited them farther down the road. A woman off-screen shouts "We don't want you here."[101] Seconds later, shooting starts—and intensifies as the marchers scatter. By the end, seventeen peasants were dead, some as they tried to swim across a stream, others as they ran for their lives while being hunted down. Another fifty wounded people were allegedly beaten on the way to the hospital.[102] "They killed us like pigs, like dogs," recounted a bandaged survivor, "I was not seen as a person in that moment, I was treated like a beast."[103]

The timing could not have been worse for the right wing. Goldberg's expulsion and the Pando massacre on the thirty-fifth anniversary of Salvador Allende's overthrow created a potent image linking what Morales was enduring to Chile's tragedy. The Morales government declared a state of siege and arrested Governor Leopoldo Fernández, charging him with terrorism, murder, and conspiracy. Racist violence had ultimately proven counterproductive to the right's agenda.[104] Most importantly, it failed to halt the determination of the peasant movements. A survivor of the Pando massacre was resolute, "We are still on our feet, because we are carrying out the total reconstruction of our country."[105]

VICE PRESIDENT ÁLVARO GARCÍA LINERA[106]

It is always extremely dangerous to revel in any victory over the right. They are more than capable of regrouping, seizing power, and reimposing their agenda. After they were weakened by our 2005 victory, we were initially pretty successful in avoiding confrontations. That changed dramatically toward the end of 2006 when we began to threaten their privileges by mobilizing to break up their huge landholdings. They latched onto regional autonomy, which stems from long-standing and legitimate demands, but distorted it to convince people to support their attempts to destroy our popularly elected government.

At first, we responded rather passively, believing that they would trip themselves up, which is, in fact, exactly what happened. Their initial misstep was the recall referendum they demanded for the president, vice president, and departmental prefects in August 2008—which we agreed to. Then the massacre of indigenous marchers in Pando meant they lost most of their remaining support. This was what I call a point of bifurcation—a moment where a political situation comes to a head and significantly changes the future course, much as it did in another September, that of 1986, when 15,000 miners were forced to turn back before they reached La Paz because the government deployed a huge number of military to block their way. Both cases, one a victory for the right that marked the defeat of state capitalism by neoliberalism and the other a decisive loss, involved not the deployment of the state's monopoly on coercion but rather the threat of force. In 2008, we seized the opportunity of the recall referendum to retake the initiative and demonstrated clearly to the right that we were willing to take aggressive action against them. We learned the hard way that you cannot leave your enemies only half-defeated.

A Second Term

The MAS handily won the December 2009 elections by the largest margin since the 1982 return to civilian rule, capturing 64 percent of the vote, 8 percent higher than in 2005. An unprecedented number of indigenous candidates stood for office, and voter participation reached 90 percent. Indigenous candidate Fidel Surco declared the process of change irreversible, "There is no way back, this is our time, the awakening of indigenous people. We'll keep fighting till the end. Brother Evo Morales still has lots to do, and four years are not enough after 500 years of submission and oppression."[107]

Ex-Cochabamba prefect and conservative Manfred Reyes came in a distant second with 27 percent, while cement magnate Samuel Doria Medina only captured 6 percent, reflecting the ongoing divisions on the right. The MAS also won a two-thirds majority in both the Chamber of Deputies and the Senate.[108]

As their power slipped, eastern elites shifted attention to regional and municipal politics, just as the left had done after structural adjustment decimated the COB.[109] The April 2010 municipal and departmental elections registered a record level of voter participation, with the MAS victorious in six governors' elections and the opposition predictably triumphing in Santa Cruz, Beni, and Tarija. While the MAS won 228 of the country's 337 municipalities, it only won three departmental capitals. The left-leaning MSM won municipal races in La Paz and Oruro.[110] Indicating a gradual breakdown of spatial polarization, the MAS won a handful of eastern mayoral races, although these were in indigenous-majority municipalities.

As the right-wing threat dissipated, dissent within the MAS's diverse coalition grew. Nineteen days of violent protests exploded in August 2010 in impoverished southern Potosí, driven by frustration over government failure to invest in infrastructure and create jobs. By the time the upheaval was over, protests had cost an estimated US$2.5 million a day in lost mineral production and ground tourism to a halt at the height of the season. In a city where roughly 80 percent voted for MAS in 2009, over 60 percent of the population occupied the streets until the government capitulated.[111]

A few months later, when the Morales administration attempted the tried-and-true tactic of slipping in an unpopular measure during the extended Christmas holiday, they suddenly had their gravest crisis to date on their hands. On December 26, 2010, they cut gasoline and diesel subsidies. Those who benefited the most from the subvention were large-scale eastern agro-industries, followed by trucking companies and smugglers who doubled the price of the below-market fuel when they resold it in neighboring countries. By 2012, the subsidy was costing the government about US$1 billion, more than all social stipends and pensions combined.[112]

The effort to rein in the allowance, however, caused fuel prices and transportation costs to spike by as much as 73 percent. People surged into the streets in protest. Morales apologized and reversed the measure, reiterating that he only "ruled by obeying."[113] Once again, protest movements proved themselves masters at limiting government policy options.

In September 2011, Bolivia was on the move again. "I haven't been marching in the streets like this since the 2003 Gas War," one marcher tells us as we huddle with other demonstrators against the nightly chill in La Paz's Plaza San Francisco, the city's largest gathering space.[114] Thousands of young middle- and upper-middle-class Paceños[115] crowd around a stage while Atajo, the rock group that was once a darling of the MAS, belted out tunes calling for power to the people.

The issue was the construction of a road to connect the Beni with Cochabamba, 32 miles of which would cut through the Isiboro Sécure National Park and Indigenous Territory (TIPNIS), the 5.5-million-acre lowland forest that straddles the Cochabamba and Beni Departments northeast of La Paz.[116] The government sought the road to better integrate the inaccessible Amazon departments of Beni and Pando as well as to facilitate hydrocarbons exploration, which Vice President García Linera calls essential to balance the country's lopsided dependence on natural gas in the Chaco.[117]

The proposed thoroughfare has been a long-standing Beni demand and in the works decades before the 1990 founding of the TIPNIS. Bolivia's paved highways can be counted on one hand, and a direct road from Trinidad to Cochabamba reduces travel distance by half compared to the journey via Santa Cruz. The project would benefit Beni's cattle ranchers, reducing the control of the Santa Cruz meatpacking industry. This could increase support for the government in the conservative region, where MAS has been gaining steadily in recent elections.

Improved roads, however, also open tropical areas to logging and expansion of the agricultural frontier by highlanders, which has been a continuing source of local conflict since the 1980s coca boom.[118] A border limiting agricultural expansion was agreed to by coca growers and local indigenous peoples when the TIPNIS was founded, yet by 2010, about 20,000 settlers, mostly coca producers, lived in the park.[119]

"Nearly all the alternative routes connecting the lowland northeast with the west traverse a territory already titled to indigenous peoples," explains consultant Rafael Rojas, who has worked in the TIPNIS. "The Amazon's richest land is where the Andes meet the plains, and this has made the area particularly attractive to highland colonizers for decades, creating a dilemma for the government as they balance the rights of an indigenous minority against the perceived needs of 'intercultural' colonizers and coca producers, who form a central pillar of MAS support."[120]

Some 800 of the approximately 12,000 indigenous Moxeños, Yucarés, and Tsimanés (also know as Chimanés) who call the TIPNIS home set off in August 2011 to march 375 miles up steep mountainsides to La Paz to protest the lack of prior consultation on road construction as required by the 2009 Constitution and the 2007 UN Declaration of the Rights of Indigenous Peoples. In Yacuma, the project's supporters blocked their route, and, on September 25, five hundred police forcibly removed the protesters, wounding seventy and, according to the independent Human Rights ombudsman, violating their human rights. Feelings ran so high that two government ministers and other top officials resigned in protest.[121] Morales apologized for the use of force, begged for forgiveness, and let the march resume. He promised to negotiate a settlement, while accusing the right wing and the United States of subsidizing the marchers in an effort to destabilize the government.

As bedraggled protesters filed into La Paz on October 12, 2011, international Indigenous People's Day, thousands lined the streets to cheer them on. One longtime MAS supporter was visibly upset: "It's unbelievable how bad the government has screwed this up. Everybody marching now voted for them in 2009. All this year Evo has made one mistake after another and blown an incredible amount of political support."[122]

On October 24, in an apparent about-turn, the MAS passed Law 180 prohibiting further road construction. However, the law also banned any economic activity in the park, effectively barring local inhabitants from continuing customary hunting and ecotourism. Road supporters were furious and threatened to cut a path through the TIPNIS in order to guarantee its completion. The dispute raged on as demonstrations broke out both for and against, including a pro-road march to La Paz, backed by the government. A consultation process mandated by the MAS in February 2012 was rejected by many indigenous communities, as it was seen as after-the-fact. Indigenous leaders complained that the government was trying to buy them off with handouts, such as outboard motors. The march's principal organizer, CIDOB, along with CONAMAQ, withdrew from the Unity Pact in protest. In the bitter struggle that ensued, leaders who supported the government plan attempted to take control of CIDOB. By 2013, CIDOB had split in two.

Increasingly desperate indigenous communities set off on another much smaller march in April 2012, but despite continued public support, particularly from the middle class, they limped back to their communities empty-handed in mid-July. By August, the government had launched its highly contested consultative process, which linked continued construction with provision of services such as health and education. The northernmost TIPNIS communities still fiercely opposed the road, some even blocking government access to their communities. Human rights ombudsman Rolando Villeno declared that "the consultation process may be legal, but it lacks legitimacy."[123]

When the results were announced, the government declared that 55 of 69 TIPNIS communities had agreed to the road. The government has pledged to build an ecological highway with both elevated and underground sections to minimize negative environmental impacts. Morales has also postponed any construction through the TIPNIS itself until after the 2014 election.

The Morales government is not alone in confronting the complex standoff between the two differing visions of economic development the disagreement represents. In early 2009, a new mining law was passed in Ecuador that grants prospecting without prior community consultation, prioritizes private company rights over collective and ancestral ones, and criminalizes those who disrupt mining operations. All these provisions appear to violate Ecuador's 2008 Constitution.[124]

In June 2012, Bolivia was rocked again—this time by a mutiny provoked by government efforts to reform the national police, widely recognized as one of the most corrupt public institutions.[125] Crime and insecurity have become primary concerns, reflecting a trend throughout Latin America, where lackluster police performance, unabashed corruption, and widespread impunity have emboldened criminal activity and violence, which have steadily increased since the 1980s. Bolivia's poorly trained police stand accused of crimes from moving drugs and extortion to kidnapping and robbery.

Low-income urban barrios suffer the worst from crime, police incompetence, and abuse, which contribute to residents' widespread feelings of powerlessness and insecurity. The police often demand payment for services, which makes the poor particularly reluctant to call for help. Often when they do, their calls go unanswered, or a response is promised that is not forthcoming. Even if they surmount these hurdles, the complex, costly, and dysfunctional court system stymies efforts to achieve justice. As a consequence, some residents of poor barrios have taken the law into their own hands.

MAS efforts at reform have never questioned existing neoliberal assumptions about citizen security favored by the police and military such as relying on a strictly punitive approach.[126] Nonetheless, the 2012 reform effort quickly led to death threats against the women leading the Ministry of Institutional Transparency and the Fight against Corruption who had spearheaded the government effort. During the June 2012 riots, police demanded a salary hike and rejected improved oversight. After breaking into their own offices and burning all outstanding disciplinary case records, the police circulated rumors of a coup. The government backed down, agreeing to modify the law and meet salary demands.

Across Latin America, police reform has made little progress under governments of either the left or right.[127] The only success has been in crime-plagued Venezuela, where the notoriously corrupt metropolitan police forces were brought under national control in 2011. Salaries were tripled, gun restrictions tightened, and police training shifted to a community-oriented model focused on crime prevention.[128]

Thrust to Power Too Soon?

The rollercoaster ride the MAS has taken since 2006 was exacerbated by inexperience, unrealistic expectations, and pent-up demands, creating a potent mix that often leaves the country teetering. Bolivians joke that the shift to a "plurinational" country means that now they are "pluriblockaded." The government's limited capacity in managing complex conflicts has led it to negotiate special deals with interest groups that often thwart its national agenda, undermine its credibility, and conflate social movement interests with those of the MAS. It has too frequently reverted to age-old forms of political deal making: clientelism, bullying, and centralizing power. The barriers to implementing change the MAS has faced are common not only to low- and middle-income countries but to any democratic society with powerful entrenched interests.

The 2010 disturbances in Potosí illustrate how the definitive defeat of the right enabled the tensions between the divergent forces in the MAS coalition to surface. As long as there was an identifiable, powerful enemy, as there was throughout Morales's first term, the government was able to keep its coalition strong. As the opposition faded, the second term became plagued by a tug-of-war between those who had supported Morales at the polls.

The TIPNIS clash fractured the MAS coalition and laid bare the contradictions between a vision of development based on continued extractive-resource-dependent growth and the protection of the Pacha-mama (Earth Mother). More fundamentally, it raises the question of what might be a viable alternative vision for a development that encompasses — and funds — the social programs, schools, health centers, roads, and job creation that social movements demand.

CHAPTER 4

"Reinventing" the State, Expanding Rights, and Navigating Dependency

The new government began debunking deeply held popular myths the moment Evo Morales became president. After five hundred years of domination by elites of European heritage, many Bolivians, indigenous or not, doubted that any First Nations person could successfully run the country. Evo and his indigenous allies, some of whom became ministers, were determined to prove them wrong. Just as in the 1994 election of South Africa's Nelson Mandela, the psychological impact of indigenous leadership, especially for Bolivia's majority, has been immeasurable.

In this chapter, we explore how the MAS's story is not just one of enormous challenges and considerable shortcomings; it's also about how the MAS as an antisystemic political movement attempted to reshape government itself. The newly elected MAS was confronted with the paradox of possessing no faith in governing institutions while having little choice but to rely on those same institutions in order to govern. The aim was to convert a historically fragile country built on a largely western liberal political culture into a "decolonized" one that embraced the traditions of the majority.[1] The first move in this ambitious agenda was installing social movement leaders in ministerial positions, a realignment not attempted by the region's other left governments and one that, in practice, has had mixed results both for governance and for social movements' ability to advance an independent agenda.[2]

Like its peers, the MAS faced three options in relating to social movements: work to co-opt them, incorporate them as partners, or keep them at a distance. More than any of the region's other governments, the MAS initially strove for partnership but steadily moved toward co-optation, arguably an inevitable tendency in the complex and highly contested terrain of building a political party.[3] Many of its initial appointees were hamstrung not only by the absence of educational and professional opportunities available to indigenous peoples and social movement leaders but also by the cold shoulder they got from bureaucrats.[4] Casimira Rodríguez, head of the domestic workers' union, was made justice minister. "I didn't receive support from the vice ministers and advisers who resented my lack of formal training. They couldn't get used to the idea of a maid being their boss."[5] A year later, Morales had switched almost half of his original cabinet. Indigenous representation dropped dramatically, their posts filled by middle-class left-wing politicians.[6] Rapid turnover turned out to be the norm: in the government's first three years, the minister of hydrocarbons was substituted annually and the state oil and gas company, YPFB, raced through five presidents. The price has been highly uneven ministry performance.

Decolonization

One of the MAS's most ambitious projects and a fundamental pillar framing its entire program is to undo the five-hundred-year legacy of subjugation brought by European conquest. "Colonization really had permeated all of the social structures of the state and the society at large," explains planner Alberto Borda. To address this, a Vice Ministry for Decolonization was set up in 2009 under the leadership of Aymara intellectual and activist Félix Cárdenas.[7]

Considerable confusion, however, has surrounded what the concept of decolonization means in practice. Anthropologist Xavier Albó worries, "If we are going to really advance on this front, we must come up with an agreed-upon definition."[8] Cárdenas promotes a vision that discards a romantic return to the past in favor of a recuperation of ancient epistemologies. "The task is to convert the state into an expression of our identity and our traditions," he states.[9] To this end, the vice ministry passed the 2010 Law against Racism and Discrimination, designated October 12 as National Day of Decolonization, and proposed a Law of Decolonization and Depatriarchalization—literally the dismantling of patriarchy—intended to reinvent institutions such as the armed forces and the police as well as policies such as those governing health and education. In 2010, a Unit of Depatriarchalization was added to the vice ministry because the two struggles were conceived as linked, particularly by indigenous women.[10] In most government discourse, patriarchy is constructed as a colonial inheritance that must be disassembled in order to achieve decolonization.[11]

When asked which postcolonial theorists from around the world most shape their approach, vice ministry employees in 2012 often stated that they had to forge their own path, based on local indigenous realities.[12] In practice, analyst Jenny Ibarnegaray Ortiz argues, scant discussion has occurred about the explicit impacts of colonialism on Andean cultures, including those generated by fourteenth-century Inka expansion. She is concerned that little understanding exists of how five hundred years of Spanish, and then Republican, domination has distorted the social order, and perceives the government as idealizing pre-Hispanic society, particularly that of the Andes.[13]

For Guaraní activist Marilyn Carayuri, decolonization is often perplexing:

> In some ways, the whole idea of decolonization comes from outside. It's not something we understand well, and we really don't know where to begin to address it. We find that what is being offered by the government is an increase in indigenous perspectives from the highlands rather than a focus on our own heroes and stories.[14]

Administrative Capacity

Undoubtedly, an Achilles heel of the MAS project is the inefficiency, disorganization, delays, and rent-seeking that have always been standard issue in Bolivia and typical of extraction-dependent governments.[15] Although it compromises institutional memory and bureaucratic efficiency, the MAS embraced a model of rotational service, following practices of rural unions and highland indigenous communities. "I see the government as the largest union and the communities as the smallest unions, and in each one you have the same principles for planning and executing projects," says former MAS vice president of the Legislative Assembly, Julia Ramos. "The village union organizes the community, and the government organizes the country."[16]

This rotational logic means that the 2002 contingent of MAS lawmakers by and large did not return to office in 2006, and only a handful of legislators were reelected in 2009. As a result, the delegation lacks the skills to function effectively. Newly elected deputies tend to cultivate personal rather than institutional relationships, much as they had as community leaders, which was evident whenever we visited government offices from the legislature to ministries. During Morales's first term, this inexperience plus opposition control of the Senate frustrated much of the MAS agenda, driving Morales to frequently resort to Presidential Decrees, which may be effective in pushing through desired policies but chip away at government legitimacy.

Failure to coordinate across ministries poses another serious obstacle. Alberto Borda, 2009 director of Planning, recounts, "We hoped to create a truly functional Environment Ministry from the three ministries involved because policies were incoherent. When we tried to move on this, turf wars erupted."[17] Ministry rivalries also stunted the National Alternative Development Fund's ability to execute coca policy.[18] "These types of disagreements directly undermine convincing farmers that adhering to government plans is in their interest," social control head Reynaldo Molina complained.[19]

Governments at all levels are further crippled because their restricted administrative capacity means they do not spend their budgeted allocations, a problem common in low-income countries.[20] But, ironically, ministries also lack adequate funding for staff. Alberto Borda recalls, "Almost everyone who worked with me in the Planning Ministry was a consultant, financed by foreign governments, not from our national treasury."[21]

DAVID ARUQUIPA, DIRECTOR OF CULTURAL PATRIMONY 2006–2010[22]

For four years, I saw close-up how the government functioned. Despite a solid ideological program, neoliberal hegemony had so thoroughly penetrated the veins and the arteries of the state that, in a certain sense, it persisted despite our best efforts. We were severely constrained by dictates from the presidential palace and by socially conservative forces within the ministry. Decolonization quickly became a slogan rather than the substantive center of all that we did.

As a consequence, the Ministry of Culture where I worked focused on the passage of laws: a cultural patrimony law, for example. Culture was reduced to the production of "indigenous" handicrafts, music, and dress. This feeds a new form of hegemony that reduces the possibilities of innovative kinds of cultural constructions and threatens to create new forms of exclusion.

Change is impossible without a shift in ideology. It is now apparent that government functionaries have been doing what is easiest rather than continuing with and engaging in more profound political struggles. The result is an emphasis on performance in the political realm with well-written scripts—you kiss a queer on the street or hug an indigenous person—which reflect political performativity rather than any substance.

The vision for what was possible with Evo's election has been reduced. How did this happen? Many of us had a vision that was broader and more vanguardist than that of the MAS, which perceived culture in strictly ethnic and indigenist terms. We sought spaces to discuss how culture—urban as well as rural, indigenous culture—is conceived and produced. There was little dialogue about the difference between "being" and "producing" culture.

I see this as a government of firefighters. They respond to crises rather than really have the time to develop and implement policies and programs and actively engage in a dialogue with the citizenry. This is exacerbated because the state has always had a paternalistic relation with its citizens, as people hope the government will solve all their problems. While social movements have played an active role as the sites to generate demands, since 2006, as many of their leaders have become incorporated into the government, these movements have relinquished some of their power to the state and, in many instances, become captured by it. That is particularly true for the leaders, as these have been steadily co-opted. Previously, the leaders were like walking sticks, supporting rather than driving social movements, because the grass roots steered themselves. Once social movement leadership was inserted into the state, they lost the capacity to maintain their autonomy because they believed the social movements now *were* the state.

Governing Style

The same characteristics that paved Morales's way to the top as a union leader—his charisma and strong leadership—undercut the government's capacity to create the solid institutions needed to guarantee change over the long run. The emphasis on personal loyalty, distrust of "outsiders," and preference for his long-term and proven disciples are all traits of Evo's administration. Describing a fellow cabinet member who had resigned abruptly, a minister highlighted her disloyalty above all else. Allegiance is not just to Evo but to the MAS as well. "When I went to work for the government," one of the few openly gay men in a high-ranking ministry job chuckled, "I was sure that sooner or later I would be fired for being homosexual. But in practice, I was under far more pressure because I refused to join the MAS!"[23] Public humiliation is part of the managing style. One vice minister told us, "You have to be very careful in cabinet meetings not to criticize Evo. If he thinks you have done something poorly, he will give you a drubbing in front of your peers that can be excruciating."[24]

The MAS claims to "rule by obeying" social movements, a concept borrowed from southern Mexico's Zapatista movement, which has sought to apply it in rural Chiapas municipalities.[25] It mandates that leaders both execute the decisions reached by the political base and answer to them if they don't. Vice President García Linera argues that to ensure the leadership of social movements, the MAS has explicitly erased much of the distinction between state and civil society.[26] Critics counter that pervasive corporatism renders ruling by obeying impossible, and that in reality the MAS endeavors to subordinate movements to its own agenda.[27]

The government tends to lurch from crisis to crisis. "It is government by reaction not by proposals and programs," Abdul Aspiazu, a former midlevel functionary, told us. "Everyone works to keep the boss happy, and we can't really accomplish anything unless there is political pressure from higher in the government, the press, or from the streets. This is frustrating, as we can see, sometimes months in advance, an issue that should be addressed, but we can't break through what functions as a highly vertical chain of command."[28]

While Morales assumed office with a strong anti-neoliberal ideology, his government has yet to meet the challenge identified by mining economist Rolando Jordan twenty years ago, to "develop the capacity to bargain successfully with the multinationals," a shortcoming in resource-rich Ecuador as well.[29] Gas contracts renegotiated in 2006 and 2007 with international firms were full of inconsistencies when presented for congressional approval.[30] Formulas for valuing Brazilian gas payments measured volume rather than energy density, allowing exporters to augment margins when "wet" gas — gas with a high caloric content — was shipped. Oversight of gas production is further hamstrung by deficiencies in verifying multinational firm accounting practices. Similar drawbacks are also evident in mining.

Consistent with governments before them, the administration has a reputation for not respecting the law when it doesn't suit them. The 2011–2012 TIPNIS crisis provides one of the most glaring examples, as the initial failure to consult the region's indigenous groups contravened the 2009 Constitution. Arguing that it was merely complying with existing laws, the government contended at one point that road construction did not fall under prior-approval requirements. The consultation process eventually carried out was, according to opposition critics, a formal rather than a substantive process, put in place after contracts for road construction were finalized.

Bureaucratic inefficiency plagues this government as it did its predecessors. While we were living in La Paz in 2012, friends were irate that the new "plurinational" state required people to stand in line for hours to get their birth certificates and other documents reissued, as those distributed by the former Republic of Bolivia were no longer valid. "Bureaucracy is unavoidable in any state," comments former MAS official Vicky Aillón, "but we all really hoped that forming a different kind of country meant a new style of governing."[31] "The face of government may have become more indigenous, mostly Aymara," reflects Javier Medina. "However, the behaviors and way of managing the state remain the same."[32]

Rent-Seeking

Bolivia is doubly cursed by chronic corruption, as it is endemic both to countries with extractive economies as well as to those affected by drug trafficking. Morales promised to end the practice, as have leaders of the region's other left governments. Yet this goal has proved elusive, and scandals remain a part of daily life as the 2005 vote-buying crisis that rocked Lula's government in Brazil and the 2011 uproar over alleged misuse of government funds involving Argentina's legendary Mothers of the Plaza de Mayo both reveal.[33]

When Morales took office, Transparency International ranked Bolivia among the most corrupt countries in the world, although its subsequent improvement has been noteworthy.[34] A Presidential Decree to bolster mechanisms for investigating public officials was in place by 2007, creating the Ministry of Institutional Transparency and Fight against Corruption. A former official there told us, "Corruption is so pervasive that we had a very hard time figuring out where to begin."[35]

Supporters expect that the government will furnish (or create) jobs, whether they are cast as patronage, decolonization, or development. Bureaucratic systems frequently function less as institutions promoting social or economic development than as sites for rent-seeking. Within the MAS government, a strong sense of "now it's our turn" prevails among many who historically have been denied the perks of office, exposing the extent that grassroots organizations, as well as both urban and rural unions, internalize the assumptions underlying patronage politics.[36]

Not surprisingly, the Morales government has not been immune from accusations—sometimes backed by hard evidence—of patronage and corruption. While the public perceives the MAS as less corrupt than its predecessors, the government has generally been hesitant to prosecute its own.[37] A notable exception is a 2008 scandal involving one of its most trusted militants, Santos Ramírez, head of YPFB and former president of the Senate, who was found guilty of benefiting from natural gas contracts and is now serving twelve years in prison. A late-2012 Ministry of Interior scandal was also aggressively pursued by the government. Taking members of sitting governments to trial, as difficult as it may be, is steadily rising regionally as well. Brazilian president Dilma Rousseff's prompt sacking in 2012 of several cabinet members accused of corruption was widely praised.[38]

While tackling at least some of the rent-seeking within its ranks, the MAS appears to have found in its early-2009 anticorruption law, which allowed for retroactive enforcement until 2012, a powerful tool to attack its foes.[39] Consequently, the standard practice of overlooking previous administrations' crimes and indiscretions has been replaced by what Vice President García Linera has called the "law of the guillotine," a reference to the French Revolution that predictably terrified the opposition.[40]

Several of Evo's adversaries hurriedly dropped out of the April 2010 departmental elections and fled the country because they feared arrest, as they stood accused of previous misuse of funds. Allegations have also been filed against former allies: both Juan del Granado, ex-mayor of La Paz, and Félix Patzi, former education minister, faced charges soon after they broke with the MAS.[41] The law is even making some MAS loyalists reconsider their political careers. One mayor commented, "I'm committed to the process, but I don't want to run [for mayor] again. Not only is it too hard to get anything done, but if anything goes wrong, I could go to jail."[42] Evo scoffed at opposition cries of persecution, "Paz Estenssoro's government went after me, followed by Paz Zamora's, and then Goni's. When Tuto Quiroga was president, he had me thrown out of Congress. I never ran away to another country."[43]

Expanding Representation, Rights, and Status

Indigenous Peoples

"We indigenous don't govern, rather a white entourage who are enemies of both indigenous people and workers are in charge, and they hold President Evo Morales hostage," decried El Alto's neighborhood association, FEJUVE, in 2010.[44] By 2012, only three of twenty cabinet ministers were indigenous. Very often these ministers either find themselves disconnected from their base or, given the confusion about the roles of social movements vis-à-vis the MAS, operate awkwardly with a foot in both the government and their organizations.[45]

Nonetheless, the Plurinational Legislative Assembly (previously Congress) had 17 percent indigenous representation in the first Morales administration, and 25 percent (43 of 173 representatives) in the second, a sharp increase over previous governments.[46] No other country with a sizable indigenous population (Ecuador, Peru, and Guatemala) has done so well.[47] The constitution ensures seven indigenous seats in the assembly: one from each department with the highest First Nations population. While this improves on previous constitutions, for indigenous organizations such as CONAMAQ and CIDOB, it isn't enough. "We did not get the representation we deserved," objects Guaraní organizer Marilyn Carayuri. "We are thirty-four ethnic groups in the lowlands, and each of us should have a seat at the table."[48]

Enhancing indigenous representation is complicated by changes in how people classify themselves. While 67 percent self-identified as indigenous in the 2001 census, only 37 percent spoke an indigenous language and 33 percent lived in self-denominated indigenous communities, begging the question of who decides who is indigenous. The 2006–2007 Constituent Assembly, where 56 percent of the delegates declared themselves indigenous, is exceptional when compared to similar endeavors in the region, for example, the largely government-controlled 2008 Constituent Assembly in Ecuador.[49]

While much is made of the symbolic importance of Morales's election, material benefits have also been substantial for indigenous peoples. Public policy has prioritized the countryside, and universal programs, such as literacy promotion, road construction, and electrification, have yielded the most positive impact there. "Even the rains have gotten better thanks to Evo!" praises sixty-year-old Nazario Condori Choque in the remote windswept altiplano hamlet of Wila Apacheta.[50]

A 2010 antiracism and antidiscrimination law authorizes criminal sanctions for public and private institutions and bars media dissemination of racist and biased ideas.[51] For the first time, all kinds of businesses have signs posted reminding customers and employees that "we are all equal under the law." However, five hundred years of racism cannot be reversed in a few years—indigenous university students are still pressured to adopt western clothing, and white people, especially older ones, continue to push to the head of the line in public offices. But change is in the air. One afternoon we entered a bakery in upper-middle-class Sopocachi behind two women dressed in urban Aymara clothing. In years past, the white shopkeeper would most likely have moved immediately to assist us first. That she didn't was noteworthy. It was for the women, too. As they turned to leave and realized we were waiting patiently, they looked a bit sheepish, clearly pleased if somewhat surprised.

Women

No one doubts the strides the Morales government has taken for women's rights. Though it opted not to create a Ministry of Gender, as many women's organizations demanded, in 2011, half of the twenty cabinet ministers were women (although by 2012, it had dropped to a third, a pattern sustained in 2013). Evo calls appointing women to high posts "a tribute to my mother, my sister, and my daughter." In 2001, not a single woman served at the ministerial level. This remarkable shift parallels that accomplished by the other new leftist governments.[52] "Very early on, we discussed gender inequality at the highest levels," explains Vice President García Linera. "We decided we could either opt for a minority or majority understanding—why should half the population be relegated to just one ministry? We felt that by creating a Ministry of Gender, we would marginalize women."[53]

Thanks in no small measure to the pressure brought by a campaign of two hundred union, indigenous peasant, and feminist organizations,[54] the Plurinational Legislative Assembly in 2013 is 28 percent female. By 2011, 43 percent of all municipal council members were women.[55] And in 2013, a comprehensive law was passed that mandates harsh penalties to prevent and punish violence against women.

Although these gains rank among the best in Latin America, which overall has seen a striking increase in women's political participation since gender quotas were adopted in eleven countries (including Bolivia) during the 1990s, what is most remarkable is the upsurge in indigenous women's involvement. Nemecia Achacollo, minister of rural development; Silvia Lazarte, president of the Constitutional Assembly; Leonilda Zurita, head of the MAS in Cochabamba; Nilda Copa, justice minister; and Cristina Mamani, head of the Magistrates Council, are all indigenous women. At the same time, the indigenous and peasant women's federation has emerged as a critical player among social movements. However, this upswing in women's political participation has been accompanied by an increase in harassment of female politicians, which reached an extreme with the murder in 2012 of two municipal councilors.[56]

Improving women's daily lives is harder to attain. On the 2012 Gender Equity Index for Latin America, Bolivia ranks just below the average.[57] Domestic violence is rampant, and men are often seen as having the right to beat their wives; rural women still have fewer land titles than men; workplace discrimination persists; newspaper classifieds explicitly advertise for young, attractive women; there is little discussion of equal pay for equal work; less than 1 percent of sexual assaults are reported; and sexual harassment is considered normal.[58] Just as elsewhere in the world, rural women remain the poorest, do the most work, and suffer the most violence.

In urban areas, 150,000 women and girls, many under the age of fourteen, labor as domestic workers, excluded from protection by current labor laws. They are typically paid less than minimum wage and are often abused, sometimes sexually, by their employers. "When I was thirteen, because we were so poor, my parents allowed a city family to take me with them with promises they would send me to school and feed me," remembers Casimira Rodríguez. "I never went to school, and for two years I never received any pay except room and board in exchange for very long days of work."[59] Under Morales, new policies have played an important role in improving poor women's lives, including stipends for women who attend prenatal and postnatal checkups, for children who remain in school, and for the elderly.

Overcoming sexist culture extends beyond laws, however. During Carnival 2012, in a public blessing of the presidential palace, Evo sang a rhyming verse, or *copla*: "This president with a big heart / will take the panties off all his female ministers."[60] Women at the highest levels of government reported not-so-subtle harassment to us, such as being cut off in cabinet meetings and feeling that their subordinates treat them as token appointees.

Labor

Bolivia manifests extremes of many characteristics typical of Latin America's labor markets: a low-skilled work force, much contractual short-term and part-time employment, inadequate grievance procedures, and unions that have little influence at the level of the firm.[61] Until the 1980s in the region's most industrialized countries, corporatist unions predominated under the sway of political parties and governments, from the Peronist-dominated unions in Argentina to those controlled by the PRI in Mexico.[62]

Neoliberalism's restructuring of industry and production increased capital flexibility, and mounting global competition converged with the informalization and feminization of work to erode these traditional unions.[63] As the number of unionized workers dropped in some countries, including Bolivia, the labor movement became a mere shadow of what it had once been.[64] We first participated in La Paz's vibrant May Day during the mid-1980s; by 2012, not only were there far fewer participants, but the tremendous spirit of collective struggle for a better society had largely dissipated, replaced by fragmented, sectoral demands.

While "pink tide" governments are universally sympathetic to workers' rights, only mediocre improvements have been registered to date.[65] Labor organizations have had the greatest success where they have actively pushed for reforms, according to political scientist Mark Anner.[66] An example is found in Chile, where the country's first general strike since the 1990 return to democracy successfully pressured the Concertación government in 2003 to include informal workers under labor laws.[67] In contrast, in Brazil, despite optimism that Lula's past as a labor leader would ensure an advance in working-class interests, the CUT's ambivalence in challenging the new government they had helped put into power meant that only modest gains were achieved.[68]

In Bolivia, the much-diminished COB had high expectations that the Morales government would create new jobs as well as substantially improve wages and working conditions. On his first May Day as president in 2006, Evo issued a Supreme Decree of considerable symbolic importance: it undid parts of the informalization of labor permitted under neoliberalism. The move was a component of a MAS government commitment to increase job security and institute a regularized system of salary increases.

But as job creation is exceptionally difficult in Bolivia's extractive economy, the MAS government has been unable to fully deliver on labor movement demands. Consequently, like every administration before it, the MAS has struggled with the trade unions more each year; in 2009 alone, over one hundred labor disputes rocked the country. Sociologists Silvia Escobar de Pabón and Bruno Rojas Callejas argue that "despite the economic recovery, and actual government policy, unemployment, low salaries and the deterioration of work quality remain among the country's most pressing problems."[69]

Much conflict has centered on the minimum wage. One of the lowest in the region in terms of purchasing power, it has steadily risen from a little over Bs. $500 when Evo assumed office to Bs. $1,200 by 2013. Once adjusted for the moderate inflation experienced since 2006, this totals a 60 percent increase for the lowest-paid workers, propelling private businesses to gripe that these raises are destroying their competitive advantage.[70] The COB maintains—correctly in the view of most economists—that the improved amount remains insufficient to feed an urban family. But their demands in 2012 that top Bs. $8,300 a month—seven times the 2011 wage—cannot realistically be met by any employer over the short or medium term. As the COB refuses to allow company owners a seat at the negotiating table, compromise is unattainable and disputes quickly end up in the streets.

An ambitious government initiative in 2009 sought to revise the labor law in place since 1939, which had seen significant modifications but never a complete revision. Only 30 percent of workers are covered by current legislation, which excludes businesses with less than twenty employees, those employed informally, and public sector workers. The preliminary proposal was roundly rejected by the COB, which prepared a proposition of its own. "This task was the most important of my life," explains lawyer Frank Taquichiri, who assisted the COB. "It was far from easy, plagued by internal and external problems, from the first draft that was successfully adopted as the point of departure rather than the Labor Ministry document. We have been working for three years to fit the proposed law within the parameters of the new constitution."[71] Such a level of union participation is not uncommon, as both Salvadoran and Brazilian unions have played an important role in formulating labor code reforms, even though the outcomes have largely not lived up to union expectations.[72]

The proposed law expands coverage to agricultural and domestic workers, firmly establishing worker protections, privileging collective rights over individual ones, prohibiting workplace discrimination and subcontracting, granting the minister of labor enforcement powers, and protecting unions from government interference. Achieving collaboration on the proposal between the government and the COB, fraught as it often is, has been undermined by ongoing annual struggles over salaries and the minimum wage. Repeated strikes, including a 2011 one that lasted fifteen days, have slowed the law's adoption.

Even if the law passes as anticipated, active enforcement seems unlikely if past practice is any guide. For example, despite a 2009 Presidential Decree prohibiting employment discrimination, little has changed.[73] Presidential Decrees are clearly easier to issue than enforce: two were proclaimed in 2012 to end short-term contracting, as this enabled employers to avoid paying benefits. They provide protection from firing to new mothers and extend labor law coverage to most workers in the biggest municipalities.

By late 2012, jobs creation got a boost with a new employment assistance program slated to furnish a subsidy and technical training to 20,000 young people over five years. The government also turned over a new national headquarters to the COB, entirely financed with public funds. While many worry that this represents a MAS attempt to buy off the labor movement, as new union infrastructure has been funded both nationally and locally, Evo argues that governments of social movements should support their base. Stressing his own union background, he insists, "We may have ideological differences, but as workers we have two paths: either unite or sink."[74]

Minority Rights

Despite often relentless opposition from many Christian churches, Catholic and Protestant, lesbian, gay, bisexual, and transgender (LGBT) populations across Latin America are steadily extending their civil liberties. After legalizing same-sex marriage in 2010, Argentina approved some of the world's most progressive legislation in 2012 when it agreed to finance sex-change operations. Same-sex marriage has been recognized in Mexico City (2009), four states in Brazil, and São Paolo (2012). In March 2012, Brazil took the lead in presenting the first United Nations resolution on LGBT rights, after the Organization of American States (OAS) had adopted an LGBT rights plank in 2011.[75] Undermining these achievements is the prevalence of violence directed at LGBT peoples, especially those who don't conform to accepted norms for how gender is displayed in public.[76]

When we marched for gay rights through downtown La Paz on a frosty night in June 2007, we were nervous at first when we saw the hundreds of people lining the route, far more than those of us in the march itself. But as onlookers began clapping enthusiastically, the fear dissipated, and we were amazed how much support this recently emerging minority already had among the population. After all, the media had only begun acknowledging the existence of local sexual minorities in 1993.[77] By 2009, many more had left the sidewalks to join the march and the event had taken on a decidedly festive air. There was a reason to celebrate: the recently adopted constitution's Article 14 expressly prohibits discrimination on the basis of sexual orientation, and the MAS government had declared June 28 Sexual Minority Rights Day. In 2013, the marchers were joined by a MAS minister, Claudia Peña.

"Our struggle is not one of complaints, tragedies, and self-victimization," Paris Galán announces. "Our country already sees itself too often as a victim. We want to work alongside other social movements to fundamentally change our society for all those who are excluded and marginalized."[78]

By 2012, MAS senator Hilda Saavedra had introduced a bill seeking to uphold the spirit of the new constitution by legalizing civil marriage for gay and lesbian couples. Communitarian lesbian feminist Julieta Paredes believes, "The process has been worth it, even though some people try to tell us nothing has changed. No, definitely not. It's not the same. We knew it wouldn't be easy, but no process of change is a piece of cake, all of it is mixed with dreams and nightmares, good decisions, errors, and betrayals."[79]

Official numbers place Bolivia's disabled population at 40,000 people, although human rights groups assert the figure is much higher because of the prevalence of preventable diseases like German measles and polio, childhood malnutrition, and scant enforcement of occupational safety regulations. As in much of Latin America, this vulnerable population faces an almost complete absence of services and accessibility coupled with widespread discrimination and often extreme poverty. "Having a disability means being marginalized, excluded, and without basic human rights," Carlos Mariaca Álvarez told the *Guardian* newspaper. "Being confined to a wheelchair comes with great stigma attached. We were hoping for more inclusion with the government of Evo Morales, because he talked about multiculturalism and multidimensionality."[80]

As with so many other aspects of Bolivian society, the problem is not a lack of laws protecting disabled peoples' rights but the lack of enforcement. Other pink tide governments have made modest gains in protecting their disabled populations: in Ecuador in 2012, a monthly benefit of $50 was granted, and in Peru in 2012, both private and public entities were required to show that they were hiring a certain percentage of people with disabilities.

In December 2011, about 120 disabled Bolivian protesters and their supporters trekked for one hundred days the 900 miles uphill from Trinidad to La Paz to demand an annual subsidy of roughly US$400, which the government said would be impossible to grant. As the protesters approached La Paz's main square, they clashed with riot police, who were later accused by Amnesty International of using excessive force. In March 2012, yet another law was passed, granting an annual subsidy of US$145, but only for those with severe disabilities, far short of activists' demands. Another march, this time with 40 people, set off in February 2013 demanding that the yearly payment be made to all disabled people, but it was suspended within a month.

Navigating Dependency

Bolivia, long dependent on international aid to finance government operations, has always had to pay particular attention to how it manages international relations. The deluge of gas revenues, however, has afforded the MAS relative autonomy from the United States, which has long treated Latin America as its domain.[81] Until Morales, the U.S. embassy vetoed cabinet appointments, maintained private landing strips, coordinated laws with senators, reprimanded officials, and even, on occasion, publicly scolded presidents. Ambassador Donna Hrinak, for example, informed the press that President Hugo Banzer "didn't have the balls to confront corrupt drug judges."[82]

Days before entering office, Morales adopted a confrontational tone with the United States, vowing to be the Bush administration's "worst nightmare." The posturing did little to enhance Evo's ability to negotiate in a historical context of extreme vulnerability. South America currently enjoys the luxury of not being a U.S. priority, which provides some breathing room. Even so, the Bolivia-U.S. relationship quickly degenerated into a nasty tit-for-tat during Morales's first term. After U.S. ambassador Philip Goldberg was expelled in 2008, U.S. officials responded in kind. Bolivia next threw out the Drug Enforcement Agency, and the United States retaliated by withdrawing Peace Corp volunteers and allowing the Andean Pact Trade and Drug Enforcement Agreement (APTDEA) to lapse. As the United States is Bolivia's second-largest market for manufactured goods, the end of the tariff-free entry agreement particularly affected clothing exports, costing as many as 12,000 jobs, mostly in El Alto, and an estimated US$150 million a year.[83]

Hopes that Barack Obama's election would create a more favorable climate were dashed in September 2009 when the new administration sustained the Bush-era refusal to "certify" Bolivia's antinarcotics program, a stand they have taken every year since, although they have publicly praised rising cocaine seizures. In November 2011, the two governments began negotiations to restore full diplomatic relations, on collaborative terms that are far more equitable than most agreements between powerful and weak countries, although as of November 2013, the countries had yet to set a date to exchange ambassadors.

Relations with Europe are more positive. The European Union (EU) is a leading regional trading partner and investor, accounting for a significant share of foreign direct investment.[84] Bolivia receives the most EU bilateral aid in Latin America, and the European Union is the largest aid source. Current bilateral programs emphasize job creation and poverty alleviation, drug control, and integrated watershed management to expand drinking water access and mitigate the effects of climate change.

Since 2006, international financial institution authority in the region has waned as country after country has profited from the commodity boom to pay off outstanding loans. By 2013, no Latin American countries depended on International Monetary Fund (IMF) standby arrangements. Bolivia loosened the shackles as well: from 1985 to 2005 the World Bank and the IMF exercised enormous leverage when the country was one of the highest per capita aid recipients, but with massive financial reserves, a standby arrangement with the IMF was scrapped in 2006. The same year, grants and donations constituted only 1 percent of GDP.[85]

Foreign debt also plunged. In mid-2006, the World Bank's Multilateral Debt Relief Initiative (MDRI) forgave 36 percent of Bolivia's public obligations. Later that same year, the Inter-American Development Bank (IADB) approved limited debt relief as part of a package for Latin America's poorest countries. Public debt in 2012 stood at a relatively modest 33 percent of GDP.[86]

Bolivia adopted a groundbreaking stance against international financial institutions when it became the world's first country to withdraw from the World Bank's international arbitration tribunal, the International Center for the Settlement of Investment Disputes (ICSID), in May 2007.[87] Morales argued that ICSID judgments consistently favored multinationals over low-income nations. Bolivia's landmark decision was followed by Ecuador (2009), Venezuela (2012), and Argentina (2013).

CECILIA CHACÓN HELD VARIOUS POSTS IN THE MORALES ADMINISTRATION, INCLUDING MINISTER OF DEFENSE IN 2011.[88]

It was very exciting to be part of this government from the beginning because we all felt like there was so much we could do. We had a great urgency to bring about change because none of us had any idea if such an opportunity would ever come again. I'm proud of everything we accomplished in reducing poverty, improving education and health, and formulating the new constitution. Remember that this process is only a few years old, and to overcome a long history of colonialism, patriarchy, and racism is far from easy. Because of the weak state we inherited and the conditions we faced, we were not able to accomplish everything we wanted. But we did some pretty unheard-of stuff: for example, the president chose me to be defense minister precisely because I'm a woman and under thirty.

Once Evo was elected, the social movements tended to leave everything to the state, thinking that now the government would solve all the problems. Alternative projects of all kinds—in local water management for example—were put aside. Many leaders also went into the government, so communities and movements lost key people.

We were able to bring voices to the table in international forums that aren't normally heard—voices from the poor countries. We broke a lot of the rules governing international protocol. Mostly we just didn't know them, so we could ignore them, often to the consternation of other governments' representatives. I remember once Evo was presented a document that promoted bio-fuels, and we are really opposed to these. So he just scratched out the bit he didn't like and handwrote a note right on the document. You should have seen the faces. This just *isn't* done.

It was great to be able to have Bolivia play a role—particularly on climate change—that small countries like ours never do. We are usually too intimidated in international conferences by the big countries, and let them set the pace and culture of meetings. We were able to act how we did in part because we weren't shaped by a lifetime of following the rules. On the other hand, we often found ourselves scrambling frantically to put something coherent together without the time or the necessary resources. This happened all too often.

Since I resigned from the government over TIPNIS, I think it is really important not to become discouraged and to remain committed to the process of change that has cost so much to achieve.

Morales also displayed little fear of multinationals. On February 10, 2007, Bolivia repeated the David and Goliath act for which it became so famous during the 2000 Cochabamba Water War when it tangled with

Switzerland's privately owned Glencore Corporation, Europe's sixth-largest firm. Controlled by billionaire commodity trader Mark Rich, Glencore is known for breaking arms embargos, paying illegal kickbacks, engaging in human rights violations, and fomenting widespread corruption.[89] Glencore purchased ex-president Gonzalo Sánchez de Lozada's holdings, including Oruro's Vinto foundry. In 2007, the government nationalized the plant, and it has expanded rapidly into the world's eighth-largest tin smelter, consistently reporting a profit.[90] In June 2012, Colquiri Mine, another Glencore property, was expropriated, and Glencore's two remaining mines were forced into a partnership with COMIBOL, which now controls 55% of the operations.[91]

Relations with Cuba as well as Venezuela intensified, and both countries have financed productive investments as well as medical training and services. In 2006, Bolivia joined the Bolivarian Alliance for the Peoples of Our America (ALBA),[92] which envisions regional economic integration based on mutual respect and economic aid.[93] "Continued cooperation with our neighbors and friends in the region—with Ecuador, Peru, Cuba, Argentina, and Venezuela—is essential," explains MAS militant Silvia Lazarte. "We need to focus less on Europe and the United States and more on each other, so that we build a new kind of diplomacy that will make the continent more able to live well."[94]

Despite right-wing alarm over Cuban and Venezuelan clout, the real regional powerhouse is Brazil, with the world's sixth-largest economy and about half of South America's territory and population. Brazil is not only the major player in Bolivia's natural gas, its firms have huge investments in soy, gold mining, and road construction. It is also the transit point, and increasingly, the destination, for the burgeoning eastward flow of cocaine, which, much as in the United States, wreaks havoc in its cities' poorest neighborhoods. By successfully forming a close bond with Lula da Silva early on, Morales may have gained greater space from the United States and better deals for Bolivia, but the reality is that dependency is shifting southward, not disappearing.

Bolivia emerged as the angry representative of poor nations at the 2009 Copenhagen climate summit, proposing a financial transactions tax to fund climate change mitigation. The issue has considerable urgency, as the country is on the front lines of global warming. Just an hour outside La Paz, 17,400 feet above sea level, the twenty-thousand-year-old Chacaltaya Glacier once hosted the world's highest ski run. Now only scattered chunks of ice remain hundreds of meters above the top of the ski lift. Even though Bolivia is among the world's smallest contributors to carbon emissions, vanishing glaciers throughout the Andes put water sources at risk, not only for residents of La Paz but also for about one hundred million people from Bogotá to Santiago.[95]

In Copenhagen, Evo was adamant, "The defense budget of the United States is $687 billion. And for climate change to save life, to save humanity, they only put up $10 billion. This is shameful."[96] He demanded reparations for countries like Bolivia, placing the blame for climate change squarely on capitalism. Disgusted with what they perceived as the lack of progress at the Denmark summit, the government organized an alternative conference outside Cochabamba in April 2010, attended by over 30,000 people. "Bolivia has had an important impact for such a small country," says activist Elizabeth Peredo. "It convinced others to stand up for their rights in face of the major powers, and supported the formation of an alternative network on climate change."[97]

La plus ça change, la plus c'est la même chose?[98]

Accomplishing greater equality through left-wing electoral wins is far from assured, as the uneven experience from South Africa to Chile bears out. Bolivia's MAS is hindered more than most others by the state it inherited, which had been further eroded by two decades of neoliberal policies.

While philosopher Luis Tapia is likely correct to assert that the MAS has perpetuated well-established patterns by guaranteeing jobs to party faithful and failing to encourage debate about the nature of the state and its relationship to its citizenry, such ambitious goals may simply not be realizable over the short term.[99] Reforms are likely to assume relatively low priority in the face of demands for immediate and visible change, economic dependence on world economic vicissitudes, and administrative ineptitude.

"The government's ambitions require planning," explains ex–vice minister of planning Alberto Borda, "but leadership was never willing to commit funds to the Planning Ministry, the main organism to integrate the entire project, with the argument that they didn't want to foster more bureaucracy. This has left us with the only planning being that which is conducted by the president himself, and this cannot deliver the institutional support necessary for this process to thrive."[100]

Yet it may not be prudent to measure the success of Morales and the MAS in the short term, since change can take generations. Nowhere is this clearer than in Evo's January 2013 speech specifying targets for the 2025 bicentenary of the republic. Revolutionizing the state is a long-term project: it will take indigenous students, for example, recently admitted to the military academy, decades to rise through the ranks to the high command. But will indigenous officers redefine military culture and everyday practices to transform the institution to one that supports the rights of the majority over the elite? Does greater participation by women and indigenous peoples serve to simply broaden access to power, or can it change the way power is used? These are the broader challenges facing Bolivia and other countries and communities that embark on processes of inclusionary transformation.

CHAPTER 5

Continuity and Innovation in the Economy

SANTUSA FLORES QUISPE[1]

Almost everyone in our community voted for Evo. But it seems that nothing has changed.

Nothing? I thought you said the road was cobbled.

Yes, that makes it easier for us to get to Tarabuco and Sucre.

What about the health post?

There's a clinic now. The doctor, nurse, and dentist are there every day. They don't charge anything to see you.

And the school?

The community next to us got a new school, which is much closer than the old one, but we didn't get one.

And what about electricity?

They just put in power to the village, so we don't spend as much on candles and kerosene or batteries for the radio.

Don't you now have cell phone coverage?

Well, yes. Not long ago we all got cell phones and can make calls from the community. But there are fewer tourists now than there were before because Evo fought with the Americans, and those who do come now don't spend as much on weavings, so we don't make as much as we did before.

Long-Term Growth: Continuity or Change?

For Santusa Flores, whose limited Spanish and indigenous dress mark her as a peasant farmer, incremental improvements designed to foster long-term development are less important than whether the government has hindered or helped her immediate need to make a living. The dissatisfaction in her Quechua-speaking community east of Sucre exemplifies the difficulties the Morales administration confronts in making a highly extractive economy better serve its population.

The failure to satisfy pent-up demand for jobs is even more acute in cities. Max Mendoza sums it up: "This government has failed to bring factories to El Alto. The demand is huge, especially among young people. It's a terrible situation—we have people turning to drugs and alcohol because they can't find any work."[2] The majority of indigenous people now live in these marginalized urban areas throughout the country. Since the middle of the twentieth century, these neighborhoods have been characterized by state neglect and deeply embedded poverty.[3]

In this chapter, we discuss how Bolivia's legacy as a landlocked supplier of raw materials to industrial nations shapes what it is able to do with the current windfall from natural gas. While income has soared, the Morales administration has proven incapable of fundamentally altering the economic structure. The reliance on gas exemplifies what Eduardo Gudynas identifies as neoextractivism, prevalent among Latin America's new left administrations.[4] The recent model differs from long-standing extractivism by granting a stronger role for the state, ensuring more favorable contracts with multinationals, and promoting efforts to add value to natural resource exports. Its continuity with the past in the face of burgeoning world demand can mean, however, as in Bolivia's case, even greater dependence on natural resources.

Recent growth has only served to recover the ground lost between 1975 and 2005.[5] A few fundamentals clarify why.

GDP per capita, expressed in current U.S. dollars, has multiplied eightfold since 1970. But when considered in constant dollars—that is, real GDP, corrected for inflation—a different picture emerges. Real per capita GDP in 2012 only slightly surpassed its 1975 level. The bottom row of Table 5.1 provides the explanation: Latin America's 1980s debt crisis and subsequent inflation wiped out the gains. While Bolivia has faced only modest inflation in recent years, and real income (US$2,232 per capita in 2012) has doubled since Evo took office, it lags its neighbors in Peru, Brazil, or Argentina, where World Bank figures place 2011 per capita income from US$5,500 in Peru to US$10,400 in Brazil.[6]

Table 5.1. Bolivian per capita Gross Domestic Product (GDP) 1970–2012[a]

Year	1970	1975	1980	1985	1990	1995	2000	2005	2012
GDP in Current US$	240	504	654	688	731	899	1,011	1,044	2,232
GDP in Constant US$ (2010)	1,349	2,041	1,733	1,397	1,221	1,286	1,284	1,169	2,110
2010 US $1.00 value	5.62	4.05	2.65	2.03	1.67	1.43	1.27	1.12	1.00

[a] Source: United Nations 2012.

The Legacy of Potosí and the War of the Pacific

Why has the country done so poorly? At first glance, it is especially puzzling, as the city of Potosí, in what was then Alto Peru, probably generated more export earnings in the early seventeenth century than Paris or London. Part of the answer is simple. Spanish colonialism demolished sophisticated Andean production and distribution systems. Not only was the wealth from the mines hauled away, but the focus on mining stalled other forms of economic development.[7] After the 1825 liberation from Spain, indigenous people were held as chattel or escaped to areas beyond colonial control, similar to patterns that James Scott documents in Southeast Asia.[8]

These conditions prevailed in neighboring Peru as well, but it always fared better, due in no small part to its access to the sea. Economists note that landlocked countries grow at a rate between 0.6 and 1.5 percent per year slower than those with a seacoast,[9] which may not seem notable, but when compounded over 130 years, accounts for all of the income difference between the two countries.[10]

The Paradox of Plenty

In the past decade, resource extraction, driven by increased global demand, especially from China and India, has boomed throughout Latin America. In Colombia alone, foreign direct investment (FDI) jumped more than 500 percent between 2000 and 2010, mostly in mining. Trade between China and Latin America, just US$10 billion in 2000, surged to US$241 billion by 2011, helping the region weather the worst of 2007–

2008 financial crises.[11] Latin America's resource wealth has turned it into the world's leading destination for mining and mineral exploration, and there is no sign this will slow, as international companies from Canada to Japan are continually escalating investments. A similar growth pattern can be seen in hydrocarbons, timber, and soy. Accompanying this explosion in extractive investments are rising concerns about environmental consequences, a new round of foreign domination, and inadequate consultative processes with local communities.[12] From Mexico to Chile, vulnerable indigenous peoples are under assault as they struggle to hold on to what remains of their lands and some vestige of their traditional way of life.[13]

Within this regional context, Bolivia is a minor player. Nonetheless, it is currently the second-largest natural gas producer in South America, with investments led by Spain's Repsol followed by Brazil's Petrobras and France's Total. Production has skyrocketed since 1999, when most of Bolivia's gas began flowing eastward to fuel Brazil's industrial heartland of São Paulo. In 2013, almost 70 percent of Bolivia's gas supplies about one-third of Brazil's needs.[14] About 20 percent supplies northern Argentina, and the remainder is consumed domestically. Since the boom began, Bolivia has struggled to keep up with its contractual commitments to its energy-hungry neighbors as well as to its own citizens.

Almost all current production originates in the desert scrubland of the Chaco in the southeastern department of Tarija, which has been transformed by the latest boom.[15] By 2012, gas accounted for 45 percent of total national exports, increasing government income ninefold from 2002 to 2008.[16] The bonanza isn't over yet: the government has announced that it plans to double production by 2015.[17] But despite the impressive surges in income, gas remains a capital-intensive industry that produces few jobs.

Mining, particularly cooperative mining, is the one sector that has created employment, although Carlos Monge argues that increased mining has little impact on reducing poverty in the Andes.[18] Total production — almost all in zinc, silver, and tin — has shot from US$346 million in 2005 to around US$3.5 billion in 2011. Sixty percent of this stems from large mines, controlled primarily by growing Bolivian private sector investments followed by multinational corporations. Marginally productive cooperative mines absorb the most labor, generating some 80,000 low-paying jobs where life expectancies are twenty-five years less than the national average. With the government stalled principally by cooperative miners from passing a new law that would increase government revenues, the 2011 state share from mining was a modest US$350 million.[19] This dropped about 20 percent in 2012 as world prices declined and production slowed. With 2012 the most conflictive year yet between cooperative and state miners, the uncertain playing field has scared large investors away. Neither COMIBOL nor the cooperatives have the capital to develop any sizable new operations.

JOSÉ PIMENTEL, EX-UNION LEADER AND MINISTER OF MINING IN 2010–2011[20]

President Paz Estenssoro announced that "mining is dead" when he shut the COMIBOL state mines in 1985. But mining didn't die—it fell into the hands of cooperative miners and private companies. That is what we inherited.

Our plan was to industrialize mining and recoup mines rented to private companies.[21] But we quickly found that our biggest obstacle is the cooperative miners. They produce 30 percent of all minerals in miserable, archaic working conditions. Almost all the rest is produced by largely industrialized private mines. So we found ourselves with these two polarities in mining—one where almost everything is done by hand and the other the complete opposite.

We can't transform the cooperative mining sector into an industrial one because they lack the skills, and the way the work is organized doesn't permit large-scale production. But also twenty years of neoliberalism has changed their consciousness. The wealthy few who control and benefit from the cooperative mines will fight us tooth and nail to maintain things as they are. Our only hope is that the current system generates such inequality that subcontracted workers will organize. The government can encourage a culture of collaboration, but it has to be the miners themselves who struggle to improve their situations. After all, if there's anyone capable of changing their lives, it's Bolivia's miners.

We've made virtually no progress toward industrialization because of the political power the cooperative miners wield. I'm waiting for mineral prices to fall, because I think this might well oblige the cooperative miners to reflect that current methods require huge sacrifices and are very inefficient.

Our other frustration is trying to recuperate the highly profitable rented mines. In some cases, the operators are only paying a small amount of rent—Glencore-owned Porco Mine, for example, provides the government a ridiculously low 8 percent of the gross value of production. We want to nationalize these mines, but our first difficulty is with the private sector miners themselves. For example, when COMIBOL ran Colquiri, there were three thousand miners; when it was privatized, it dropped to only four hundred, but productivity tripled. They had better salaries and working conditions than before, so they were reluctant to return to state control. We did recuperate Huanuni, but the company running it had done such a poor job that the miners welcomed a return to COMIBOL. Recouping mines from the cooperatives is almost impossible.

Currently five thousand miners work in Siglo XX. In an industrial mine, we couldn't possibly absorb that number, so new jobs would have to be created, an almost inconceivable task because we just don't have the funds. Situations such as these completely tie the government's hands.

The workers in the cooperatives don't have a sense of where their future lies. Many of them don't have any sense of a future, because at any moment they could die in an accident and they are all dying from black lung. If we are going to industrialize mining to benefit the country, our only hope is to convince them to give up their neoliberal form of thinking.

The third-largest export by volume is soy and soy products, part of a massive regional expansion that has swept across neighboring Paraguay, Argentina, and Brazil as well. Wholesale bulldozing of forests and displacement of indigenous people characterize this latest round of agricultural growth, which is led by agribusiness but benefits some highland migrants as well. Fragile tropical soils are so quickly exhausted that soy production is more akin to strip mining than to sustainable agriculture.[22]

Together, these sectors plus the mushrooming construction industry make up the bulk of traditional Bolivian elite investment. After their initial shock at Morales's election and their failed rebellion in the east, many now accept that their historic control over the public sector has ended. Their acquiescence stems in no small measure from the substantial benefits they have accrued during the recent boom and the fact that their economic privileges have not been threatened. As opposition leader and business owner Samuel Doria Medina explains, "This government has expressed since the beginning that business people are welcome as long as they don't get involved in politics."[23]

In the altiplano, a much smaller-scale boom involving campesino producers has occurred in quinoa production, estimated at US$85 million for 2013, as Bolivia is firmly established as the world's largest producer of the increasingly popular vegetable.[24] The National Association of Quinoa Producers (ANAPQUI) and strong campesino unions have successfully kept middlemen and multinational agricultural corporations out, increasing farmer income. Prices have risen dramatically since 2006, and highland farmers are dedicating more and more land to the lucrative crop, in some places threatening the delicate altiplano ecosystem. While production remains family based, with plots ranging from 2.5 to 37 acres, and

90 percent is organic, in some areas rising prices have aggravated existing local land conflicts and made quinoa too expensive for some local people, particularly in urban areas.[25]

This reliance on resource income—silver, tin, gold, and now natural gas, minerals, and soy—to drive growth has created what development economists often refer to as the paradox of plenty. Some scholars contend that an abundance of natural resources can even provoke a country's poverty. Stunted manufacturing, rent-seeking, unstable governments, a poorly educated workforce, and economic inequality are all significantly higher in resource-dependent countries than in those with more diversified economies.[26]

While Bolivia exhibits most symptoms of this "resource curse," a more nuanced approach suggests that path dependency—how previous decisions and social and political processes shape and constrain subsequent ones—can complicate economic diversification, because extractive industries typically out-compete others for state attention.[27] Recent research suggests that dependence on resource rents is not the cause of low economic growth and persistent poverty.[28] Where state institutions are accountable and competent, a resource boom can substantially benefit society.[29] Norway has proven particularly successful in using revenues from North Sea oil to subsidize social democratic improvements for its citizens, while small states like Qatar have effectively diversified their economic, if not productive, activity.[30] Bolivia and countries like it, however, are often caught in a vicious cycle. Their dependency on extraction undercuts the evolution of the institutional capacity necessary to take full advantage of those same resources.

Extraction-based growth also has a limited multiplier effect. Development sociologist Brent Kaup argues that resource dependency has not only shaped the orientation of Bolivia's physical infrastructure but has contributed to a specific institutional and regulatory configuration—laws, taxes, contracts, policy making, and scanty administrative capacity—that constrains internal economic diversification and growth.[31]

Constant social unrest adds another level of risk for businesses, both large and small. "We lost our chicken business during the Cochabamba Water War," Losel Ramírez told us. "We just couldn't get our eggs to market."[32] To compensate for the risk, national and international investors seek higher returns than common in lower-risk settings. In the case of oil and gas, this risk premium was and continues to be enormous—until the 2006 partial nationalization, companies like Petrobras anticipated making ten dollars for every dollar invested, some of the world's highest returns.[33]

Is Economic Stability Enough?

Bolivia's current macroeconomic strength is unprecedented in its recent history. With government coffers overflowing, the value of the currency, the boliviano (Bs.), against the U.S. dollar has shot up. Loans are now made in bolivianos, not dollars, reducing the cost of imports but also lowering the competitiveness of exports. The cash influx has financed a nationwide construction boom.

An hour's drive north of La Paz, the imprint of the infusion of cash is visible on the landscape. Brick and two-story houses dot the high, largely treeless plateau where once rough adobe predominated. Electric wires now run to the houses rather than by them. More recent houses boast oversize TV antennas and occasionally satellite dishes. A sign for Lácteosbol, the new state-owned milk-processing plant, welcomes visitors to the Aymara heartland of Achacachi, famous for its combative history and now boasting a recently constructed multipurpose sports facility.

Conservative economists worry that such extraction-based government spending is not sustainable. Yet despite all the new projects, the country had an astonishing US$14 billion in reserves in January 2013,[34] leading progressive critics to denounce government expenditures as far too conservative. The disappointment was palpable when we talked to Planning Ministry consultant Juan Téllez: "Even after the tremendous win in 2009 elections, the MAS allowed the Ministry of Finance to dictate policy. Rather than increase investment to create jobs, the minister convinced Evo to hold massive fiscal reserves. We—in the Ministries of Planning and Education—fought unsuccessfully in the cabinet, insisting that a former banker shouldn't dictate social policy."[35]

Finance Minister Luis Arce Catacora counters that current policy is exactly where it should be and that "macro-economic stability is the point of departure, not the goal."[36] To test how well this newfound stability plays internationally, Bolivia ventured into the international credit markets for the first time since the 1920s with a successful $500 million bond sale in October 2012.[37] Government economic strategy has been described by Vice President García Linera as seeking to stimulate internal markets and reduce external dependency by expanding public enterprises and promoting redistribution to the most disadvantaged peoples. Purchasing power is up 41 percent since Morales took office.[38]

EDWIN ROJAS, VICE MINISTER OF PUBLIC FINANCES, TREASURY AND PUBLIC CREDIT[39]

Our most important achievement has been to show that a left government can create economic stability efficiently. From the beginning, this government was regarded suspiciously throughout global financial circles, as revolutionary and left governments in general are not known for sound fiscal management. What we learned from the hyperinflation of the UDP [1982–1985] was that without economic stability, it's impossible to do anything.

Given this legacy, we have had to do a lot of rebuilding. For decades, Bolivia has had one of Latin America's highest rates of U.S. dollar use. The country was about 90 or 95 percent dollarized, but that's changed. That 70 percent of all current loans are in bolivianos is a clear sign of confidence in our currency and the process of change as a whole.

Neither the constitutional reform nor the ongoing state restructuring would have been possible without a solid economy. We can see the link between stability and progress in social areas. We have made great strides in health, services, and education—all thanks to our economic strength.

Our monetary policy rests on three pillars: (1) promoting the use of bolivianos; (2) an exchange policy that inspires trust in our currency; and (3) a sound fiscal policy. Together, these form a durable base that allows us to develop economic sovereignty. Clearly our policy was made possible because of gas nationalization, which makes our resources benefit the country not just the multinationals. Before nationalization, we lacked the ability to really have an effective monetary policy. The growth of our reserves is one indication of this success. When we came to office we had a little less than US$2 billion set aside, or about 20 percent of our GDP. Now we have about half of our GDP in reserves, which admittedly is higher than in most countries. Having strong reserves provides a level of economic security and increases the use of the boliviano nationally, which adds to stability.

There have been criticisms that if we made more money available for investment we would grow faster, and indeed, we might do better if we had slightly smaller reserves, say eight to nine billion, given the opportunity costs of holding the cash. But this level allows us to monitor and set interest rates, which we couldn't do otherwise. And this feeds into expanding investments, both by the state and the private sector.

Over the short and medium term our biggest challenge is to promote industrialization. We're doing pretty well. During the world financial crisis in 2008–2009, we had the best growth in the region and among the highest in the world. Of course, we need to be careful to use our reserves for investments that will lead to further growth rather than for operational costs, like pay hikes for government employees.

From Resource Extraction to Industrialization

Adding value to natural resources exports has been the perpetual, and unfulfilled, promise made by every government since the 1952 revolution. Bolivia is not alone in its limited ability to broaden the economy. In Venezuela, for example, after twelve years in power, Chávez's government had largely failed to extend the country's productive capacity beyond that of oil and gas exports.[40]

Favorable economic circumstances have not come along often in Bolivia's history, and analysts make a strong case that this is the perfect time to diversify the economy beyond simple extraction. The government, however, has been inclined to prioritize soccer fields, paved roads, and union buildings, partly because it's easier and partly because public works provide tangible signs of action. Critics contend that investing in "nonproductive" projects represents a lost opportunity to encourage the economy to branch out.[41]

The upswing in revenue has not meant a seamless expansion of state-financed public investments. After all, 65 percent of income is needed just to cover basic administrative expenses, exactly as under previous administrations.[42] Fifty percent of earnings now come from natural gas, compared to 35 percent derived from gas and oil in Ecuador, almost 40 percent in Mexico, and roughly 50 percent in Venezuela.[43] Foreign direct investment equaled 37 percent of GDP in 2010, 10 percent higher than the South American average, and by 2012 it had grown to double the 2009 amount.[44] This puts a left-wing, anti-imperialist government in the awkward position of relying heavily on the very foreign firms it publicly disparages.

In 2007, the government instituted a National Development Plan (NDP), built on three pillars: macroeconomic and financial stability, stable employment growth, and social inclusion.[45] Central to the plan is what García Linera calls "Andean capitalism." He justifies the approach as based on theories of stages in building socialism, contending Bolivia is not yet ready for a socialist economy.[46] Andean capitalism "reflects our reality," explains the vice president, "not what we might want it to be, not what our idealism makes us want to believe, but what it really is. This is a country of small producers and family enterprises. However, it also has deeply entrenched communitarian systems and relationships, although these have weakened over the past sixty years. We must construct a strong state that mobilizes its resources to strengthen community organizations and communal forms of production."[47]

This idealized communitarian economy, purportedly practiced on a small scale in rural areas where peasants control their labor and the fruits of their production,[48] we believe, represents an oversimplification of the complex economic reality of indigenous society. Critics point out that much of the so-called communitarian economy is rooted in forms of exploitation and self-exploitation far worse than that in formal capitalism, raising questions about how this model can be successfully linked to an emancipatory project.[49]

Investments to diversify the economy have proven uneven. State control of the economy had mushroomed from 8 percent in 2005 to about 34 percent by 2013.[50] The declared goal of the new public enterprises is to generate state income to invest and reallocate rather than to create jobs.[51]

An exception is the faltering textile industry, which before the 1980s was an important source of good urban jobs. However, the contraband that flooded across the borders in ever-increasing amounts after neoliberal policies were adopted asphyxiated local manufacturing. "It's gotten so bad that about 70 percent of the economy not related to minerals and gas now runs on contraband," said Business Federation president Daniel Sánchez.[52] While producing hundreds of jobs for small-scale smugglers and street sellers, contraband has taken a huge toll on the formal economy.

In June 2012, the biggest textile exporter, AMETEX, was forced to suspend production, shedding 1,700 jobs. The MAS government interceded to save the workers' positions by setting up a new state-owned enterprise to rent the factories. Teresa Morales, minister of productive development, is exploring increasing tariffs beyond the 35 percent adopted in 2009 in order to give the industry a chance. "It will be a new era for textiles," she announced optimistically.[53]

Aside from hydrocarbons, the state runs profitable businesses such as a telephone company and a new airline, BOA.[54] A sugar refinery is slated to be inaugurated by 2015 in tropical northern La Paz, and a cement factory is on the boards for Potosí. A considerable accomplishment was bringing silver and lead smelter Karachipampa outside Potosí online in early 2013, but in March, technical problems shut it down again. Paralyzed for twenty-eight years after its initial construction, once it is fully operational, the new plant is expected to absorb 30 percent of national production.[55] Despite these initiatives, the new enterprises are sometimes accused of responding more to local political pressure than to any coherent plan.[56]

"It didn't make any sense to put a paper factory in the Chapare, but they did it because they had to respond to grassroots demands. With the constant rain and humidity, the costs are going to be astronomical simply to keep the raw materials dry. I inspected the machinery, which because of delays hadn't been put to use, and it had already rusted. I heard they spent $6 million for the plant, and from what I saw, they should have been able to do it for less than half that amount," noted a development worker.[57] A May 2012 audit by PricewaterhouseCoopers found that the contractors had been paid $12 million even though the factory was never put into operation, setting off a minor corruption scandal.[58] Such rent-seeking is common in attempts to create new ventures in low-income countries.[59]

How can natural resources foster broader development? The ill-fated attempt to establish an industrial facility at Mutún, among the world's largest iron-ore deposits, is particularly instructive. The government signed a forty-year contract with India's Jindal Steel to develop 50 percent of the site, located close to the Brazilian border. An investment of US$2.1 billion was to generate 6 million tons of sponge iron, 10 million tons of iron pellets and 1.7 million tons of steel per year—quantities that would have made Bolivia the world's twelfth-largest steel producer.[60]

Legal problems and inadequate infrastructure plagued the project from the start.[61] In October 2011, Jindal pressed the state hydrocarbons company YPFB to guarantee 10 million cubic meters of gas per day by 2017—equal to one-third of current exports to Brazil—refusing to order reduction furnaces until the gas supply was assured. As the situation deteriorated, Jindal filed for arbitration and, in June 2012, rescinded the contract. A month later, company officials fled the country when faced with a government-initiated lawsuit, and the military "occupied" the site.[62] The government put the contract out to tender again, assuring the public that its half of the mill will manufacture a modest half a million tons of sponge iron by 2015 and begin exporting iron ore in 2014.[63]

The project with Jindal was supposed to be Bolivia's biggest direct foreign investment. But the government signed the contracts before resolving underlying issues of landownership. Necessary energy and transportation infrastructure didn't exist—not only was there no gas supply, but the country has neither the rail nor the barge facilities to transport the promised 17.7 million tons of iron per year, an amount that would fill about 650,000 trucks or, if there were a rail carrier, on the order of five 100-car trains every day. Furthermore, the plant would have directed 90 percent of its production to relatively low-value-added pellet and sponge iron, while the high-value-added steel and its products were, at least over the short term, manufactured elsewhere.[64] Even so, the project was likely to have had a huge economic impact with the potential to fuel regional industrial growth and generate thousands of jobs in eastern Santa Cruz.

In an ideal scenario for Mutún, iron-ore exploitation would combine with the construction of a steel mill to fabricate the rails for the track and the plate steel to build the cars to export the finished products. Bolivia could have been able to not only export iron and steel products but also cut the transportation cost of everything that flows through the country, making its products more competitive by taking advantage of its location in the heart of South America to cement a position as a continental trans-portation hub. Mutún steelworks could have induced what economists refer to as a "virtuous cycle" and the possible creation of a twenty-first-century industrial growth pole in the east.

But it was not to be, which, in fact, may be the good news. "The received wisdom about growth poles in Latin America is that they produced unbearable social costs, consumed inordinate amounts of public and natural resources, and failed to develop beyond isolated boomtowns," writes sociologist Amy Hite. She points out that after forty years, Ciudad Guyana in Venezuela, probably the most successful project of its type, which was "to 'sow' oil windfalls . . . still experiences dependent development similar to that plaguing projects in its cohort, demonstrating the structural constraints of growth-pole strategies and their limited viability in a global economy."[65] If Venezuela, with its comparatively substantial economic, institutional, and educational advantages, failed to overcome the structural constraints in Ciudad Guyana, it is unlikely that Bolivia would succeed in its attempts to develop Mutún.

Extraction's Price

Relentless resource extraction from silver to soy has saddled Bolivia with an inheritance of destruction so severe that environmental organizations consider as much as a quarter of the territory or 60 million acres degraded and an additional 17 million acres under immediate threat.[66] "At some point, there has to be a day of reckoning," Marco Octavio Ribera of the environmental coalition League for the Defense of the Environment (LIDEMA) warns, "and every year that day comes closer."[67] Ministry of Environment and Water analyst Giovanni Altuzarra agrees, "To remedy these environmental problems, many from mining operations dating back to colonial times, would take a massive investment and many years of work."[68] Throughout Latin America, as mining accelerates, local struggles increasingly focus not only on the site-specific toxic tailings and destruction it leaves but also on the amount of local water mining consumes and contaminates.[69]

The MAS government faces an endless tug-of-war between its stated commitment to protect the environment and the pressures to expand extractive industries to fund its ambitious programs. On the one hand, environmental monitoring has been strengthened. Mirso Alcalá of the Environment and Water Ministry, who served in previous environment-oriented ministries, insists, "For the first time we have a committed government and are actually able to formulate and carry out plans."[70] But on the other, the Environment Ministry carries little weight in the cabinet and is never consulted when economic issues, such as oil and gas extraction, are discussed.[71] In the Chaco, this means that "the hydrocarbons companies have come onto our lands without respecting or consulting us," laments Guaraní Peoples Assembly (APG) spokesperson Teófilo Murillo. "For the most part, our reports and our complaints have been ignored."[72]

By 2012, this had shifted, as the consultation provisions of the new constitution enabled the APG to stall thirteen new projects with demands for compensation. This has caused considerable government consternation and fueled efforts to separate the current environmental impact reports from the consultation process so as to reduce bottlenecks in strategic state projects. Officials also note that the poorly defined consultation process is full of legal inconsistencies.[73]

The MAS government has claimed that the decisions reached by the constitutionally mandated consultation process are not binding. Morales complained in July 2011, "When we want to build roads there's no lack of Indigenous brothers and sisters, influenced by some NGOs, who don't want them. When we want to explore for oil, they don't want it. When we want to build dams they also oppose. . . . It is a necessity to have more oil, more gas, more roads, industry. . . . Consultation does not exist so that Indigenous brothers and sisters can extort the government and [private] companies. Consultation serves to avoid environmental problems."[74] Repeating strategies employed by neoliberal governments, the Morales government has often bypassed regional indigenous organizations to negotiate directly with affected communities, fomenting internal divisions and discord.

An environmental catastrophe is looming in Bolivia's vast woodlands, the Americas' fifth largest. With almost half of the country wooded, the lowlands are full of spectacular trees with indigenous names like *jichituri-qui*, *ochoó*, and *curupaú*. But the diverse forests—from the dry woods in the Chiquitanía east of Santa Cruz to the wet Amazon jungles in northern Pando—are being cut down at one of the fastest rates in the world. Just when Brazil has slowed its violent destruction of the Amazon, deforestation in other parts of lowland South America has gathered speed, with an area in Bolivia the size of Delaware (1,400 square miles) now estimated to fall under the ax every year.[75] The proximate causes are the explosive expansion of agriculture and growing illegal logging as well as smallholder colonization.[76] Policing illegal logging is close to impossible in remote areas.[77] Yet thanks to NGO[78] and bilateral efforts, Bolivia is also a leader in certified natural forests under the voluntary Forest Stewardship Council process, with more than 3 million acres of its forests verified as meeting international standards, ranking it third in the region.

When Morales came to power, forests were under the jurisdiction of a 1996 neoliberal-era law that had sought to extend regulatory control and increase market incentives to encourage sustainable forestry. Forestry in the 1990s was expanding slowly and focused on selective extraction of the most valuable species, although the country was judged as having enormous potential.[79] By the end of 2005, seventy legal forest concessions harvested almost 10 million acres, providing work to approximately 60,000 people.

As of 2013, a comprehensive forestry law still had not been written. However, a controversial amendment to the 1996 Forestry Law was put in place in January with the stated intention of improving food security and "restitution of forests" through allowing an estimated 12 million acres of illegally deforested land to be used for agricultural production. Environmentalists were irate. Marco Octavio Ribera calls the move "perverse . . . because it expands the agricultural frontier and rewards export agro-industrialists who are a principal cause of our environmental destruction."[80]

The law forgives illegal deforestation between 1996 and 2011 in exchange for owners paying a small fine and increasing productivity, planting crops the government deems strategic, and engaging in reforestation.[81] Julio Roda, of the Eastern Agricultural Chamber of Commerce (CAO), once staunchly opposed to the Morales government, enthused that this agreement would allow producers to expand agriculture fivefold to 35 million acres. "Many producers whose operations had been halted can now ask for permissions to clear land and begin cultivation again," applauded Roda.[82]

In May 2013, Vice President García Linera announced that the government would permit hydrocarbons exploration in Bolivia's twenty-two national parks, many of which curve around the fertile base of the Andes where oil and gas are commonly found. Hydrocarbons concessions already exist in eleven parks, although most are inactive. The vice president assured the public, "We have to use what nature has provided us, but we mustn't destroy nature in the process."[83]

These types of setbacks have discouraged environmentalists, many of whom felt until recently that this government had done more, even if not enough, than previous ones. "For government after government, sustainable development and environmental protection have been nothing more than a slogan. At least this government is taking on some initiatives," Sucre activist Apolonia Rodríguez told us in 2009. But she added, "Unfortunately, it is too little too late. We are being devastated by uncontrolled forestry, mining, hydrocarbon extraction, and ever-expanding soy cultivation."[84]

Initiatives like the Law of Mother Earth, signed in October 2012, which grants rights to nature for the first time in world history, do not address the fundamental contradiction that the Morales government faces. A landmark piece of legislation, it bans genetically modified organisms (GMO) but clashes headlong with the $800 million soy economy, which relies almost completely on GMO seeds. Soy producers were immediately up in arms, arguing that they could not compete internationally if forced to comply.[85]

People as the Foundation for Development

The difficulties confronting long-term economic development were made abundantly clear at a planning meeting in Betanzos, an hour outside Potosí, where, on a crisp Saturday morning in 2012, twelve rural municipalities discussed priorities. About a third of the audience was women, mostly in *polleras*; the men sported clothing from a U.S. Postal Service jacket with Ché embroidered on the front to a Brazilian national team soccer shirt topped by a New York Yankees baseball cap. Flash drives around necks completed the semiotically contradictory wardrobe, which seems indicative of what appeared to be the desires of the audience: retaining their rural way of life and values while embracing global cultural icons and their own version of modernity.

The desperately poor communities are assaulted by mining pollution that destroys their crops, land, and water supply, but the discussion that morning proffered few solutions. The meeting made evident that while the state has resources to embark on national and regional planning, no one has yet figured out how to convert the natural resource boom into the type of local economic development that generates jobs or remediates the dire consequences of mining.[86]

With public expectations that the government will spearhead job creation substantially higher in Bolivia and other parts of Latin America than in Canada and the United States, the pressure on extraction-based governments is acute, as their economies do not easily produce the necessary forward and backward linkages to create many jobs.[87] Labor productivity in Bolivia is the region's lowest, as is its investment rate.[88] Although the country had twenty-two treaties in place to adjudicate disputes over investments by the end of 2011, in practice, it struggles to provide the secure legal environment that private capital, whether national or international, demands.[89] In early 2012, the government became more proactive, proposing to invest 10 percent of national reserves to foment production, particularly of textiles, wood products, food, and mining.[90]

Bolivia supplies low-cost, largely unskilled labor to global markets. An estimated 2.5 million people, about one in five since the 1980s, have emigrated.[91] Argentina attracts the bulk of them, about 1.5 million, where Bolivians occupy a space similar to Mexicans in the United States, although very often under better legal conditions, as since 2006, Argentina has made it relatively easy for immigrants to gain permanent residency and citizenship rights.[92] About 300,000 are in Spain, with a similar number in the United States, although in both places many face the hurdles affecting undocumented workers. In 2009, migrants sent about one billion dollars a year home to their families, an enormous injection of cash that matches almost one-fifth of exports and is second only to Ecuador in South America as a proportion of GDP. Most of the money was spent on basic necessities: school fees, clothing, health costs, and house construction.[93]

Out-migration affects the quality of the local labor force. "I haven't been able to keep any mechanics," protests Carlos Ramos at a small motorcycle repair shop in Cochabamba. "I hire a helper for two or three years, and after I train them, they're off to Spain or Argentina. I've trained five mechanics who have emigrated. It's good for them, and it's clear that even if life is hard, they are doing well—at least most of them—the ones that get to Spain or the United States do best. When they come back to visit after a few years, it's like their software has changed. They are more responsible, work harder, and have better skills. Paco, who went back to Spain, told me, 'Don Carlos, I can make more there in a weekend than you paid me in a month.' I'm glad that they are getting ahead, but I spend a lot of time teaching new guys." He laughs, "Spain should be paying me for training technicians."[94]

Emigration has been holding steady at between 1 and 1.5 percent annually for over twenty years. What are the prospects for those left behind? Most job growth occurs in what is commonly called the informal sector[95]—the unlicensed street vendors, woodshops, garages, and other small firms that account for almost 70 percent of all employment. These firms typically are highly local, often organized at the family level, labor intensive, with minimal access to capital, marginally productive, and incompletely regulated. They offer the advantages of providing easy entry to the market and, most important, a way to make a marginal living. It is far easier, for example, to encourage people to set up a small woodshop or a hot dog stand than to mount a steel mill or a national rail system. In rural areas, the lack of mechanization keeps labor productivity low, and off-farm employment opportunities are few except in highly exploitative small-scale mining or as agricultural laborers on large estates.

JOSÉ LUIS PEREIRA, NATIONAL VICE DIRECTOR OF MICROFINANCES FOR PARASTATAL BANCO UNIÓN[96]

We're interested in using our bank as a financial institution that can drive the process of change and foster economic development through democratizing access to capital and financial services. Bolivia is a big country with services concentrated in a few cities. As gas nationalization has allowed us to increase social benefits, rural people need access to financial services and education so they can use their new cash income to improve their lives. In parts of the Amazon or the Chiquitanía, it's still necessary to travel as much as two or three days to cash a government check. We see access to financial services not only as a right but also as an economic development tool.

As we work to extend services, we're beginning to understand the country differently as well. Unlike other countries, we just don't have reliable statistical information to inform policy making, so it's more based on experience. In the Amazon, for example, there aren't any roads, but it's obvious that the possibilities for river transport are excellent, so the government established a public transportation company that offers people who live along the river access to health services, a way to convey their goods to market as well as a means to integrate them with the larger country. These kinds of changes, particularly for people who live in remote corners where there was never any state presence, have been transformative.

I've worked in rural development for over twenty-five years and I think only now are we beginning to see real structural changes. We've not done everything—the impact on health and income is just beginning—but we are bringing people into the national economic sphere who were excluded before. The process isn't as fast as we would like, but things are happening. Just a few weeks ago, for example, we passed the country's first ever law on agricultural credit. It's based on one developed in Brazil, and while it may not be perfect, it is an important start.

Without exaggerating, I can say that I have worked under a dozen different ministers. They keep moving us around in terms of which ministry we're under. What surprises me most about these constant changes is that very often the new minister is given a different mandate, so projects that began under one person are dropped midstream, and everything begins over again and then over again once more.

I think you have to look at the process critically because, unfortunately, errors have been made, but also optimistically because the changes are irreversible. The rights that people who were second-class citizens have won, and the recognition and respect for our diversity of cultures, that is what will remain over the long term. The rest is just details.

Conclusions: Breaking Beyond Extraction

No matter what the political orientation of the government in power, Bolivia's persistent challenge is to escape from simple extraction of natural resources to transform infrastructure, foment productivity, generate jobs, and create sustainable social benefits that decrease inequality.[97] Unfortunately, but unsurprisingly, under Evo, the economic structure remains unchanged. The government still fundamentally relies on gas revenues, making modern development dependent largely on foreign capital and extraction. The best jobs are found outside of the country, and at home the informal sector still dominates. The economic elites retain their privileges; contraband remains uncontrolled and, some would say, uncontrollable; and the government struggles to reshape the bureaucratic culture of the state.

Soccer fields and union buildings aside, the substantial investments in physical infrastructure such as roads, electric grids, schools, and clinics, as well as social investments in health and education, are essential if Bolivia is to propel itself into better economic conditions over the long term. In the next chapter, we look more closely at how the government is attempting to turn the definition of development inside out, in its efforts to help the majority "live well" rather than simply increase macroeconomic growth.

CHAPTER 6

Living Well/Vivir Bien: Government Transfers, Health, and Education

On the broad expanse of altiplano outside La Paz, the newly paved road sports a sign to make sure you don't forget that "Evo *cumple*"[1]—the president fulfills his promises. In tiny Pisca Ajira, brand-new classrooms in the recently expanded school sit ready for students. A local man proudly tells us, "We have two teachers for twenty students; in the city, sometimes you get forty-five in a class. And the teachers are good, too!"

"The changes I have seen are extraordinary," says Marta Arévalo, director of the Swedish Cooperative Centre,[2] who counts twenty years' experience in rural areas throughout the country. "Not like anything we've ever seen before—the stipends, the schools and health post, the electrification, and the improved roads. For rural people, this government has made a huge difference."[3]

From north to south and east to west, people agree with Marta's assessment. In southern Tarija valleys: "My parents live almost at the Argentinean border. A big change has happened since Evo got elected. My mother, who is now eighty-six, has running water and electricity for the first time, and the community has a new school," relates taxi driver Juan Ramos.[4] In the Oruro highlands: "Ever since Evo entered office, everything has gone better. In our village, we have a new municipal office, and recently we got electricity," reports llama herder Filomena Condori Condori.[5] In rural Santa Cruz: "We have titled land for sixteen communities during this government," landless leader Eulogio Cortés explains proudly.[6] In highland Potosí: "My community now has electricity and running water. I really appreciate what Evo's government has achieved," states María Rivas, whose family was driven by near destitution to Santa Cruz fifteen years ago.[7] Bolivia is not alone: poverty has fallen sharply throughout Latin America since left-leaning governments have come to power.[8]

City dwellers, however, frequently complain that the government has failed to prioritize urban unemployment and chronic poverty. Ibeth Garabito, director of the small organization MUSOL that works with desperately poor miners' widows in Potosí,[9] voices a typical complaint, "We had high hopes for change. But the widows and their children are either no better off or the change is so slight that it makes little difference."[10] In Sucre, small shop operator Doña Teresa belonged to a knitting cooperative that folded after the APTDEA trade agreement with the United States collapsed in 2008. "Things have just gotten worse since Evo. There's less tourism, and when I make clothes for the local market, they can't compete with cheap goods from China."[11]

In 2005, 60 percent of the population lived in various degrees of poverty,[12] two-thirds of them rural and most of them women and children. The southern departments of Potosí and Chuquisaca and northernmost Pando registered 60 percent of their people surviving on less than a dollar a day. Latin Americans don't want such a high degree of inequality in their societies: 75–85 percent believe current income distribution is unjust.[13] While it remains South America's poorest country, by 2007 Bolivia was scoring better than Haiti, Honduras, Nicaragua, and Guatemala.[14]

Living Well: Vivir Bien, Suma Qamaña, Sumaj Kausay, Ñande Reko, Teko Kavi, Qhapaj Nan

The foundation underpinning the new social programs is the concept of Vivir Bien (Living Well),[15] a philosophy that gauges well-being differently from the usual economic indicators, even those such as the Human Development Index that take into account access to health, housing, running water, and education. Vivir Bien seeks harmony, consensus, and good governance, prioritizing community values of self- and mutual respect, redistribution of wealth, and elimination of all kinds of discrimination within a framework of valuing diversity, community over individual rights, and the natural environment.[16] For Guaraní leader Marcia Mandepora, "Thinking deeply about knowledge, nature, and 'living well' requires a profound engagement with socially, historically, and spiritually embedded realities of indigenous people's relationships to nature."[17]

With similarities to Bhutan's Gross National Happiness Index, and drawing from the UN's International Labor Organization convention 169, the 2007 UN Declaration on the Rights of Indigenous Peoples, and the 2009 Constitution for its legal framework, Vivir Bien was largely conceptualized by Aymara intellectuals. The concept renounces capitalism, war, imperialism, and colonialism, recognizing basic services as a human right while valuing local consumption and moderation.[18]

Philosopher Javier Medina explains why it offers a better measure of human well-being, "The erosion of communal values and organization combines with spiritual alienation to harm people more than material deprivation. . . . Overcoming poverty is more than simply improving income and public services."[19] However, other observers worry that the notion is poorly theorized and understood differently across varying ethnicities, and that its advocates are consistently clearer about what it stands against rather than what it means.[20] Karen Lennon found in a rural Chuquisaca community that while Vivir Bien is not part of the local vernacular, many aspects of the concept are evident in how people live their daily lives, such as engaging in reciprocal practices and a deep respect for land and place.[21]

Despite its flaws, President Rafael Correa was inspired to adopt Vivir Bien for the 2008 Ecuadorean Constitution. "Reducing the enormous gap between rich and poor through Vivir Bien is fundamental," says Evo Morales. "Knowing that we are gradually achieving it encourages me to deepen my commitment to its goals."[22]

In this chapter, we examine how the MAS government has employed Vivir Bien, a concept that challenges teleological notions of development, in its efforts to improve the quality of life in Bolivia. Critics argue that the focus on living well is simply rhetoric and the result of fuzzy thinking, but we suggest that incorporating an alternative vision of what development might be has contributed to programs that reflect new, albeit imperfectly executed, perspectives in health, education, economic development, and social welfare. The evidence shows that, to date, these have had positive material impacts on people's lives.

Transfer Payments: *Bonos*

The MAS government's most fully executed poverty-alleviation measure revolves around financing small but significant conditional cash transfer payments, reflecting higher social welfare spending throughout the region over the past ten years.[23] Similar programs are now under way in nineteen countries, reaching almost one-fifth of Latin America's population.[24] While falling short of universal programs common in Europe and Canada, and on a more limited basis in the United States, the plans are generally favored by pink tide governments over more difficult and contentious projects such as combating wage inequalities.[25]

Poverty alleviation is further inhibited by leftist governments' reluctance to aggressively tackle wealth redistribution through restructuring taxes. Only Uruguay and Ecuador have made any progress on this front. More typical are Brazil, which retains low income-tax rates, and Central America, where particularly regressive taxation perpetuates the region's inordinately high concentration of wealth.[26] In Guatemala, an antagonistic and powerful private sector was able to prevent Álvaro Colom's government from implementing moderate tax reforms despite the mandate the measures had under the 1996 peace accords.[27]

Although most transfer programs have grown roots under left-leaning governments, they were pioneered under conservatives, originating in Honduras in 1990, and later extended to Mexico in the late 1990s through the "Opportunities" program that offers cash incentives to decrease school desertion and augment health care participation. Brazil's Bono Familia, instituted in 2003, covers over 50 million participants (a quarter of the population), and is conditioned on school attendance and vaccine compliance, as well as pre- and postnatal care. In one of history's most remarkable social welfare triumphs, Brazil's poverty rate plummeted from 43 to 29 percent and its Gini coefficient (the most common indicator of inequality) plunged 17 percent in just five years.[28] Conditional cash transfers have now become so entrenched that even right-wing politicians recognize that they must publicly commit to them to stand a chance of winning office.

Are the programs offered by left-wing governments different from those of their conservative predecessors? Overall they are, as most are complemented by some combination of expanded public pensions, health care, and land reform, providing a policy coherence that proves more effective than simple transfer payments.[29] Their long-term viability, however, has been questioned, as many rely on current high commodity prices and the expansion of extractive industries for financing.

Similar to other initiatives, Bolivia's three programs include an annual stipend for children who stay in school, an old-age pension, and a supplement for women who attend pre- and postnatal care. The bulk of the money allocated for these programs finances the Renta Dignidad,[30] in an expansion of a late-1990s program, which now reaches over 750,000 women and men over sixty.[31] British NGO HelpAge International representative James Blackburn is impressed, "Renta Dignidad is significant for such a low-income country. Certainly there's a long way to go to protect the elderly here, but if you compare it with Peru, which is not as poor overall, the results are remarkable."[32] While it amounts to only about US$29 a month, the disbursement substantially shrinks elder poverty and plays a part in making the state more accountable to its citizens.[33] "It isn't enough to live on," an elderly Cochabamba man clarifies, "but it pays for staples like rice, pasta, sugar, and oil for almost the whole month, so it's a big help. My wife gets it, too, so it means we always have enough to eat."[34]

The previous partially privatized pension scheme was a huge drain on state resources, a common difficulty throughout Latin America.[35] Returning to a version of the preprivatization "pay-as-you-go" arrangement had the potential to significantly slash these pension burdens, but only Argentina has embraced this option to date.[36] Bolivia, however, is moving in that direction.[37] The Morales government recouped pension funds that cover 1.2 million workers from foreign banks, convinced that the state could better administer the assets. The retirement age was dropped from sixty-five to sixty, and minimum benefits were extended to self-employed people. By 2010, bucking the global trend, all Bolivians became eligible to retire at fifty-eight, and miners at fifty-six. The system has also been enlarged to include those who work informally and currently lack pensions.[38]

The Bono Juancito Pinto[39] provides an annual payment of Bs. $200 (about US$29) for each child enrolled up to the fifth grade in an effort to reduce dropout rates. By 2008, it had broadened up to the eighth year of schooling. An independent evaluation at the five-year mark concluded that not only was the Bono meeting its goals, it had a particularly positive impact for the poorest students.[40]

A 2008 program named for nineteenth-century indigenous leader Juana Azurduy granted pregnant and nursing women a modest subsidy.[41] Standing in a long, hot line in the Cochabamba tropics, surrounded by other women with babies strapped to their backs in colorful striped *aguayos*,[42] Florinda Vallejo says the wait is worth it. "It does take time away from work, but I know it's good for me and my baby. The money also helps buy milk and bread for my other children."[43] The *bono* played a significant role in cutting the high maternal mortality rate by more than half in just four years.[44]

When Morales took office, twenty years of erratic attempts to stem childhood malnutrition had largely failed, and under-five malnutrition, mostly in rural areas, had remained constant at 26 percent between 1998 and 2005.[45] In 2007, an ambitious five-year goal of reaching zero malnutrition in at least half the municipalities by integrating specific nutrition-oriented budget items was inaugurated. After initial success, high-level commitment fell off, and hampered by inadequate coordination, improvements have slowed.[46]

For the poorest, these social policies, taken together, have often been life-changing. UN representative Yoriko Yasukawa lauded Bolivia's reduction of extreme poverty by 2011 from 38 to 26 percent in cities, and from 60 to 50 percent in the countryside.[47] Such steep declines are also evident in Venezuela and Nicaragua, where similar policies are in place.[48]

In a country that is home to one of Latin America's most imbalanced societies in the world's most unequal region, income inequality has also diminished, although optimistic claims by Vice President García Linera that the proportion the richest 10 percent earns has dropped by half[49] are disputed by sources such as the UN and the World Bank.[50]

Education

"Come and see the swearing-in of our new governing board," urges Eulogio Laura at Indigenous University "Tupak Katari," north of La Paz. Hidden among tall eucalyptus and pines, a rarity on the desertlike altiplano, the ex-hacienda is bustling with life. A student in veterinary medicine, Eulogio exudes an enthusiasm that is contagious, and we soon join the throng of students in the large, newly constructed hall. The four hundred young people all have noticeably Andean features, with many young women in long braids and *polleras*. One by one, students and professors, almost all Aymara and recently elected to the university governing board, solemnly take their place at the front of the auditorium. On this gentle slope that descends to the marshy, deep blue of Lake Titicaca, they are shaping a new kind of education.

In 2006, rethinking educational policy had gotten off to a roaring start when Aymara activist and educator Félix Patzi was named education minister and declared that all government employees must study an indigenous language. Education policy was framed as part of a broad commitment to decolonize society, put indigenous and western knowledge on the same footing, and make education community based and participatory. Patzi's proposal to require state schools to teach indigenous languages

frightened the urban middle class, whose deep-seated fears of an indigenous takeover were manipulated by conservatives claiming that Spanish
would be displaced as the national language.

Patzi ignited further controversy, this time with the Roman Catholic
Church, when he proposed substituting a "History of Religions" class
based on Catholic mores for a course that integrated indigenous beliefs.[51]
By January 2007, protests against Patzi had become vociferous, and Morales first overruled and then sacked him.

Controversies over public education are nothing new. Before the 1952
revolution, only 31 percent of the population was literate[52] and 60 percent
had no access to schools, with almost none available in the countryside.[53]
The 1955 Education Code ambitiously called for a system that was "universal, free and obligatory, as well as national, democratic, revolutionary,
anti-feudal, anti-imperialist in nature; progressive, co-educating, global-
izing, and scientific."[54] Then, as now, reform was driven by the role that
education plays both in forming ideology and training students for the
workforce.[55]

Weak educational systems act as a significant brake on economic development not only in Bolivia but throughout Latin America, where students
lag behind much of the world on standardized tests.[56] While education expenditures are substantial and rising, performance hasn't kept pace.[57] All
the pink tide governments prioritize improving education as part of improving standards of living: school repairs and a standardized minimum
curriculum have been the thrust in Ecuador;[58] educational access and a
spectacular growth in universities serving the poor has been the focus in
Venezuela;[59] increasing teachers' salaries is the priority in Brazil;[60] and
nutrition and free school supplies programs, infrastructure repair, and
community involvement are the crux of Salvadoran policy.[61]

While Bolivia's 1955 Education Code emphasized creating a national
identity and an engaged citizenry, a 1994 neoliberal-era reform focused
on grooming students to join the labor market, in some cases as young as
fourteen. Parents could formally participate in teacher and curriculum
evaluation, materials were to be made more culturally appropriate, and
learning processes were highlighted as equally important as content. At
its core was a pedagogically progressive western educational philosophy
with multicultural and neoliberal components.[62]

By the start of the twenty-first century, the country still suffered from
the highest adult illiteracy rate in South America,[63] the result of decades
of lackluster state-sponsored literacy campaigns.[64] Women were three

times as likely as men to be unable to read and write, particularly in rural areas where illiteracy, at 40 percent, was double that of cities. The MAS moved quickly to prepare a program based on the Cuban model, which has also been adapted for Argentina, Nicaragua, Ecuador, and Venezuela.[65] The "Yes I can" campaign commenced in March 2006, and over 500,000 people graduated from literacy classes in Spanish and indigenous languages. By 2009, Evo claimed illiteracy had been conquered, although the World Bank expressed doubts, contending their research showed only a 5 percent overall decline.[66] "Not being able to read and write is like being blind," Cochabamba's Margarita Pérez recalls. "Now I feel like a real person for the first time."[67]

Education reform has been slowed, just as it was under neoliberal governments,[68] in part by the objections of the powerful, militant urban teachers' union. Throughout Latin America, teachers, often on the front lines of struggles for social change, resist reforming education, usually because of concerns about their abysmal salaries, poor working conditions, limited voice in decisions affecting them, and often punitive teacher evaluations.[69] Bolivian teachers objected to the 1994 reform for political as well as cultural reasons, effectively painting the measure with a neoliberal brush and referring to it, as union leader Mario Quintanilla told us, as "that damn law."[70] The situation is complicated, as teachers' unions often disagree and clash with school committees, the Juntas Escolares, which were mandated as early as 1955 to involve the parents of schoolchildren. By the late 1990s, they numbered over 11,000 groups.[71]

Composing the largest contingent of public sector workers, teachers' salaries start low but rise more rapidly than any others.[72] Nonetheless, almost a third of urban teachers live below the poverty line, and more than half hold a second job to make ends meet.[73] Salomé Magne Ayala teaches thirty-nine four- and five-year-olds for four hours every afternoon and only occasionally has an assistant. Sometimes, she has disabled children in her classroom. "I work in a private school in the mornings for three hours just to cover my expenses. And I don't have any children of my own to support." In 2012, with ten years' experience, she earned a little less than US$400 a month working two very demanding jobs.[74]

Education has also struggled to overcome its neocolonial legacy. Ministry of Education's Victor Pinaya recalls growing up, "I remember my school book . . . it said, 'Mother eats cake.' First of all, I didn't know what cake was. Second, there was a drawing of a mother, but she was blond, with a white complexion, and in a dress and shoes. But when I looked at my mother, she was brown-skinned with braids, short with sandals, with worn, swollen feet . . . Where did that type of education lead us? To admire that type of mother and look down on our own."[75]

To address this complex scenario, a broad-based educational congress was convened in July 2006 to draft a new law. The unions, the universities, and the Catholic Church representatives soon stormed out, largely for the same reasons they balked in the 1990s: teachers resisted parent participation, decentralization, and a revision of their pay raises; universities objected to any public oversight; and the Church protested making education secular. The government had little choice but to back down. "The new law is condemned to fail," says La Paz teachers' union official José Luis Álvarez. "This government is just repeating the mistakes of the past."[76]

Taking a different tack, the Ministry of Education supported the formation of Indigenous Educational Councils (CEPOs), which drafted a new law based on consultation with local communities. Named after the founders of Warisata, a pioneering 1930s effort to provide indigenous education,[77] and inspired by the liberation pedagogy of Brazilian Paulo Freire, the Avelino Siñani y Elizardo Pérez Education Law was signed into law in December 2010. Every child is obligated to learn an indigenous language and culture alongside Spanish and western subjects. The new model is both intracultural and intercultural, fortifying culture within indigenous communities and between indigenous and western cultures as equals.[78] "We dream of a decolonizing education," Morales announced when the law was enacted.[79]

JIOVANNY SAMANAMUD, DIRECTOR, PEDAGOGICAL RESEARCH INSTITUTE, MINISTRY OF EDUCATION[80]

We are committed to the idea of plurilingual community knowledge generation. But what does this mean exactly? We want to recuperate traditional indigenous knowledge in formulating a new educational system. But the problem is that this knowledge varies enormously and operates differently in distinct contexts. For example, in mathematics, some think we should learn the ancient *khipu*[81] as a counting system. But how do we integrate this into western mathematics? How do we make this useful and pertinent while reconstituting indigenous knowledge? Its utility must go beyond the purely cultural because we want to ground it within a socioproductive community project.

What we are talking about is not substituting one type of knowledge for another, but making different kinds of learning relevant to current reality while reinforcing cultural identity. It is a new way of looking at education.

One of the biggest tasks is to improve teacher quality. Many teachers are steeped in a colonial mentality, which is how they were trained. We need to work with young teacher trainees, because we have a better chance at transformation when they are just beginning.

We hope to construct a new educational proposal from below, something that has never existed. But people don't value this much, they seek a magic bullet that will address their immediate needs. We don't want a system designed by professionals. Rather we seek to gather existing experiences and translate these into concrete plans. Rural teachers have made several interesting proposals. Unfortunately, people conceive of these ideas as just for the countryside. But we have gotten really interesting proposals from people from the urban periphery and marginal public schools as well. It is important to comprehend urban experiences because, after all, education is life, it is about life and for life. It's not just about reducing knowledge to its practical uses, nor is it just about celebrating and romanticizing some "indigenous" past.

The socioproductive community model requires that math and social science teachers flesh out projects oriented to local problems. This enables students to learn physics, chemistry, and mathematics. For example, if a place has contaminated water, how can the schools help address that problem? Students can learn biology, chemistry, and physics while also supplying clean water to their community. Given that we have a state without strong institutions, schools should fulfill an important community role. This is productive in the sense of responding to concrete problems, not just in the sense of improving production.

This is a new methodology, a novel way of communicating knowledge. At this point, we are changing education's orientation, but we still haven't gotten very far, and people are often left to their own devices. Now is the time to systematize experiences and see what it will take to get to where we want to go.

The new curriculum remains under construction, a state that Minister of Education Roberto Aguilar Gómez insists should remain permanent. "Community participation in enriching educational processes must never end," he believes. "This is the only way that education can truly respond to people's needs, aspirations, and expectations."[82] Designed to draw from social movement struggles and indigenous values, the model seeks to assimilate the school and learning into the community, as well as striking a balance between traditional and western systems.[83]

Three indigenous universities,[84] one in the highlands, the second in the Chapare, and the third in the lowland Chaco, were launched in 2008, mirroring a trend toward indigenous-oriented education throughout the Americas.[85] Students receive assistance from both their organizations and government subsidies, which are financed by a special tax on natural gas. Nineteen-year-old Leni Machis studies textiles in highland Warisata, "Being here is both an amazing privilege and [an] opportunity because nowhere else would I be given a full scholarship that covers everything, and without the support I couldn't possibly go to university."[86]

Programs focus on strengthening the communitarian economy, emphasizing subjects such as forestry management, veterinary medicine, and fisheries. Even though she recognizes the toll from extractive activities on indigenous communities, Marcia Mandepora, first rector of the Bolivian Indigenous University of the Chaco, argues for "engagement rather than opposition . . . so we can restructure how extractive activities are carried out in indigenous territories . . . [W]e now possess the power to prevent oil companies from acting as they please. Training could help our peoples monitor, mitigate, and participate in all aspects of extraction and commercialization with more concern for environmental and social impacts. . . . If we are just training our youth to be like the rest, we are doing nothing for our people."[87]

Mandepora worries, however, "We are caught in the contradiction confronting us as a country: how to reorder the extractive economies that worsen rural poverty and environmental degradation, while relying on these same activities to generate revenues to revolutionize our society."[88]

Health

The disjointedness of Bolivia's health care—typical of many systems from the United States to Argentina—meant that attempting reform soon thrust the government into what was often a baffling quagmire. The state system, split between public services, which encompass state-run health posts and hospitals, and universal maternal, infant, and elderly insurance, covers less than half the population and was judged one of the region's most hierarchical. Administrative incompetence, an obsolete and contradictory legal framework, and profound dependency on international donors characterized the fragmented and incoherent system.[89]

The new government expressed determination, just as Latin America's other left-wing governments did, to extend health coverage. Only Costa

Rica had a functional universal system. Without the resources to move toward universal coverage, as Chile had done with Plan Auge or Venezuela with Barrio Adentro, the MAS government focused on the immediate goal of expanding basic coverage up to age twenty-five.[90] The Ministry of Health and Sports became the most important player in setting standards, initiating innovations, and coordinating the decentralized system.

Health status, like income and poverty, differs enormously between rural and urban, rich and poor. For example, only about 20 percent of rural people can count on access to safe water and sanitation. The country sits close to the bottom of the region's health indicators, with only about half the doctors per capita, most of them ensconced in the cities. "Seventy-seven percent of the population is excluded in some manner," explained Morales's first health minister, Dr. Nila Heredia, in 2006[91] when the government initiated a noteworthy service expansion to the country's poorest people.

The new system's foundation is the 2006 SAFCI,[92] based on the primary health-care principles of the 1978 Declaration of Alma-Ata, promoted by the WHO and UNICEF.[93] It advocates community participation in planning and implementation, recognizes the social underpinnings of illness, and proposes integrating traditional medicine. Medical students are compelled to commit to three years in an underserved health facility, and their new curriculum encompasses traditional medicine and intercultural sensitivity.[94] Both theoretical and operational complications, however, have constrained implementation. Local health committees are mandated to have considerable influence, but these committees, which have been slow to form, have encountered resistance from health-care providers and authorities in some districts. As well, committee members typically lack the training necessary to fulfill their roles.[95]

Discursively at least, as the hemisphere's earliest government-led effort to unite traditional and western medicine,[96] SAFCI elevates indigenous healing to the same plane as biomedicine, necessitating an as yet largely unrealized philosophical shift among medical practitioners. Integration efforts have been most successful in Oruro and Potosí, where central hospitals offer postgraduate degrees in intercultural health as well as certification for indigenous healers. Traditional medicine practitioners are also being accredited in Chuquisaca and Tarija, where healers must verify their experience and community recognition, as well as furnish recommendations from local authorities. Nonetheless, poor coordination, sparse funding, and constant staff turnover have kept traditional medicine at the margins, guaranteeing the abiding power of westernized medicine, which continues to dictate day-to-day operations in most places.[97]

The country's health programs have been funded for decades by international agencies, such as the Pan American Health organization (PAHO), and bilateral aid from the United States, Japan, and Europe. However, USAID funding stood apart from the rest, as the agency often directly designed Bolivian government health policy. USAID initially responded to the MAS victory by shifting resources away from existing highland projects to those controlled by the lowland opposition. Parallel scholarship programs, set up in coordination with the anti-Morales College of Physicians, also privileged eastern students. In 2008, USAID did an about-turn as tensions between the United States and the MAS government escalated. In an effort to minimize disputes, and in the hands of a health programs director more sympathetic to MAS goals, USAID endorsed the SAFCI model.[98]

Cuba sent about nine hundred nominally paid doctors and eight hundred paramedics to work in the country's most impoverished municipalities, which particularly distressed U.S. officials. Cuban-run eye clinics had provided free cataract surgery to over 600,000 people by 2011, including the soldier who had killed the last Cuban-based doctor he had laid eyes on—Ché Guevara.[99] The government obtained full scholarships for five thousand low-income Bolivians to study medicine in Cuba, ten times more than previous administrations.

DR. DANIEL FLORES QUISPE[100]

I first heard about the scholarship from my godmother who is a street vendor in Sucre. I had finished high school close to home in rural Chuquisaca, and I knew I wanted to become a professional, but I wasn't sure how I would do it because my family is very poor.

I thought perhaps this was my chance. So I filled out all the forms and, much to my surprise, I was accepted. Almost all of us who went, from all over the country, were from low-income families. That was the purpose of the funding.

Cuba is a beautiful place. I found people very generous and keen to help and share. There was a real sense of solidarity that people showed toward us. People have a great level of education there, and I think that helps them to understand how to be good to each other. People are much more competitive here.

The medical training was excellent. It will take twenty or thirty years for us to establish a medical system as good as Cuba's. Cuba has eradicated all kinds of diseases, like tuberculosis, that we still have here. All medical services there are free, while here everything costs so much. I have worked in a clinic in Bolivia's lowlands, and if people showed up without money, we couldn't do anything for them.

I would like to get a specialization in internal medicine. I'm interested in the other side of the coin and would like to study a specialization in the United States. But I'd have to get another scholarship.

Traditional medicine is very important, and we need to figure out how to integrate it into our health programs. People really believe in it, and, consequently, it plays a critical role in curing all kinds of illnesses, including psychological ones.

Even if I eventually get a job in the city, I will always help out in my community. I did a bit of medical work there when I returned from Cuba at the beginning of 2012, and the need is very great, so I will always help my people.

The Cuban influence encouraged the MAS government to emphasize a socialist health model, but Cuba's system is largely western, doctor-centric, and hierarchical.[101] Given the resistance of many Bolivian doctors to both Cuban socialism and traditional medical practitioners, marrying the two systems is proving far more difficult than the Ministry of Health ever imagined.

An example is found in the plan to revamp the medical school curriculum, which has been strongly resisted by many faculty members and has consequently stalled. Broad antagonism from public sector doctors came to a head in March 2012 over government insistence that they work eight hours a day rather than the six they were accustomed to, so as to improve coverage and cut patient wait time.[102] "Sometimes, you see people waiting hours in line just to get an aspirin," says physical therapist Hernán Vallejos Calle, who works in the Beni. "Most doctors work two jobs—they should do the one that serves the people instead of worrying so much about making money."[103] After fifty-two days of often violent confrontation, the doctors finally agreed to return to work when the government rescinded its plans for eight-hour days and agreed that the conflict be presented to the Inter-American Human Rights Court of the Organization of American States.

Despite the hurdles, services have seen an impressive, if uneven, expansion. In short order, the Morales government opened twenty new hospitals, and in 2009, sixty rural health posts were rehabilitated in La Paz Department alone. Two-thirds of municipalities had no health posts in 2009; by 2012, that number had dropped by half, as the government doubled the number of health centers and hospitals.[104]

On the Road to Vivir Bien

The MAS government's greatest achievements grow from its embracing goals to diminish poverty and expand basic public services—health, education, and infrastructure. Paralleling a process seen under other left-wing governments, the impressive gains in poverty alleviation are reshaping the region. Conservative critics claim these initiatives are driven by government self-interest in shoring up support among the poor, but as Vice President García Linera points out, "In northern social democracies, such benefits are viewed as a legitimate part of the state's role, but here we are accused of buying votes."[105] Conservatives tend to ignore that historically they have consistently been the primary beneficiaries of government largesse.

But the reforms do not go far enough to secure structural change, as the distribution of wealth, income, and opportunity remains highly skewed. The generalized reluctance to strengthen the long-term financial base through fundamental tax reforms exacerbates reliance on natural resource income, putting the sustainability of reforms in question. Alleviating poverty through modest redistributive programs masks the structural changes needed to fundamentally revamp society.

While agreeing on little else, development economists concur that growth is faster in countries with a healthy, well-educated citizenry, and in 2013, the Morales government continued to enlarge the health and education budget.[106] Over the long run, perhaps the most important contribution made by the new programs and the focus on Vivir Bien will be the formation of an engaged citizenry capable of holding governing officials accountable and able to frame alternatives to traditional "more is better" development models.

Comanche, La Paz. Typical altiplano landscape with the Andes in the background.
Photograph by Benjamin Kohl.

Encampment of disabled protesters near the Plaza Murillo in La Paz, April 2012. The signs say "Strike" and "We want a solution or death." Photograph by Benjamin Kohl.

Álvaro García Linera (third from left), Evo Morales (fourth from left), and two military officers in the parade to honor the Day of the Sea, March 23, 2012. Photograph by Benjamin Kohl.

Santa Cruz. The wall on the left reads "Yes to federalism, no gas price hikes FSB." FSB is a fascist political party formed in 1937. "Evo = Goni. No to gas price hikes." Photograph by Benjamin Kohl.

Harvesting coca in the Yungas. Photograph by Linda Farthing, 2009.

Anti-MAS mural in Santa Cruz, April 2012. The top line roughly translates as "Persecuted politicians"; the bottom line, as "Don't be indifferent, you could be next!" Photograph by Benjamin Kohl.

Vendor selling ice cream during protests, La Paz, May 16, 2005. Photograph by Benjamin Kohl.

A Sunday soccer game in a rural community on the altiplano, Provincia Pacajes, May 8, 2005. Photograph by Benjamin Kohl.

CHAPTER 7

Land and Territory: The Enduring Struggle

When Evo Morales stood on the balcony of a restored ex-hacienda in the semitropical Yungas in May 2009, the symbolism couldn't have been greater. As union representatives walked one by one up to the wide veranda, Evo dispensed titles to land that had recently been expropriated from one of Bolivia's richest and most unpopular men, ex-president Gonzalo (Goni) Sánchez de Lozada.

Two thousand people strained to see above the crowd, as the ceremony granted land to a mix of about 280 Afro-Bolivians and Aymaras. Suddenly, anything seemed possible, and the crowd buzzed with the longtime dream of building a regional hospital on the communally held portion of the land. "Mission accomplished with the Afro-Bolivian community that has suffered so much humiliation and exploitation for so long," Evo told the delighted crowd.[1]

"Before the 1952 revolution, we had to work on the hacienda three days a week without pay," recalled José Iriondo Torres Chijchpa, an elderly union executive, with tears in his eyes. "We could barely survive on what we grew for ourselves."[2] With the 1953 Agrarian Reform, most haciendas were designated "medium-sized" properties, which made it possible for their owners to retain the house and any land they actually cultivated. Goni bought the property, about three hours' drive east of La Paz, from the former hacendado[3] and promptly started to acquire surrounding properties. By the 1990s, he owned 1,128 acres, an enormous spread in a region where average holdings are less than 7 acres and some families work as little as an acre.[4]

"This is a historic day for us, a dream come true," beamed Torres Chijchpa, who is also one of the beneficiaries. "I never thought I would live to see it. We have our president to thank." The next day, the community celebrated with dance and song that ricocheted off the walls of the narrow surrounding valleys, reminding nearby villages of what had been achieved.

In this chapter, we consider land tenure, one of Latin America's most contentious and, in Bolivia's case, contradictory issues. Not only was Morales's government's new land reform slow to take off, but a host of fundamentally different visions of how land should be used competed both within and outside the government. Highland migrants to the lowlands, now called *interculturales*, often aspire to individual ownership, whereas lowland indigenous groups usually seek communally controlled territories. This is further complicated by the economic dependence on escalating resource extraction that places minority rights to territory and livelihoods in conflict with the majority rights to share in resource rents.

Land

Land has generated conflict in Latin America since the conquest, when huge tracts of indigenous territory were granted to loyal servants of either the Spanish or Portuguese Crowns. Land grabbing has mushroomed in recent years, whether perpetrated by paramilitaries in Colombia or heavily armed landowners in isolated parts of the Brazilian Amazon.

Most of the region's landholders work small farms with a chronic deficit of credit and equipment. Their position stands in stark contrast to a minority who concentrate medium- and large-scale holdings linked to global commodity markets. Policy makers generally recognize that successful landownership redistribution has shrunk poverty and spurred economic growth in places as diverse as France at the end of the eighteenth century and Japan and Korea after the Second World War.[5] However, they disagree on how to reallocate land (state or beneficiary led), how to acquire holdings (market-rate purchase by the state, compensated expropriation, outright confiscation, or a negotiated price between buyer and seller), and how to determine beneficiaries. But one thing is certain: substantial redistribution of land has rarely occurred without the massive upheaval associated with revolts, revolutions, and conquests.[6]

When Latin America won political independence in the early nineteenth century, the new republics inherited huge estates known variously as *latifundios* or *haciendas* in Spanish and *fazendas* in Portuguese. Largely rural societies clamored for reform early on as peasants, many of them at least partially indigenous in origin, labored in serfdom and semislavery. Western conceptions of private, individual ownership were often foreign—in Bolivia, half of indigenous holdings in 1825 were held communally[7]—and few peasant farmers had the resources to acquire legal title.

Latin America's first reform was short-lived, enacted as part of the independence struggle by José Artigas in 1815 in what is now Uruguay and parts of Argentina and Brazil. It took until 1910 for the next attempt in Mexico, where 95 percent of peasants had no land while some 11,000 haciendas controlled more than 50 percent of all landholdings.[8] Forty years later, Guatemala's 1952 Agrarian Reform sought to overturn United Fruit's control of 62 percent of arable land.[9] Subsequent reforms followed at an accelerated pace: ten more by 1980, including one of the most far-reaching in Bolivia in 1953.

Most state-initiated efforts focused first on redistribution and secondarily on titling and recognizing the claims of the poor.[10] Almost all the schemes originated with left-leaning governments, who faced nonstop, often violent resistance from conservative elites, who frequently reversed the even limited gains once they regained political power. Two hundred years after Uruguay's first faltering steps, ownership throughout Latin America remains highly skewed. In some cases, reforms were poorly formulated and failed to dispense the credit, legal, and technical support that would have permitted smallholders to retain their titles. In others, ill-conceived colonization schemes couldn't launch successful settlements or suffered from elite manipulation.[11] Bolivia has experienced both.

A relentless process of land concentration, driven by growing world demand for sugar, coffee, cotton, and, most recently, soy, has offset reform gains. The pace accelerated during the 1980s and 1990s, prompted by neoliberal governments that extended land markets and slashed ownership restrictions. Land has also reconsolidated during the region's recent upsurge in extractive industries. Property speculation is now rampant: in Uruguay, for example, prices multiplied sevenfold in ten years.[12] Foreign ownership is also on the rise. Taken together, these trends reveal how resilient the skewed land tenure patterns the Spanish and Portuguese established centuries ago have proven to be.

Charting a different course is, discursively at least, a high priority for the region's progressive governments, as struggles over land have always been central to left-wing agendas for increasing equality. But granting title is never enough. "If the agrarian reforms under way in the region don't become oriented to improving productivity, very quickly they will generate new frustrations among rural peoples, who are key supporters of progressive governments," cautions Bolivia's Miguel Urioste, a land rights activist for over thirty years. Peasant farmer Mauricio Rodríguez agrees, "We are fifteen families on a communal holding that we got thanks to the MST[13] and this government. The land is far from the road in northern La Paz, and we would like to grow rice, but we have never been able to get any assistance from either the government or NGOs."[14]

Urioste also worries about the "lack of operational mechanisms and public support to carry out the laws, especially in the face of the violent reactions of powerful landowners."[15] This muscle was displayed in the June 2012 battle over land in neighboring Paraguay that forced left-leaning president Fernando Lugo out of office.[16]

The most noteworthy transfers of land have occurred in Brazil, where Lula bolstered resources to the faltering program he inherited. Thanks to constant pressure from the MST and other advocates,[17] 77 million acres were parceled out to 361,000 families (one-third of the acreage originally promised), the bulk through compensated expropriation.[18] In Venezuela, where some 70 percent of all holdings lay in the hands of 3 percent of the population, the often top-down, uneven effort under Hugo Chávez suffered from entrenched bureaucracy and disorganization. Peasants have been killed by paramilitaries, even in states with Chavista governors.[19] Nevertheless, considerable land has been successfully reallocated through compensated expropriation, even though landowners complain bitterly that it is virtually impossible to actually get paid.[20]

Reform is also a high priority in Ecuador and Nicaragua, although as elsewhere, landowner resistance has slowed it. When local peasant organizations are not strong enough, or feeble and corrupt bureaucracies frustrate what is often a piecemeal process, reforms can appear primarily designed to create photo opportunities to enhance presidential popularity. Bolivia's often torturous road to restructuring land tenure highlights just how deep-rooted the obstacles can be.

Land to the Tiller

By the mid-1930s, long-standing struggles for land equality in Bolivia found expression through newly formed agrarian unions that spread across the country from modest beginnings in the Cochabamba Valley. The three-quarters of the population who had no property rights at all were fighting against the country's 615 haciendas that controlled almost half the arable land.[21] Serfs labored three days each week without pay, and also had to provide domestic—and sometimes sexual—services, gather firewood, spin wool, care for livestock, work for others at the *patrón's* whim, and occasionally even make cash payments.[22]

Empowered by the April 1952 revolution, these Quechua-led unions rallied around the cry of "The land to those who work it," mirroring Latin America's widespread adoption of land's "social function" and productive use as the basis for ownership claims. Peasants drove rural landowners off their haciendas and seized land, livestock, and equipment.[23] The government had little choice but to recognize the de facto land reallocation in the valleys and highlands and signed an Agrarian Reform bill on August 2, 1953, under the watchful eyes of 50,000 peasants in the dusty Cochabamba village of Ucureña, home to the first agrarian union.[24] While the unions interpreted the reform as restoring land to its original inhabitants, just as in other parts of Latin America, the middle-class government saw in the measure a mechanism to modernize the highly inefficient agricultural economy and convert *pongos*—bonded laborers—into campesinos, or rural citizens.[25]

Enraged landowners immediately petitioned the government to break up the rural unions, restore their lands, and disarm peasant militias. They deployed one of the customary arguments against agrarian reforms: that the measure lowered production because so many small producers turned to subsistence farming and grew little for urban markets. In some areas, this has proven the case, largely because government abandoned the former serfs to their fate, providing no technical assistance or production and marketing support, but overall, by the 1990s, peasant farmers grew 70 percent of the country's food, about average for low-income countries worldwide.[26]

The Agrarian Reform Commission quickly proved an unwieldy bureaucracy, with few resources to complete the enormous task of transferring titles to the new owners. By trickery, delays, and intimidation, landowners manipulated the process, especially with older peasants, who had lived their entire lives under their *patrones*.[27] The gains that were made relied on strong, united unions, although the poorly implemented process also led to land grabbing, competition for inheritances, and illegal dividing of communal lands among peasants themselves, an outcome exacerbated in communities with corrupt union leadership.[28]

About 25 percent of arable land was completely expropriated, and the remaining large landholdings were designated either small or medium enterprises, which allowed owners to keep significant shares of their pre-1953 holdings. By 1967, 263,000 individual and collective titles had been bestowed, covering some 45 percent of peasant families, but a thorough titling process was never finished, a common shortcoming in many reform efforts, and one that would complicate control over land in the decades that followed.[29]

The reform also failed to anticipate changing demographics. In 1950, the rural highland population was half what it is today, and, as the populace grew, plots were divided and subdivided with each subsequent generation. By the 1990s, landholdings around Lake Titicaca were often the size of suburban lots. Increasingly, young people migrated, uprooted as often to outside of the country as to urban centers. Typically, migrants maintain ties with the land, making a rational consolidation of plots into economically viable–sized units almost impossible. Despite the reform, 77 percent of the 2007 rural population remained poor, South America's highest rate.[30] Although production and living standards rose quickly after 1953, these benefits soon receded, as credit and agricultural extension never reached peasant farmers.[31]

Worldwide, rural peasant women remain the poorest, in no small measure because they customarily lack control over the land they work. As in many low-income countries, in Bolivia, inheritance traditions that favor sons, peasant unions that consider men heads of households, and male control of community governance have combined to marginalize and impoverish women.

Land in the East

Together, the northern tropical Amazonian forests, the central grassy wetlands and dry forests, and the semidesert scrub farther south make up two-thirds of Bolivia's landmass. Marginalized, largely indigenous populations, often facing extermination, were not sufficiently mobilized to force application of the 1953 agrarian reform. Their lands were neither titled nor clearly demarcated, and low population density led them to be considered "abandoned" by the western logic of land use.

Lowland indigenous conception of space also differs appreciably from that of Andean peoples who have lived in settled communities for thousands of years. Lowland groups tend to combine agriculture with hunting and harvesting of forest products. Communally held territory is privileged over that held by individual title, and biodiversity is prioritized in a worldview that does not necessarily place human beings at the center.

As the agricultural frontier has advanced deeper into the tropics, land and territory claims based on these values have grown throughout Latin America.[32] Vice president of the original CIDOB, Nelly Romero, explains, "Our dream is to consolidate and expand collectively managed indigenous territories. There we can exercise self-government."[33]

By the early 1960s, highland peoples driven off ever-tinier plots fled east to the less densely populated lowlands. To a lesser extent, and similar to programs in other parts of Central and South America, state-planned colonization schemes paralleled this spontaneous process and granted from 45 to 95 acres to thousands of Quechua and Aymara settlers.[34] Such migration programs were often designed to circumvent the thorny problem of redistribution with the politically easier solution of dispensing "unoccupied" state lands.

As agrarian reform entered the 1970s, its original purpose was increasingly corrupted. During what Miguel Urioste calls the Agrarian Counter-Reform, some 100 million acres in the east were transferred to about six thousand owners, with the forty-two largest gifts accounting for over 10 million acres. This largesse to friends, family, and political associates of military regimes shifted nearly 90 percent of the country's arable lands into the hands of 10 percent of owners, ironically conferring on a country with one of the most radical land reforms one of South America's most inequitable distributions.[35]

Many large estate owners are of foreign origin. After World War II, Canadian Mennonites formed self-contained colonies and Okinawans arrived after a U.S. military base displaced them from their Pacific island homes.[36] They were followed a generation later by Brazilians. Together these groups now control 20 percent of arable land and 70 percent of soy production. At the other extreme, two million rural families average 6 acres each and another 250,000 peasants are landless.[37] The conversion of forest into vast fields of soy or the running of cattle on hundreds of thousands of acres of grasslands brings agro-industrialist models into direct conflict with traditional indigenous land use.

By the 1980s, the trickle of highland migration had become a flood, and some of these new farmers became quite successful during the soy boom. "With neoliberalism, the highland invasion began," says the MST's Eulogio Cortés. "They used to say that the statue of Jesus in downtown Santa Cruz shows him with his arms outstretched welcoming all. Now we joke that he is really trying to block the road to the lands farther north, saying, 'No more highlanders.'"[38]

From Land to the Tiller to Land to the Taxpayer

Neoliberal politics introduced a different kind of relationship to the land. Echoing similar initiatives elsewhere across the region, in 1996 a new Agrarian Reform Law created private markets for commercial holdings, with the argument that this model was essential for agricultural modernization.[39] The tricky issue of titling was deemed the top priority, to be resolved within ten years, as some parcels had as many as seven overlapping claims.[40] The National Agrarian Reform Institute (INRA) was charged with resolving conflicts, determining whether land had been granted legally and was socially and economically productive, and distributing state-owned property to land-poor and landless peasants.

The 1996 law exempted subsistence farmers and indigenous communities from property taxes, created eight lowland indigenous territories,[41] guaranteed women equal inheritance and property rights, designated peasant colonizers and local indigenous peoples the only eligible recipients for future public land donations, and reverted abandoned properties to state ownership. Paradoxically, these progressive measures were wedded to a guarantee that absentee landholders, as long as they paid minimal taxes, would not face expropriation. In effect, the 1953 "land to the tiller" was converted into "land to the taxpayer." Absentee landlords paid a 1 percent annual property tax on the value they assigned to their own property. This meant the owner of a 25,000-acre spread could value the holding at US$25,000 and pay US$250 a year in taxes to prove that the land had not been deserted.

For indigenous communities, the titling requirement created two kinds of risk. Not only did many communities lack sufficient resources to undertake the process, but as anthropologist Nancy Postero reports, communal lands have on occasion been sold without the consent of community members, since the very existence of a title transforms land into a marketable commodity.[42] Indigenous and agrarian organizations denounced rampant corruption, an absence of community participation, and a bias toward the largest landholders.[43] By 2006, only 10 percent of eligible land had been titled.

Land Reform Redux

Despite the euphoria following Morales's election, almost seven months of sustained peasant marches and roadblocks were necessary to obtain the one vote needed in the Senate to pass a land bill. Rumors of last-minute government payoffs to opposition senators so that they would support the law were widespread.[44]

"We will fight for our lands, and I welcome a Defense Committee to protect them from this government," José Céspedes, president of the Eastern Agricultural Chamber of Commerce (CAO), announced in May 2006 to his well-heeled constituents, including ex-government ministers.[45] Owners claimed they were efficient entrepreneurs under government attack and adamantly refused to participate in the reform. "They and their grandparents have stolen our lands for five hundred years," retorted Morales. "They have to give it back."[46]

Formulated in close consultation with indigenous and peasant organizations, the 2006 law reallocates state lands; enhances access for peasant women, as has been done in Nicaragua through an equal land purchase program;[47] expropriates underutilized lands; and permits seizures of property from landowners employing forced labor or debt peonage.[48] Provincial councils composed of peasant, indigenous, and women's organizations negotiate with producers and ranchers to ensure "social control" and transparency.[49]

The same sun-baked Cochabamba Valley town of Ucareña that kicked off the 1953 reform was chosen to launch the measure. Once again, the region was mobilized: while in 1953, 150,000 campesinos rallied, in 2006, the crowd was a modest 20,000 hardscrabble peasants with worn-out sandals and patched clothing. They watched while a flower-garlanded Morales handed out 2,300 titles and fifty tractors amid much fanfare. With the *wiphala* fluttering behind him, Morales declared that his government would "not only seek a simple distribution or redistribution, but also an agrarian revolution, a profound transformation in agriculture." Peasants, much as they did in 1953, cheered. "We have waited a long time for this," one onlooker said. "This government understands our lives, how hard we work to survive."[50]

INRA and the Vice Ministry of Land quickly swung into action: in the first seven years, surveys and title clearing for 157 million acres was complete, benefiting one million people. One-third of the new titles were held collectively.[51] By 2013, about 60 percent of land had clear titles, and 321,000 titles had been granted to mostly indigenous people and peasants, a stark contrast to the 26,000 titles granted between 1996 and Evo's election.[52] Women's rights advanced as well: 46 percent of the new titles included women's names by 2013.[53] "After working on other peoples' property for twenty years as a laborer, it is amazing to me to work my own land for the first time in my life," marvels Santa Cruz MST member Ángel Estrada.[54]

ALEJANDRO ALMARAZ, FORMER VICE MINISTER OF LAND[55]

I am very proud that we achieved an important formalization of both indigenous and campesino lands, some 60 million acres, most of which are designated indigenous territories. The rest is divided almost equally between communal holdings and individual land titles for campesinos. Of this total, some 10 million acres are actually properties that were expropriated: some came from expired and expiring logging concessions and others from large landowners.

It's important to understand why we didn't push for passage of a complete and integrated agrarian reform law. We were afraid that we would lose our political momentum, so we thought it more important to do something partial than risk not being able to get anything through. I calculate that if we had been able to expropriate another 100 million acres, it would have been a complete reform.

The biggest limitation is the lack of technical and productive support. This is exactly the same problem that occurred in 1953. We just haven't had a real public investment in agriculture, much less agriculture at the community level. We have a long history of corruption in agricultural administration, which undermines any efforts at change. This is compounded by frequent attempts by some of the campesino leadership to break down communal ownership and permit the growth of a land market for the benefit of their members.

Although the law limiting landownership to only 12,500 acres [per person or legal entity] is not retroactive, it limited the land controlled by state institutions. No longer can the armed forces or universities, which manage thousands of acres of unused land, keep these holdings, which have only served as sites of corruption over the decades. The state can grant land to a public enterprise, but if this land is not used productively, it reverts to the state with a specific mandate that it be redistributed.

The reform process has slowed since 2011, and we are faced with the challenge of avoiding the reversion of community titling. My feeling now is that the expansion of community control will only occur under different political conditions and with a different government. From my perspective, this government is following too closely in the footsteps of the 1952 revolution by promoting state capitalism and individual instead of collective titles, rather than pushing for a profound transformation in economic and social relationships.

In keeping with the region's other leftist governments, the administration has proceeded very cautiously with actual redistribution of expropriated lands.[56] For the 2009 Constitution, the government promoted a 25,000-acre private ownership limit rather than the still generous 12,500-acre figure insisted on by indigenous organizations. In the congressional compromise, the lower maximum was approved but was not applied retroactively to economically productive properties. Nonetheless, by 2012, tenure had shifted profoundly: for the first time since the Spanish Conquest, smallholders controlled 55 percent of the land. But perhaps even more astonishing is that the state controls almost 59 million more acres than it did in 2006. These include not only land available for distribution to individual citizens and indigenous communities but also forests and protected areas.[57]

The scale of the reform challenge is illustrated by the conflict in Alto Parapetí, deep in the arid southeastern Chaco. Over half of its vast lands are in the hands of just fourteen owners.[58] As late as 2010, some 600 Guaraní families toiled in captivity on cattle estates, working over twelve hours a day for a pittance, sometimes receiving only food and secondhand clothes for pay, with debt slavery and child labor unchecked.[59] "These cattle ranchers abuse us," denounced local Guaraní Grand Captain Félix Bayanda. "We insist on an end once and for all to the servitude and enslavement of our people."[60] The Guaraní People's Assembly (APG)[61] had demanded state-owned territory for fifteen years, but the petition was ignored until early 2008 when the Agrarian Reform Institute committed a total of 375,000 acres for an indigenous territory.[62] But when government surveying teams showed up, they were attacked and kidnapped by gun-toting ranchers and right-wing youth gangs, who sacked a land reform office and assaulted indigenous peoples. It took almost three years for 750 families from nineteen Guaraní communities to be awarded land from three large owners, including a U.S. citizen, who were all accused of holding families in debt peonage. Soon after, a government-funded program had enabled the local communities to double their corn production.[63]

The Chaco is also where the landless peasants' movement, the MST, got its start in 2000. Inspired by its powerful and often successful Brazilian counterpart, it quickly took hold in Tarija's eastern plains, where 80 percent of peasants had no titles. The wretched conditions facing landless workers fueled the MST, which in just ten years grew to over 50,000 members. Its first major victory was in 2004, when five hundred campesinos seized the hacienda of Rafael Paz Hurtado, whose family controlled over 185,000 acres throughout Santa Cruz. Nine months later, armed men attempted to expel the occupiers, compelling the military to take over the ranch, in the process displacing the landless until Morales's government granted them title in late 2006. The MST has also seized land in the highlands: in June 2003, just months before Goni fled, three hundred landless peasants occupied the 16,000-acre Collana plantation, south of La Paz, known for its excellent cheese and owned by Goni's sister-in-law.[64]

Expanding Indigenous Autonomy

The long-standing goal of achieving greater indigenous autonomy is intimately linked to land and territory. "Our goal is to consolidate our autonomy based on the structures we already have," Chiquitano leader Rodolfo López announced optimistically after the 2009 Constitution passed.[65] Much to his disappointment, the autonomy process in Lomerío, his home northeast of Santa Cruz, like so many others, has stalled.[66]

When Bolivia made the 2007 United Nations Declaration on the Rights of Indigenous Peoples binding as national law, hopes for greater autonomy ran high in the most indigenous parts of the Americas—primarily Mexico, Central America, and the central Andes. Limited autonomy had been won by the Kuna people in Panama almost a hundred years earlier after a 1925 uprising, followed by some success in Nicaragua under the Sandinistas (1984–1987), Colombia (1991), Ecuador (1998), and Venezuela (1999). As indigenous identity reemerged as a crucial organizing frame during the 1990s, autonomy claims have come to serve as an articulating structure for all other demands, and they are strikingly similar throughout the region.[67]

CIDOB's first cross-country demonstration, the 1990 March for Dignity and Territory, forced the government to create four indigenous territories. Between 1996 and 2009, the state granted indigenous groups title and administrative responsibilities to a total of some 26 million acres, in the process drawing indigenous peoples into adopting a logic of land tenure legible to the state and inevitably transforming the way they frame their demands.[68]

The 2010 Law on Autonomies and Decentralization (LMAD) permits autonomy through municipalities or indigenous territories and commits state resources on a per capita basis.[69] Efforts to date, however, have been hamstrung by enormous disparities in land tenure and titling, cultural heterogeneity, grinding bureaucracy, and contradictions within and between the constitution and subsequent laws.[70] Political scientists Jason Tockman and John Cameron argue that, in practice, the new laws effectively inhibit rather than promote indigenous rights to self-governance.[71]

Autonomy Minister Claudia Peña has publicly acknowledged how pains-takingly complex the process is.[72]

Although an estimated 140 of Bolivia's current 339 municipalities con-tain more than 90 percent indigenous peoples, only 11 have sought au-tonomy and of these, 5 have approved the required statutes. Disagree-ments center on what precisely "traditional" community norms and procedures consist of, as well as how to define physical boundaries and different competencies.[73] This can generate "deep and perhaps irreconcil-able conflicts" that often reflect long-standing local wrangles over power and resources, and for women and younger men, a questioning of past practices that marginalized them from decision making.[74]

Beyond the commitment evident in the Ministry of Autonomy, the broader MAS government has become increasingly ambivalent about the issue. "If there were a massive conversion to indigenous territories," con-tends Cameron, "the government might lose easy access to nonrenewable resources as well as the strong political ties between the MAS and its rural indigenous base."[75] The process has become so unsettled that CONA-MAQ's former head, Rafael Quispe, worries that it will become nothing more than "putting a poncho on the municipality," rather than fundamen-tally redefining indigenous relationships with the state.[76]

MARILYN CARAYURI, GRASSROOTS EDUCATOR, FORMASOL; ASAMBLEA DE PUEBLOS GUARANÍ[77]

I'm Guaraní from the city of Santa Cruz, but my roots are south of here in the Chaco. My family moved here in 1986 when they came to work in the sugar and cotton harvests but also to try and make a better life because there were more schools available. We urban Guaraní comprise about thirty communities totaling some 30,000 people on the outskirts of Santa Cruz, but over the years we have been incorporated into the city itself, and as a consequence, we are gradually losing our language. Before the 1990 CIDOB march, no one ever admitted they were Gua-raní because the discrimination was so intense. We never spoke our language in public. But we have overcome this shame, and now you hear it everywhere.

Things have definitely changed since Evo was elected. My parents recall that in the early 1990s our primary goal was to be recognized as citizens through devel-oping a new constitution. And now, through the alliance with the MAS, we have achieved this. Unfortunately the constitution didn't turn out how we had hoped, particularly in relation to land and territory, prior consultation, and the structure of government.

We had to fight and march in order to get indigenous autonomy recognized, and we are still struggling for it. In all of Santa Cruz, there are only two places currently trying to establish autonomy because it has not been an easy process. The 2010 law put up yet another barrier. I think the government is doing this because they are afraid of losing power or perhaps because they don't understand eastern indigenous movements. I have been active in supporting the autonomy process in Charagua, but it has become really polarized. People ask me all the time, "Are you on the government's side?" I always respond, "I'm working for the people."

We struggled so hard to get a person into office who we thought would represent our interests, and there are those who believe Evo has betrayed us, but I think that we can still find a way forward. It seems like a lot of the problem is poor administration and so much bureaucratic red tape. I'm not sure if it's always been this bad, but it certainly is a problem now. It is frustrating to have fought so hard only to not benefit much.

What we want more than anything is the opportunity to sit down and talk with government officials. I think it is critical to have a serious discussion about what economic development means, and particularly what it signifies to us as indigenous peoples. We, as a people, don't have clarity on this issue.

Nonetheless, we recognize momentous things have been achieved. For us as Guaraní, one of the most important was the freeing of captive families. We couldn't have achieved that without government support.

Land and Territory on Balance

The strains between migrating highland peasants and lowland indigenous peoples only set more hurdles in the ongoing tensions over land. Land-poor highlanders often look with resentment at the huge amounts of territory granted to lowland peoples. "Many of us only have a few rows to plant, and our lands are exhausted," says CSUTCB leader Rodolfo Machaca. "We need government grants in the east, accompanied by technical support and services, so we can feed ourselves and the country."[78] Esteban Sanjinés of the research organization Fundación Tierra[79] worries that "the view that 'lowland indigenous people have so much land and we have none' is gaining force among highlanders. We heard this view commonly expressed as 'How is it that they are given huge amounts of land for just a few families and they can't share with their campesino brothers, who only need 100 or 50 acres for each family?'"[80] On the other hand, Sanjinés explains, lowland peoples frequently see the settler from the highlands as an invader and an enemy, and that's going to have negative consequences, sooner rather than later."[81] "We are still being colonized," Marilyn Cara-yuri told us, "this time by people from the highlands."[82]

One barrier is that highland migrants often insist on individual title. "If land is titled individually to campesinos, it enters the market," complains the MST's Eulogio Cortés. "After making a few improvements, some of them then sell their holding, move somewhere else, and demand more land, which they in turn sell to other recently arrived peasants. They're small-scale land traffickers—the biggest piece they get is about 50 acres. For this reason, we are against individual titles."[83]

The MAS government has carried out more restructuring of land tenure in six years that in the previous forty, even though questionable compromises have been made with eastern agro-industrialists. This pattern has been replicated in various forms elsewhere in the region, although the latest round of reforms has not come close to what peasants had dreamed of. Every year, it seems pink tide presidents commit to do more: in 2013, Brazil's president Dilma Rousseff reassured supporters that future efforts would surpass lukewarm reforms to date.[84] These governments are caught in a difficult dilemma, as intense pressures to further expand extractive agriculture, mining, oil and gas drilling, and timber harvests bring them into conflict with the needs of land-poor peasants and the rights of indigenous peoples to territory.

Bolivia's "second" agrarian reform lacks the same force of organized peasants behind it as the first, which may explain in part why it has only managed to title about 60 percent of what the 2006 law mandates. Many of the most difficult disputes are still ahead in the five more years the government calculates it will need to complete the process.[85] But the widespread hope of peasant farmers remains that fifty years from now, their grandchildren won't have to travel back to Ucareña to listen to unfulfilled promises that yet another government will grant them access to the land of their ancestors.

CHAPTER 8

The Sacred Leaf at the Center:
Reconceptualizing Drug Policy

The cheapest and safest way to eradicate narcotics is to destroy them at their source . . . We need to wipe out crops wherever they are grown . . .
FUTURE PRESIDENT GEORGE H. W. BUSH IN A 1988 CAMPAIGN SPEECH

¡Kausachun coca, wañuchun Yanquis! *(Long live coca! Death to Yankees!)*
COCA GROWER SLOGAN

After two decades of abysmal results in the U.S.-financed War on Drugs, it was time for a radically different approach. Not only had the policy failed to stem the flow of cocaine northward, but it had bred profound social unrest, perpetuated human rights violations, and consistently undermined sovereignty.[1] The MAS government, with its strongest early support base in Chapare coca growers, was determined to make a sharp break with the past.

"Coca yes, cocaine no" is the new policy's name, the region's first to successfully split from Washington's emphasis on police and military repression. By 2008, Morales had allowed the U.S. Agency for International Development (USAID) programs to lapse in the coca-growing Chapare, and several months later, accused of political interference, the Drug Enforcement Agency (DEA) was ordered to leave. "Welcome to Villa Tunari: territory free of USAID," a rather dilapidated sign now greets visitors as they approach the Chapare's largest town.

In this chapter, we look at the simultaneous role of the hardy, disease-resistant coca bush as the heart of indigenous culture and the center of an illegal global trade. Coca provided the focal point for mobilization against neoliberalism, even though it is the perfect neoliberal product and successfully absorbed surplus labor in the late 1980s and 1990s. It offers few barriers to entry for workers who otherwise have little role in the global economy; it has a high value to weight ratio and is undamaged by bumpy roads and rain-choked rivers when hauled to market. Perhaps most importantly, while "prices may fluctuate," Yungas farmer Lucio Mendoza explains, "there is always a market for coca." Behind Colombia and Peru, Bolivia is the world's third-largest producer; however, given its comparatively small economy, coca and the cocaine derived from it have always had a greater impact on Bolivia than on other Andean countries.[2]

Coca has flourished on the eastern slopes of the Andes for at least four thousand years, serving as both an essential trade good and a key facet of Andean life. While Spanish colonization almost entirely eliminated consumption in Ecuador and Colombia, chewing remains common in both Peru and Bolivia. Coca's mild stimulants dull hunger and fatigue, aid digestion, reduce altitude sickness, and offer vitamins and minerals lacking in local staples. For miners, it is an article of first necessity to survive their brutal work conditions, and agricultural workers laboring in the hot, humid lowlands consume large quantities as well. Coca is ubiquitous in highland and valley rural social interactions, as people perceive it to encourage wisdom, reflection, and introspection.[3]

In English we speak of chewing coca leaf, the most common way to consume it in the Andes, but that's a misnomer. The Aymara word *pijchar*, or *akullikuy* in Bolivian Quechua and *chacchado* in Peru (*acullico* in Spanish), refers to placing one leaf at a time in the mouth to form a wad tucked tight into a cheek. A small amount of lime or other base is added to extract the alkaloids. Some of the Andes' best coca for *acullico* grows on the highly terraced Yungas mountainsides east of La Paz. Coca from Bolivia's other major growing region, the Chapare, a semitropical lowland east of Cochabamba comparable in size to New Hampshire or Wales, is most likely to end up as cocaine. Both on the steep, verdant Yungas slopes and in the scrubby flat forests of the Chapare, families employ manual labor, cultivating fields as small as a third of an acre that yield four harvests a year. Coca is the main cash crop, complemented with rice, bananas, citrus fruits, and a few cattle and chickens.[4] This peasant economy mirrors Peru's, where an estimated 120,000 people grow coca, principally in indigenous communities on the eastern slopes of the Andes and in tropical zones settled by land-poor highlanders.[5]

In the Yungas, 30,000 mostly Aymara-speaking families form six agrarian federations. Entrenched political patronage and inter- and intra-union rivalries, however, undermine their cohesion. Cleavages run particularly deep between producers from the Yungas "traditional" coca-growing zone, who are anxious to avoid any limits on cultivation, and the much larger group that has steadily expanded into fertile frontier areas, where the leaf is more often destined for conversion into cocaine and fields are legally subject to eradication. The Yungas now surpasses the Chapare in total volume, as well as in the quantity of coca that ends up as cocaine.

Approximately 44,000 families, primarily Quechua speakers, some of whom participated in 1960s government colonization schemes similar to those promoted during the same period in Peru's tropical Alto Huallaga, settled the Chapare. They brought with them a mixture of indigenous cultural forms that mesh unevenly with what has emerged as a largely market economy.[6] Organized into seven hundred diverse unions, along with nominally separate women's organizations post-1994, these farmers protested the U.S.-financed War on Drugs almost nonstop during the 1990s. The constant upheaval and their agility in linking leaf eradication to broader issues of sovereignty transformed them into the country's principal resistance to neoliberal structural adjustment.[7]

The almost complete absence of state institutions made growers' unions inordinately influential. They served as local governments after the 1953 dismantling of haciendas in the Yungas and from the 1970s on in the Chapare.[8] Usually highly participatory, the unions tend to mirror highland and valley campesino organizational forms. Their centralized male leadership (although women exert considerable informal influence) takes responsibility for assigning land for settlement, resolving disputes, directing community projects to build schools or roads, and disciplining antisocial behavior.[9]

The Boom

Coca production in Bolivia and Peru skyrocketed in the 1980s with the surge in northern demand at a time of profound political and economic crisis in the Andes, triggering another of the region's cyclical commodity booms. In Bolivia, hyperinflation, severe drought, and structural adjustment provoked a dire situation for thousands of the poor. Small farmers and displaced miners flocked to the Chapare and, to a lesser extent, the remote reaches of the Yungas to weather the crisis. At its late-1980s peak, cultivation almost equaled the legal export economy, and output estimates ranged from 225 to 725 tons in 1990, when the industry absorbed as much as 12 percent of the country's labor force.[10]

Drug trafficking in Bolivia stretches back to the late 1940s, but its deep roots within the country's political and military structure were most brazenly displayed during what was called the "cocaine coup" in 1980.[11] Throughout the following decade, leaf was processed into paste in-country and then transported to Colombia for conversion to cocaine. The "king of cocaine," Roberto Suárez, a Beni cattle rancher, amassed a fortune so large working for the Medellín cartel that in 1983, he offered to pay off the US$3 billion national debt in exchange for the release of his imprisoned son.[12] This audacity demonstrates what ideal entrepreneurs traffickers can be: flexible and creative, with huge amounts of cash, and able to adapt to changing circumstances at lightning speed.

By the early 1990s, as much as a third of Bolivia's paste was manufactured into cocaine in-country, as costs were cheaper, police surveillance was less stringent, and the supply of leaf was more reliable. The European market was expanding rapidly, which drove prices higher and encouraged traffickers to move cocaine eastward along land-based export routes through Brazil. A 1992 law designed to dismantle local cartels offered traffickers a partial amnesty, short prison sentences, and no extradition to the United States, a policy similarly employed in Colombia. The laws had little impact in either country, as dealers continued operations uninterrupted from their jail cells. Extended families of wealthy ranchers; rubber and Brazil-nut traders; and cotton, sugar, or soy estate owners steadily extended networks with traffickers as far afield as Mexico, although Colombians were almost always ultimately in charge.[13]

U.S. policy makers wrapped a moralistic stance around drugs, attributing an intrinsic evil to illegal substances and their users that played well with their domestic constituents while conveniently sidestepping the role money laundering plays in the global economic system.[14] The focus penalized the weakest links in the chain: farmers in the Andes and inner-city youth in the United States. As it did throughout the region, by 1985, the United States threatened to pull badly needed development aid unless the Bolivian government endorsed military participation, which not only violated national law but also threatened sovereignty and decreased political stability.[15] It wasn't the first time the United States tried to "fix" coca: a hundred years earlier the U.S. ambassador had insisted that since the practice of *acullico* was so clearly responsible for the country's woes, U.S. companies should donate "plain American chewing gum for everyone."[16]

Policy hinged on harsh antidrug legislation (Law 1008), written in 1988 under U.S. guidance, which was similar to a 1978 U.S.-directed law passed in Peru.[17] Criticized by human rights organizations because it hampers mounting a full defense, prevents provisional liberty, and dispenses unfair penalties, the law designated the Yungas a "traditional" zone where 30,000 acres of "legal" coca could be cultivated for domestic consumption.[18] The Chapare and Yungas frontier became either "illegal" or "surplus," where the leaf was slated for destruction or substitution. A specialized antidrug police, the Mobile Rural Patrol Unit (UMOPAR), was formed and proceeded to constantly harass, rob, and generally mistreat growers, triggering fear and loathing.[19] Grover Vallejos remembers the police hauling his father off to jail when he was eleven. "I was filled with terror every time I saw men in those uniforms," he recalls. Eradication was supposed to be followed by crop substitution to replace lost income, although economic development was a poorly implemented afterthought that absorbed only a fraction of the overall budget.[20]

By 1991, the six Chapare federations began to unify, emerging as a major force in the national peasant union, the CSUTCB, and through it, the much-weakened labor confederation, the COB. Evo Morales was elected leader of the combined federations in 1996, a post he still holds. "Defense of the coca leaf is what tied the Chapare unions together," contends former senator and MAS adviser Filemón Escobar.[21] The federations also built effective alliances with leaf consumers by forging a discursive synergy that cast coca as the defender of indigenous culture and national dignity.[22]

Undoubtedly the worst period for Chapare farmers occurred between 1998 and 2001, when, under U.S. embassy pressure, President Hugo Banzer adopted the Dignity Plan,[23] launching forced eradication in exchange for promised U.S. funding that never materialized. The ensuing military and militarized police action plunged the Chapare into severe economic crisis.[24] Security forces killed 33 growers and injured 570, provoking retaliatory attacks that led to 27 military and police deaths.[25] When Banzer attempted the same tactic in the Yungas, troops faced such fierce resistance that the government had no choice but to back down.

During the 1990s, two initiatives broke the U.S. stranglehold and laid the foundations for future policy innovations. The 1994 Law of Popular Participation legally recognized over 15,000 grassroots organizations nationwide.[26] Chapare farmers were unexpectedly thrust into formal government when union candidates swept the 1995 elections in five newly created municipalities. These were soon heralded for achieving the most successful participatory planning in the country.[27] In the Yungas, the new municipalities served not only to strengthen rural unions but also made their officials more accountable.[28] A four-year EU municipal support program got under way in 2001 with sharp contrasts to the U.S. approach, as it had no preconditions requiring eradication.[29] Illegal drugs at the farmer level were understood primarily as a problem of poverty, and coca growing as a subsistence issue, a perspective shared by the growers' unions and, since 2006, the MAS government.

The overall emphasis on police-military repression persisted until Carlos Mesa was pushed into the presidency in October 2003, vowing to respect human rights. Mesa faced down vocal U.S. opposition, and after two growers were killed by U.S.-financed eradication forces, adopted the *cato* agreement,[30] which permitted a limited amount of coca per family (a *cato*) in already cultivated areas. Protest subsided almost immediately. "The *cato* accord brought us real stability. We are seeing greater economic diversification, less out-migration and greater security," praised compliance official and union leader Delfín Olivera Borja in 2007.[31]

To qualify, farmers had to measure and then register their coca fields, a process the Chapare completed by 2008. This resulted in the legally recognized cultivation of 20,000 acres. In the Yungas, where the *cato* agreement began in 2006, registration lagged, taking until 2011 to finalize in the nontraditional zones. Moreover, the accord there has often proved counterproductive to controlling production. As union leader Franz Caravedo explains, "Young people are forced to migrate because plots are too small in traditional areas where the *cato* doesn't apply. They can't grow in *cato*-controlled zones because that would result in excess production. So they set up their own coca farms in expansion zones."

In 2007, the government announced that 50,000 acres of coca would be permitted, a sizable expansion of the 30,000 acres allowed under Law 1008. The figure was more realistic, the government argued, and necessary to supply projected alternative coca products. In 2013, an EU-funded study to quantify legal consumption was completed, setting local demand at 36,000 acres. The MAS government contends the previously allocated higher quantity should be retained as it reflects anticipated future demand.

Making Coca Legal

The Morales government scored an important victory in January 2013, when the United Nations Single Convention on Narcotic Drugs recognized the traditional use of coca in Bolivia after sixty years of categorizing the leaf a narcotic. It was a particularly significant triumph, as presidents since the early 1990s had tried and repeatedly failed to alter the leaf's international status.

The 2013 success was precipitated by a bold move a year earlier, when Bolivia became the first country ever to withdraw from the UN 1961 Convention. Signed by 184 countries, the agreement, and a subsequent one in 1988, mandated the eradication of leaf consumption worldwide within twenty-five years, a goal clearly not realized in either Peru or Bolivia. "How can we forbid coca?" questions Foreign Minister David Choquehuanca. "It's an integral part of our culture."[32]

The Morales government's first decriminalization attempts in 2006 had been discouraging. Armed with a 1995 World Health Organization study confirming that coca has no harmful effects, the government was initially optimistic. But the negative reaction at the 2006 Vienna meeting of the UN's Commission on Narcotic Drugs stalled the initiative. The commission has done its best to block every proposal since. But the MAS administration was determined. Morales chewed coca leaves at a 2009 UN meeting (and every subsequent year) to make his point. "If it's a drug, stop me," he challenged.[33] Hundreds of Bolivians held coca chew-ins, including one outside the U.S. embassy in La Paz. Despite garnering the support of the UN's Permanent Forum on Indigenous Issues, a European Parliament committee, and all South American countries, Bolivia was reproached for threatening the viability of drug control worldwide.

The demand for the leaf is certainly there. "Every week a flood of international Internet requests come in asking for coca tea," reports Ricardo Hegedus, manager of the country's largest tea producer, Windsor Tea. "Our long-standing dream is to grow the legal market. In its natural state, the leaf is a marvellous gift of nature, providing a moderate stimulant—like coffee without the jitters—that also packs a generous dose of vitamins and minerals."[34]

Yungas grower Lucio Mendoza is convinced that decriminalization is the only real solution. "Legalizing coca won't happen if we have extra production that is going to drugs," he acknowledges. "We want to sell the leaf worldwide for the medicinal value we know it has. This would provide us legitimate income from coca and be good for the world, which will benefit from access to our sacred leaf."[35]

DAVID CHOQUEHUANCA, FOREIGN MINISTER[36]

A country that doesn't respect its culture is destined to disappear. We have an obligation to defend coca, and I think that no Bolivian will permit the continued vilification of the leaf. We have no interest in changing the spirit of the UN 1961 convention on drugs, rather we want to correct the historic injustice committed against coca. We will not rest until traditional consumption is legally recognized internationally.

We had no option but to denounce the UN convention because so many countries have objected to our efforts to have the prohibition against coca lifted. The convention is a direct attack on our culture, and besides it is contradictory. On the one hand, the 1961 version prohibits consumption of coca, while the 1988 one permits traditional uses. We have been chewing coca for thousands of years. Even our monuments chew coca: at the Tiwanaku archaeological site, stone statues carved over a thousand years ago have coca bulging in their cheeks!

I have traveled to Europe to teach people about coca. People need to know its nutritional and medical benefits, and that we use it as part of spiritual practices. Coca has more calcium than milk, according to a Harvard University study, and so I think we should explore how to incorporate products such as coca flour into school breakfasts and lunch.

Social Control: Anchor of the New Policy

On the heels of his 2006 victory, Morales announced that a social control program, designed by the growers themselves, would be introduced in the Chapare.[37] Grounded in indigenous practices for controlling deviant behavior, the program was conceived as a locally managed means of ensuring respect for the *cato* agreement, and reducing police- and military-driven violence. It hoped to ensure a subsistence income, maintain a high price for the leaf, and reassert sovereignty. Economic development initiatives and joint military-police action to curb drug trafficking are designed to complement grower efforts.[38]

Although the United States initially, albeit reluctantly, accepted the policy shift, Washington abruptly switched gears after the 2008 expulsion of the U.S. ambassador and DEA. U.S. officials—many holdovers from the Bush and Clinton era—are adamant that "more coca means more cocaine." Every year since 2008, the United States has "decertified" the country for failing to meet its Washington-defined counternarcotics obligations.

Rather than relying on state-applied sanctions, social control encourages farmers and their unions to exercise informal and internal controls. Given that police enforcement of the *cato* is virtually impossible in the vast and often inaccessible Yungas and Chapare, social control is conceivably the most viable, nonrepressive option: certainly it is the most innovative.[39]

"We initiated social control because we just couldn't take any more violence," explains Marcelo Terrazas, a former grower who was the program's first head.[40] "This is really different—not just for the communities, but for the government as well as the international community. Ideally, coca unions will monitor each other to ensure that they are all living up to national and international commitments."[41]

Despite a fitful start, since January 2009, the small, EU-funded staff has spent long hours in community meetings convincing farmers to comply with the *cato*. Grower federations staff compliance offices that perform routine farm visits, and, if they find excess coca, notify the antidrug police, who eradicate it. Surplus coca means to Delfín Olivera that "we will take the whole union's *cato* rights away for one year. So the social pressure to conform is intense." The new rules also allow for the government to seize land from repeat offenders.

Grover Vallejos, who belongs to the same union as President Morales, describes how it works, "Every three months, the union visits all the farms, and if they find extra coca, they eradicate it. We have to show the union receipts for all the leaf we sell. Social control works here because we comply with our unions' agreements and fear both drug traffickers and government sanctions."[42]

The novel policy requires considerable farmer sacrifices in support of national policies.[43] This is offset by economic incentives, argues social control expert Karl Hoffman, for if all growers respect the *cato*, prices rise. "From the unions' perspective, social control prevents flooding the market with coca," explains Tomás Inturias Rejas, ex-union leader and Chapare coordinator of the EU-funded Program to Support Social Control of Coca Leaf Production (PACS) project.[44] Building the necessary mutual trust and regard in communities is not easy. The compliance achieved to date stems from a combination of a deep-seated allegiance to Morales (particularly in the Chapare), a sense that social control is "theirs," respect for their unions, a fear of a return to repression, and reverence for coca.[45]

Where unions are strong, cohesive, and committed to the MAS, social control has shown considerable success. Vallejos was adamant that his union carefully manages coca leaf sales and that farmers sell only to the legal market.[46] During a June 2009 union assembly, five growers argued that social control is more cost-effective and efficient than previous U.S. programs, and all highlighted that the new respect for coca was critical for them. Three farmers praised the policy's role in improving Bolivia's image as a responsible international partner rather than a drug producer.[47]

However, pressure to expand cultivation remains intense. Grover Vallejos notes that "we just can't support our families on this."[48] Delfín Olivera concurs, "The *cato* does not meet union members' income needs, but we in the government believe growers need to concentrate on diversifying production."[49] In Yungas traditional zones, social control is often perceived as a government imposition and really doesn't function at all.[50] Some farmers argue that they should plant as much coca as possible, because they anticipate a return to repressive policies once Evo leaves office. An ex–government employee worried that "once your *cato* has been checked, inspectors won't return for at least another two years, so if your union is weak, you can replant without fear of sanction."[51] This had changed by 2013, as in situ inspection now occurs several times a year and is cross-referenced with satellite data.[52]

Long-term success hinges on agricultural diversification and development. Because the introduction of new crops faces the same difficulties it always has—a lack of roads, technical assistance, and markets and, most important, the hurdles of competing with coca's reliable income and ease of transportation—some growers initially petitioned for another *cato* by "selling" part of their land to a family member.[53] To counteract this in the Chapare, unions early on encouraged their members to grow 2.5 acres of rice, channeling US$500 in government support for agricultural loans and housing grants to those who voluntarily limited their coca.[54] Such efforts, however, have been stunted by rivalries between vice ministries and a political reluctance to condition programs on coca reduction as the United States did. The resulting policy incoherence has meant that, in certain cases, some agencies will fund projects where the *cato* accord doesn't function and others won't.[55]

Efforts to manufacture alternative products such as teas, flours, and toothpaste have been slow to materialize. A Chapare factory churning out goods from traditional Christmas breads to coca liquor took almost four years to open.[56] In the Yungas, two revitalized 1960s factories manufacture bagged coca tea and baking flour, but a new plant was postponed for years because of inter-union disagreements over its location. Karl Hoffman is not optimistic: "The industrialization of coca is a myth. There just isn't the local demand, and without international legalization, there won't be."[57] By the end of 2011, combined industrialization absorbed less than a ton of leaf.[58] In an eerie repetition of how they perceived 1990s U.S.-financed projects, Chapare farmers said in November 2011 that they didn't believe the government takes industrialization and economic development seriously.[59] In the government's defense, the six federations have been squabbling about both the administration of the plant and where the coca for it will come from.[60]

But by 2013, industrialization initiatives finally became concrete with the opening of the delayed tea factory in the Yungas and the finalization of plans for cereal and medicine production. In both the Yungas and the Chapare, government training has led to more organically grown coca with an eye toward industrialization, particularly since the victory over the UN convention. When Evo traveled to the UN drug control conference in 2013, he requested international support for alternative coca products.[61]

For the first time, other crops have proven capable of competing with coca. In the Yungas, USAID's development of specialty coffee markets merged with soaring prices in 2011 and 2012 to boost production. Although the US$20 per pound that small-batch coffee can command in exclusive stores in Europe or North America doesn't come close to the street price of cocaine, farmers do get a larger share of the sales price. Coffee in the Yungas in 2012 outpaced coca in value and acreage under cultivation, but by early 2013, an abrupt international price drop undermined coffee's long-term viability as an alternative crop.[62]

Even though many growers are persuaded that *cato* limits prop up prices, and leaf prices have risen sharply, the association between prices and social control is uncertain at best. Vice Minister of Social Defense Felipe Cáceres admits that the price spike is most likely due to greater trafficker demand rather than government ability to control supply. How much coca cultivation social control has prevented is hard to measure, although the UN Office on Drugs and Crime (UNODC) figures disclose that overall production has dropped 12 percent, a striking advance over the first years of the Morales administration.[63]

DR. GODOFREDO REINICKE, FORMER CHAPARE HUMAN RIGHTS OMBUDSMAN AND EX-DIRECTOR OF PREVENTION IN THE MAS GOVERNMENT[64]

In our modern world, coca and cocaine may have become inseparable, but they are certainly not the same. One is natural, and the other is completely transformed by human intervention. Drug addiction is not an important concern for us Bolivians— we rank last or close to last in rates of addiction compared to neighboring countries. Our drug problem is with alcohol.

Coca has been alternately demonized and deeply respected. Cocaine is intimately linked to poverty, and the lure of quick money will always attract people. Effectively limiting it requires sustained long-term efforts to improve incomes, education, and health.

With this government's emphasis on coca's cultural value, significant advances have been made, as growers are no longer labeled as responsible for drug problems in other countries. Not criminalizing farmers has fostered their understanding of the damages caused by coca that ends up as cocaine, and allowed the government to achieve far higher rates of eradication than in previous repression-oriented administrations.

Results from a new and innovative policy like social control are not going to be immediate. It is a process that will have its successes and failures, ups and downs, but it needs to be given sufficient time to see if it can provide a different and sustainable approach to reducing drug-related violence.

We need to develop a different attitude toward the whole issue of drugs in our society—a relatively poor country that has always been dependent on foreign assistance to interdict the cocaine that is produced in it and flows through it. I believe we need to more seriously consider taking a harm reduction approach, and ask how can we reduce the problems that drugs and drug trafficking cause. We need rational discussion and debate rather than the polemical, ideologically driven discussions and imposed policies of the past.

Cocaine

Curbing drug trafficking globally has proven impossible. European demand for cocaine has doubled in the past ten years, as has consumption in Bolivia's neighbors Brazil, Argentina, and Chile. The seemingly unstoppable fascination with the white powder has fueled a rapid-fire spread and dispersion of production. Given Bolivia's strategic location, it has become a major transit country as well as the world's third-largest manufacturer of refined cocaine. Production remained steady from 2004 to 2007 and then shot up in both Peru and Bolivia in 2008 when Colombian export volume tumbled due to mounting interdiction.[65] Brazil, now the world's third-largest consumer, buys between 60 and 80 percent of Bolivia's production.[66] The shared two-thousand-mile-long border between the two countries, through sparsely populated Amazon rainforest, scrubby woodland, and vast unpopulated wetlands, makes successful control unlikely.

"We make more seizures of larger amounts of refined cocaine and paste every year," reports ex–national commander of Special Forces in the Fight against Drug Trafficking Oscar Nina.[67] A notoriously corrupt police force, extensive contraband networks, insufficient money-laundering controls, porous borders, and an impoverished population all facilitate trafficking.

At the base of the cocaine pyramid are people who stockpile coca leaf and divert it to paste production. Cocaine labs, once confined to remote lowland areas, have adopted new, simplified techniques that allow mobile paste and cocaine labs to spring up anywhere—from rural communities to city neighborhoods. In the Chapare, workers are usually uneducated, landless young men. "The money goes as quickly as it comes," UMOPAR Chapare operations chief Major Julio Velásquez observes cheerlessly. "For most of them, it is a life of drugs, alcohol, and violence."[68]

Velásquez's patrols discover eight to ten hastily constructed paste labs a day, six days a week. Bending over a mound of chopped leaf only a mile from the Chapare's main highway, he points to a square blue metal box, "We call this chipping machine the Colombian method. Fewer people and less time are needed, and more alkaloid is extracted." Velásquez scoops up a shovel of ground leaf and dumps it into a blue plastic barrel. "It's mixed with gasoline or kerosene and water. The excess is thrown into the streams, poisoning animals and people, and what's left is dried to make paste. Each lab manufactures a few kilos a month—usually the operators don't have the capital to produce more. They sell to intermediaries who move the paste to wherever the cocaine labs are."[69]

"Whenever we find signs of drug production or trafficking, we call the police," insists compliance director Delfín Olivera.[70] This trust in the antidrug police is something new. Twenty years of police failure to distinguish between growers and traffickers had translated into well-documented human rights abuses.[71] Since Evo's election, the police have changed their tune. "The only effective way to rein in trafficking is through social control and educating peasant farmers to inform on drug dealers," says Colonel Nina. "This is our hope: that more Bolivians will understand that trafficking only leads us to a precipice we can't climb back from."[72]

The cocaine industry's middle echelons are composed of family clans who move paste and run small cocaine laboratories, particularly in and around El Alto.[73] The majority of labs, and to date, all the big ones, however, are found in Santa Cruz, where drug production and violence have flourished. The large labs and international marketing are largely handled by foreigners—mostly Colombians, Peruvians, and Brazilians. Unlike in Peru, Bolivian government officials insist that no Colombian or Mexican cartels operate in the country, even though there is acknowledgment that their representatives come and go.

When asked how much cocaine and paste his 180-man unit intercepts, the Chapare UMOPAR commander gives a weary smile. "Each time we figure out how traffickers are hiding drugs, they invent something new," he explains. "But we do know that half comes from Peru. In one truck alone, we discovered almost 1,200 pounds of coca paste and 825 pounds of cocaine under false panels and in wheel wells. But we can't check every truck—hundreds go through here every day. It's an unwinnable battle. As long as money can be made, there will be drug trafficking."[74]

Interdiction funding from the United States has plummeted since Morales assumed office—from some US$41 million in 2006 to US$3 million for 2013, a drop significantly greater than similar cuts in Peru.[75] U.S. lawmakers accuse the Morales government of a lack of seriousness. "Drug traffickers may have felt emboldened along border areas when DEA intelligence dried up," clarifies Kathryn Ledebur of the watchdog Andean Information Network, "but the 2011 drug control agreements with neighboring countries, and subsequent joint arrangements, show MAS government commitment to addressing this."[76] Even with funding reductions, seizures have risen sharply since the DEA left.

Bolivia is clearly doing more with less. Vice Minister Cáceres stated in late February 2012, "Both Colombia and Peru have greater financing and logistical support, but we are surpassing our interdiction goals."[77] The 2010 hiring of additional antidrug police has shown results: records have been set for the eradication of coca, maceration pits, paste and cocaine labs, and chemical processing plants.[78] The US$20 million spent in 2011 to control trafficking was upped in 2013 to US$34 million,[79] and police have stepped up raids in Santa Cruz. With Brazil's assistance, Bolivia is purchasing combat aircraft intended for monitoring its borders.

More seizures mean more arrests, and jails are jammed with people awaiting trial in a dysfunctional judicial system that moves at a snail's pace.[80] In 2012, 28 percent of all prisoners were incarcerated for drug offenses, and 75 percent of detainees have not been tried, let alone sentenced.[81] Jails are still run by inmates themselves.[82]

SAN SEBASTIÁN WOMEN'S PRISON IS A NOISY PLACE JAM-PACKED WITH WOMEN, CHILDREN, DRYING CLOTHES, AND FOOD STALLS. JULIA CHOQUE HAS BEEN HERE EIGHT YEARS.[83]

When my husband and I fell on really hard times about nine years ago, we scraped together a little money to transport blankets from the highlands down to Santa Cruz because they sell well on the streets when cold southern winds blow in. Someone approached us about taking a backpack there for US$20, which is about how much money the two of us could make in a week if we were lucky. We didn't give much thought to what was in the bag and didn't even look in it. We just thought it would be an easy way to make a bit more money.

As soon as we arrived in Santa Cruz, we got arrested. The police, dressed as civilians, burst in and immediately started pushing my husband around. They threatened to pistol-whip him if he didn't confess to the crime. It turned out the people who were really moving the drugs, who have lots of cars and houses, never got arrested. They just paid the judge off. We had public defenders, and they couldn't do anything, so I got thirteen years. Once I got to jail, I realized that everyone here is poor. The rich always buy their way out.

I come from a little village in the north of Potosí. My parents had thirteen children and we barely had enough to eat. So when I was ten, I was taken by a woman to Sucre to take care of her children. I didn't go to school because I was working, so I've only studied for three years. I can sort of read and write. Then I married and we came to Cochabamba, where I worked in the market selling food. Other times I worked as a washerwoman. We have five children and live in rented rooms. My husband managed to get out of prison and now works driving a taxi.

If I ever get out of here, my dream is to open a small workshop making clothes. I'm head of the clothing workshop in the prison, and I am very good at it. It's really hard being here—my husband and children can only manage to visit every couple of weeks. My oldest daughter is married now with her own baby, and my oldest son is working as a construction laborer, so they don't come so often.

Corruption related to the cocaine trade remains entrenched. In 2011, former police commander René Sanabria was extradited to the United States, where he was sentenced to fifteen years for running drugs to Chile, and a 2008 study found that Bolivia had Latin America's highest percentage of bribe solicitation by the police.[84] In early 2011, the government fired 144 officers for corruption and drug-trafficking links. At least 40 of those police officials are in prison.[85]

In 2012, Bolivia and the United States agreed to enhance coordination within a context of mutual respect. But no one denies that curtailing cocaine is an uphill battle. As FELCN commander Félix Molina put it, "Fighting drug criminals is difficult, but what is even more difficult is fighting people who are trying to get out of poverty."[86]

Limited Options

While social control and the 2004 *cato* accord have lowered violence and help protect vulnerable populations, they are not designed to reduce drug trafficking. Prices, demand, and availability of cocaine are shaped by forces beyond Bolivia's borders. Even if coca cultivation could be limited to only domestic consumption, cocaine's staggering profits would convince intermediaries to divert legal coca to cocaine, or cultivation would expand to meet demand.

MAS government efforts to forge a different kind of drug policy, one that focuses on harm reduction, are unique among the pink tide governments, and have achieved some real success.[87] In Peru, President Ollanta Humala announced a temporary suspension of eradication after his 2011 election in order to explore policy alternatives, but sustained U.S. pressure and the urgency to solve mounting natural resources disputes saw the program reinstated within a month. Peru's coca crop rose for the sixth straight year in 2012, and the country recently surpassed Colombia to become the world's largest cocaine producer.[88]

Bolivia's novel policy is often overwhelmed by the mercurial and explosive drug trade. President Morales acknowledges that traffickers have "more modern" technology, "more sophisticated" weapons, and "better communications" than the police and the army combined.[89] While Bolivia has asserted greater sovereignty and established larger drug-control budgets, insisting to international donors on shared consumer-producer responsibility, spiraling international demand threatens to erode the country's stability and security.

Where the government has had greater success is in upgrading the status of the leaf that is so much a part of Bolivia's culture. Former grower Marcelo Terrazas expressed it this way: "My hope, shared by all coca farmers, is that we can clean up the negative image the world has of our sacred leaf. Our greatest desire is to achieve zero drug trafficking."[90] While Morales defended coca in front of the UN drug commission during one of his annual pilgrimages to Vienna, thousands of growers filled La Paz streets in support. Yungas grower Mateo Nina Apaza explained why he was there, "Coca is life," he said. "We have used it since the times of our ancestors, and we will defend it to the death."[91]

CHAPTER 9

The Path Ahead

By the end of 2012, Evo's government had lost much of its glow, both in Bolivia and beyond. With the country racked by protests from Tarija to TIPNIS, citizens expressed the same complaints they had with previous governments: concentration of power, corruption, incompetent bureaucracies, and disrespect for civil liberties. Expectations had been high that, somehow, Evo, Álvaro, and their cohort could erase five hundred years of exploitation, create jobs, industrialize the country, and improve health and education overnight. So unrealistic were the projections that both rich and poor Bolivians, particularly in the cities, often overlooked what had been achieved.

The middle class has soared by a million people, roughly 10 percent of the population, economic growth is greater than it has been in decades, and remarkable gains have been made in civil and social rights, as Table 9.1 shows.[1] Our travels in early 2013 to majority indigenous Oaxaca, Mexico, brought home just how impressive MAS's achievements are. Even given the considerable differences in context, substantive change for the indigenous poor in Oaxaca appears a remote dream, reinforcing the fact that Morales's election marked the end of an era just as surely as the 1952 revolution or the 1985 adoption of neoliberal policies did.

But social change is more than just a laundry list of programmatic successes. The MAS government's project was the first and most extensive in the region to commit to putting indigenous and rural peoples first. International spokespeople, such as the president of the European Parliament, Ricardo Cortés, have noted "the extraordinary advance that indigenous peoples have made in participating in state decisions."[2] Yet just as the 1952 revolution was "unfinished," Morales and the MAS are perhaps,

Table 9.1. Major Accomplishments of the MAS

Legal	New constitution in 2009 approved with record levels of indigenous and popular participation; judicial reforms that included an increased number of indigenous and women candidates for judges.
Land	Significant land distribution to 900,000 individuals and communities and the formation of 190 indigenous territories; established squatters rights. Land surveying, titling, and distribution at three times the rate of previous administrations. Awards of territory to indigenous communities and peasant farmers.
Poverty Reduction	An estimated million people have escaped poverty.
Education	Education reform; increased school attendance; three indigenous universities created; widespread literacy campaign.
Health	Significant hospital and rural clinic construction; extension of rural medical services.
Coca/Cocaine	Innovative social control program; record level of drug seizures despite reduction in external funding; international recognition of traditional consumption.
Military	Indigenous students admitted to officer training; first woman defense minister; changed the mission of the army to reflect broader definition of security.
Industrialization	Initial efforts to add value to natural gas, iron ore, and lithium.
Environment	Groundbreaking Law of Mother Earth; significant role in international climate change negotiations; improved monitoring of illegal logging and coca in national parks.

as Aymara historian María Eugenia Choque describes it, only "a transitional stage."[3] For former MAS official Cecilia Chacón, "the government doesn't own the process of change, the people do, and we need to rebuild from the base up to push change forward."[4] But as the MAS has successfully taken so much air out of the room, it is hard at this point to imagine what might replace it. Who will come after Evo provokes worries across the political spectrum, although there appears little doubt that the MAS will continue in power for some time.

RAFAEL PUENTE, FORMER NATIONAL DEPUTY, DEPARTMENTAL PREFECT OF COCHABAMBA, AND VICE MINISTER OF INTERIOR AND POLICE DURING THE MAS GOVERNMENT[5]

The experience of six years of MAS government has taught us that even a small, weak, and marginal country like Bolivia can take charge of its own destiny and free itself from the controls wealthy countries have always imposed. This dramatic recuperation of national dignity is most significant for the indigenous majority.

We have also learned the painful lesson that power is the same contaminant as always and can destroy everything involved in a project of social, human, and cultural emancipation. The MAS has become intoxicated with the complex sensation that power transmits—of being above others, above reality, above political contradictions. The cost has been a serious deterioration of the process and an alarming drop in social participation.

Knowing what you're against is insufficient as a basis for building a viable alternative. Without a coherent political project, we now find ourselves at an impasse. The way out lies in what Evo said in a 2008 meeting. He reminded us not to forget that this is a process based in the people and social movements and not an imposition by anyone.

The MAS must confront its lack of internal organization. Every party is condemned to abort its own program because the project to retain power takes over. Unfortunately, the MAS has taken on all the defects we have always had in Bolivian political parties. Without self-criticism, mistakes cannot be overcome. Terrible divisions dominate internally, not along political or ideological lines, but because of power struggles over personal gain. The only choice is to dissolve the MAS, and find other mechanisms to express the popular will.

A growing part of the population is disillusioned with the process, even though Evo remains popular. But the large majority of the population is passive and uninterested. Those who support the government uncritically—Andean campesinos, for example—have little ability to make proposals and are increasingly split into defending the interests of their own sector. Their leaders tend to look out for themselves, no one else. Those of us who continue to believe in the process of change, but who believe it needs to be redirected, are a small minority.

Seven years on, Bolivia remains a lower-middle-income country with a relatively small, heterogeneous population distributed unevenly over an extensive territory, with different worldviews, different understandings of society and the economy, and, perhaps most important, different aspirations. Since 2000, economic dependence has shifted away from mining to gas and agribusiness; the majority now live in cities; Brazil has replaced the United States as the most important foreign influence; and, nationally, economic power has shifted definitively east.[6] At the same time, accelerating climate change contributes to more extreme weather events, and Bolivia has become not only a supplier but also a major transit country for drugs.

Extraction-based growth in the name of the indigenous majority increasingly clashes with local indigenous resistance to the enormous toll this model exacts. Disparities between national and subnational goals and hopes demonstrate the complexities of applying notions of indigeneity as they have historically been constructed within states and international law. Andrew Canessa suggests indigeneity as a concept that has evolved in the context of understanding conflicts between indigenous people and the state where indigenous groups are powerless minorities. But where conflict is between different groups of indigenous peoples, or between indigenous groups and an indigenous state, the framework proves inadequate.[7] The unitary indigenous identity often projected by the Bolivian state (as well as international agencies and NGOs) ignores the realities of ongoing conflicts and dissimilarities between indigenous peoples.[8]

In the cities, the urban poor have not seen the new jobs, factories, and income they fought for, and they have watched as a new class of successful traders and truckers have become wealthy while the majority struggle to survive. Growing urban violence, a problem faced by left-wing governments from El Salvador to Argentina, shaped as much by the enormous difficulty of asserting control over the police as changes in the nature of poverty, only exacerbates dissatisfaction.

CASIMIRA RODRÍGUEZ, MINISTER OF JUSTICE (2006–2007), FORMER HEAD OF THE DOMESTIC WORKERS' UNION[9]

I think the process of change is stalled. We have not been able to address some of the fundamental problems we have had for years. One example is the growing citizen insecurity and crime. It is really dangerous now, and, of course, women in particular suffer the violence. The reality is that our problems are complicated and not easy to solve.

Nonetheless, I think it is really important to recognize the tremendous advances that have been made. I go back to my community—it's four hours' drive from the nearest town of any size—and there's been a literacy campaign, a new school, and assistance to the local mining cooperative. The improved minimum wage has been really important for the sector I work with, domestic workers. Women's lives have really improved, although there is still much to do. And in terms of the racism I used to always feel, I think this has diminished.

We had expected that we could get rid of the awful corruption that plagues our country once and for all, but success on this front has been really limited. Too many of the people who went into the government sought their own personal interests over the good of the country.

When we entered the government, we had some really good ideas, but perhaps many of our hopes for big changes were just not realistic. There is a great deal of improvisation as opposed to planning. There is far too much concentration of power into a few hands, and too many decisions are top down. Evo still has enormous support in the countryside and he is very dedicated—he works incredibly long days—but he is very closed, too. Power has gone to his head in a certain sense. The mistakes keep mounting, and there is a growing lack of confidence. I often find myself in the position of defending the government and what it's achieved because there is a lot of frustration.

I think we need to go back to the grass roots and think proposals through again, and try to find new solutions. We need to have a much broader discussion about what we want. Unfortunately, I'm not convinced that the MAS is the best option for the country, but, at this point, we have no alternative.

The Revolution That Almost Happened: Why Pink Is Not Red

Longtime activists such as Domitila Barrios de Chungara were often discouraged by what they saw in the MAS. "The government lacks any clear vision based on an analysis of our historical experience," she told us in 2008.[10] Disappointment at the lack of fundamental structural change and the persistence of traditional elite economic privilege leads critics like Webber and Carr to consider Evo's government part of the "permitted left" of Brazil, Uruguay, Argentina, and Chile rather than a revolutionary project.[11] In the words of Aymara leader Felipe Quispe, the MAS government is "neoliberalism with an Indian face."[12]

Indeed, the MAS has sidestepped many of the big issues. The structures of work and economic relations, for example, have gone unquestioned, just as in the rest of Latin America. Political scientist Susan Spronk found little government appetite for comanagement in worker-occupied firms in either Argentina or Venezuela.[13] Nor have there been discussions of abolishing some forms of private property or, even less radically, the implementation of progressive income or wealth taxes. In Cochabamba, ex-factory worker and leader of the Cochabamba Water War Oscar Olivera reports: "I was involved in setting up a self-governing factory here in Cochabamba three years ago. There was absolutely no interest from the government in what we were trying to achieve."[14]

In the absence of the kind of clear collective project Domitila called for, the MAS has instead developed a patchwork program constrained in practice by continued dependence on income from gas. Bolivians' narrative that they are beggars sitting on a throne of gold has been modified by Morales's resource nationalist discourse that proclaims that the country's resources will fuel development. Yet as the perhaps unattainable vision of Bolivia becoming an industrial powerhouse through the production of lithium batteries or long steel products dominates government policy discussions, not only do more realistic plans get sidelined but so do visions of an alternative development model based on Vivir Bien.

Examples of this abound. In 2012, Bolivia spent about US$1 billion on fuel subsidies, of which a significant portion was directed to diesel consumed by major eastern agricultural producers, who, until recently, had been among the most vociferous opponents of the broader MAS agenda. This transfer payment accounts for a substantial share of the profits they derive from the US$800 million exports of soy production. Ending the subsidy would not only weaken the clout of the agriculturalists who have emerged as an important source of opposition but also eliminate an economic distortion that contributed to current land use. But cutting the subsidy across the board, as attempted in 2010, would have also meant that local bus fares in poor neighborhoods, along with everything else, would have soared. The measure was never conceived as part of an integrated policy that offered measures such as transportation subsidies or other compensation for the poor.

Finding solutions to the impasse in the mining-sector split between the modern, capital-intensive large firms, the much-reduced state sector, and hundreds of supposedly cooperative mines is even more complicated. The big mines, operated by transnational companies, may contaminate less and provide safer working conditions, but they employ far fewer workers. Mining corporations influence policy without taking to the streets with dynamite in their hands, as the *cooperativistas* do every time the government raises the possibility of imposing new regulations or taxes. But international companies also provoke bitter struggles with local communities, not only in Bolivia but throughout Latin America.[15] Faced with this contentious panorama, Bolivia has yet to substantially increase the state's share of mining revenues or significantly control environmental damage.[16]

The potential development of Bolivia's massive lithium reserves, as of 2013 the world's largest, is also problematic. Their location in a remote highland salt flat and, perhaps more important, the chemical characteristics of the deposits themselves increase the cost of extraction, processing, transport, and marketing.[17] With new projects coming online as lithium fever spreads around the world, it appears that current capacity will outpace supply at least for a decade, leading one group of analysts to contend that only the most competitive low-cost producers will survive.[18] For Bolivia, in the short and intermediate term, lithium will likely have a greater impact on the country's imagination than the economy. More importantly, it will do little for the perennial political challenge to increase economic growth and job creation. Constraints such as these, as well as those plaguing reform efforts in health, education, and the police, have effectively derailed many of the MAS's proposals and left the "new" Bolivia looking more like the "old" one as the government reels from one political crisis to the next.

Moreover, continuities with previous models suggest that the modest changes the MAS has achieved can perpetuate neoliberal multiculturalism. Linguist Fernando Garcés contends that the new constitution may signal deeper indigenous participation in the state but without changing the structures of the state itself. Anthropologist Bret Gustafson characterizes the regime as one deeply influenced by the multicultural neoliberalism embedded in NGOs, academics, and development aid.[19] Innovative ideas from grassroots movements, such as decolonizing government and creating indigenous autonomies within a truly plurinational state, have been more discursive than transformative. "I think that it will be up to another generation to implement a real change," says María Eugenia Choque.[20]

Critics often argue that the MAS government has simply returned to 1952 revolution–era policies through repeated nationalizations rather than forging a radical new path. The government's inability and reluctance to tackle the underlying extraction-based economic model and the inequality it produces reflect the ways that capitalist dominance of global systems shapes both the options available and Bolivia's five hundred years in a dependent role within that system. As well, the widespread caution even in the region's more powerful and stable left-led countries, such as Brazil and Argentina, to redistribute wealth through reforming tax structures or supporting worker-owned businesses, for example, shows how difficult the process of building more equitable societies is in practice.

JUAN DEL GRANADO, HUMAN RIGHTS LAWYER, EX-MAYOR OF LA PAZ (1999–2010), LEADER OF MOVIMIENTO SIN MIEDO (MOVEMENT WITHOUT FEAR)[21]

We are living our second chance to write our history in a different way, to construct a different kind of country. When Evo was elected, it was a moment of profound hope, with new actors at the fore to resolve the accumulated problems that plague us. What was promised was the leadership of the excluded, the transformation of the old party system, a true pluralism and more democracy, more inclusion, and the reestablishment of our sovereignty and dignity before the whole world, particularly before the planet's most powerful countries.

Despite our initial concerns—that the MAS pro-indigenous discourse was excessive, that government action was improvised and not planned, that corruption was still rampant, that the private sector was being excluded and pluralism squashed—we in the MSM believed there was more light than shadows. We became more worried as we saw evidence of populism, with power concentrated in the hands of a few, unnecessary regional polarization between east and west, and intolerance of divergent ideas. From our perspective, the MAS broke with us because they were convinced they didn't need our support, but by the 2010 municipal elections, it became clear that the MSM had become the second left-wing force in the country. Unfortunately, the attitude in the government—that "now it's our turn"— is contradictory to the construction of a new society, and it smacks of vengeance. It also prevents us from undertaking a real project of decolonization.

We see four principal challenges: first, the construction of a productive economy based on a new model of accumulation that replaces the extractive model, generates valued added, industrializes our natural resources, and creates alliances with the private sector to generate permanent employment; second, the construction of autonomy, which would involve a profound decentralization in terms of responsibilities and resources; third, the need to construct a strong legislative body to reshape public institutions and take charge of formulating national legislation and policies—this is particularly important when the role of the state is increasing in both the economy and development policy—fourth, the construction of a plurinational state that is one of equals, with respect for different cultures and peoples.

Twelve years after the MSM was founded, we reaffirm our commitment to the left because our struggles are for equality, liberty, justice, and self-determination. To be a leftist is to struggle for an egalitarian society. But we do not believe in a one-party system, strong-man politics, intolerance and lack of respect for dissent, bureaucratic centralism in the economy, extreme statism, or an almost monarchical political succession.

Rule by Obeying? Governance, Social Movements, and the State

The MAS has proven that it was not going to be immune from dirty politics. Although charges of populism are often used to dismiss and delegitimize a regime,[22] strong, charismatic leadership in Latin America has historically not been a recipe for transparency, accountability, or longevity of a progressive agenda. Although the MAS has converted itself from a political "project" to a party, it has generally failed to consolidate as other parties born in social movements—such as the Workers Party (PT)[23] in Brazil—have.

This drawback, combined with the fragmented but centralized and hierarchical state apparatus inherited from a rarely democratic country, has made it difficult for the MAS to establish decentralized decision making. The resulting governing style, just as political analyst Julia Buxton predicted in Venezuela, restricts institutionalizing changes deeply enough within government structures that they can't be easily reversed.[24] The concentration of decision making upward is likely pragmatic as well, as the government is notorious for its lack of coordination.[25] What is remarkable is that with little internal democracy, the MAS has nonetheless given voice to sectors that have never before had any say in how the country was run.[26]

The controversies around the rule of law and liberal democracy versus communitarian or participatory democracy are muddied by a lack of clarity about how governing from below actually functions.[27] Vice President García Linera claims it requires "an elevated concentration of power in the president but with broad participation of social movements."[28] More recently he has said that the MAS achieves internal democracy through two mechanisms: internal debate that creates a consensus that is then enforced by democratic centralism—that is, strict adherence to the decision reached.[29]

JOSÉ ANTONIO QUIROGA, DIRECTOR, PLURAL EDITORES[30]

Evo is an electoral machine. Every day he visits small isolated rural communities to consolidate support. This personal contact with the people is more important for him than building government institutions.

The MAS came to office to consolidate power, not to build a new state. They can pass one hundred laws, but they can't enforce them. This is no way to run a country. There's a new social and political establishment that backs Evo and that is doing very well economically. These new elites are concerned with occupying, rather than administering, power. So the change is that of the player not the game. The old ways of doing things in terms of corruption and inefficiency are the same as before.

The MAS advertised a refounding revolution, but that's not been the case. There's not been the change in interactions with the government or in daily life that people had hoped or expected to see. The new constitution may recognize rights in the broadest range that we can imagine, but, just as with previous governments, the state doesn't have the ability to guarantee these changes.

The MAS lacks vision. The homogeneous social subject assumed by the MAS— of an indigenous, First Nations, campesino person—doesn't exist in reality. There are poor and rich campesinos and big differences between the highlands and low-lands. We are witnessing the strengthening of certain campesinos and indigenous groups, who constitute an emerging bourgeois class engaged in a savage capitalism and are associated with the government.

The MAS took power but cannot govern: governing means creating conditions that can be reproduced beyond the current administration. This is the contradic-tion. At one level, they may be around for a while, but they've not created insti-tutions that will last. So the changes are in personnel not in state structures. It's important to have a project that goes beyond merely holding on to power. Instead, they've generated the conditions so that those in power before don't return.

A good example of the failure to institute change is the police: they threatened to strike and were able to ensure that their corrupt structure remains untouched. The result is that the middle class has private police and the poor take justice into their own hands. Unfortunately, the corporatist logic continues.

This model doesn't lead to development. While there's lots of money around, neither the informal nor the formal sector is generating jobs. Those with the most to lose are the most vulnerable—those without unions, without land—who will defend them? The state? No, it's got a different project.

This concentration of power and democratic centralism of the MAS's National Directorate, personified through Evo, runs headlong into the rhetoric of ruling by obeying, which suggests a broadly participatory, on-going debate between the ruled and the ruler.[31] These countervailing tendencies are framed by the reality that social movements have the power to mount protests that make it impossible for this highly centralized style to function in practice. Policies that are defined by a small group of trusted insiders are announced without much consultation, causing people to take to the streets to force the government to back down. It is enough to suggest, for example, new controls on contraband to unleash a popular fury. Historian James Dunkerley, drawing on Bolivian philosopher René Zaveleta's observation that "Bolivia is conflict . . . that is the natural form of the nation," asks if disorder is so prevalent, might it not be order itself?[32] Certainly given the MAS's predominant policy-making style, the answer is a resounding yes.

The incongruence between concentrated decision making and vocal demands for popular participation propels the MAS toward co-opting social movements whenever possible. They strive to bring them into the government through mechanisms that range from clientelism to appeals for loyalty. While the TIPNIS conflict convinced two key indigenous movements, CIDOB and CONAMAQ, to split with the MAS, the CSUTCB, the confederation of peasant unions, continues to support Morales even as they increase their criticism of the government. CONAMAQ and the COB have announced that they will each form political parties that will inevitably fragment the left,[33] giving weight to the MAS's argument that they alone have the ability to forge a national movement to defend popular interests. Certainly some social movements still firmly believe this, as they were adamant in late 2012 that government proposals be discussed with supporters in order to build consensus before they are launched.[34]

Accusations that the MAS government employs repression, disqualification, and sectarianism abound, and the government has had limited success in promoting open dialogue even with its own supporters. This political style is, of course, common in Bolivia, and the hopes that the MAS would be able to change that over the short term were unrealistically optimistic, given its inexperience and the weak and fragmented bureaucracy it inherited. But despite the repeated cries that democracy is being eroded, political scientist María Teresa Zegada and her coauthors conclude that "representative democracy continues to articulate the political terrain,"[35] which is manifested by the widespread focus of the MAS on winning elections.

Even with its tremendous limitations, the Morales administration has made impressive strides toward reinventing the state, which include instituting the most innovations in the military since 1952 and institutionalizing nonwestern models of disease and health. Many initiatives, often at the margins of government policy, such as establishing a gay television show on the state channel and attempting a completely new approach to limiting coca cultivation, point to the exciting and creative changes an effective MAS administration might achieve.

Bolivia's experience also points out how complex it is to substantively transform a state's administrative structure, especially a poorly consolidated one. Even with the best of intentions, the tendency is to reproduce the familiar. Bureaucrats, regardless of ideology, are loath to take risks. While increasing roles for women and indigenous people in the state may improve equity, their growing presence does not guarantee any fundamental change in how the state works.

Power and the Persistence of Neoliberalism

Evo's December 2009 victory with 64 percent of the votes was a resounding exclamation of support for the process of change. In 2002, the electoral map showed MAS support only in rural areas, but by 2009, Morales won by impressive margins everywhere but the departments of Santa Cruz, Trinidad, and Tarija. Even in Santa Cruz, the heart of the opposition, Morales won heavily in poor urban neighborhoods and some rural municipalities.[36] After the election, it looked as if Morales and the MAS had consolidated control of the country. Yet a year later, with the aborted attempt to remove gas subsidies, contentious politics reemerged with renewed force.

From 2011 on, almost every day, somewhere in the country, someone was blocking a road, whether a single street in the city or a highway that linked a region with the rest of the country. But the tenor of the protests was different. Rather than coalitions with tens if not hundreds of thousands of people joined together to make collective demands, the new configurations were fragmented and represented increasingly narrow self-interests. At one point, a couple dozen families blocked a section of the principal highway to Chile to demand that the government improve the road to their tiny community. In early 2012, a few hundred bus drivers insisting on increased fares parked their buses across intersections throughout La Paz, grinding the city to a standstill for two days. Cooperative miners were in the streets constantly, retooling their militant organizational experience against exploitation and global capitalism into block-ades for "freedom" not only from taxes but also from environmental and labor regulations. Indigenous groups and their allies numbering in the hundreds embarked on one march after another, both in support of and opposition to the road through the TIPNIS, with each group arriving in La Paz after hundreds of miles to smaller crowds as residents showed signs of demonstration fatigue. The marchers camped out and negotiated, first to stop (or restart) the road and then for bus fare home. Textile workers, teachers, and even privileged doctors—the list goes on—all have brought the country to a halt.

How can we understand this mounting social conflict when Evo Mo-rales won by a landslide? The changing frequency and the scale of dem-onstrations, we suggest, may be the convergence of three processes. First, the 2009 electoral triumph arguably persuaded some in the MAS that they were unbeatable and that time-consuming negotiations with social movements just distracted from their agenda. Second, economic changes fueled by commodity booms of gas, minerals, soy, coca, and quinoa have given rise to a new indigenous economic elite who support the MAS and its social programs. Many in this group come from and have deep ties to the informal sector and will take to the streets to fight against increased regulation and taxation. Third, twenty years of neoliberalism has con-tributed to an internalization of values that limit the ability of the state to promote a communitarian project.

The changes in governing style can be seen in the difference between how the MAS worked for passage of the land reform law and its failed effort to end fuel subsidies. In 2006, the MAS engaged in extensive con-sultation with grassroots organizations to determine their priorities and then, when the land reform was stalled in the senate, called on them to take to the streets to exert the pressure necessary to get the law approved. But after the 2009 victories in two successive elections (for the constitu-tion and in the national election), and with no other viable political party on the horizon, some in the government began to speak of staying in power for a decade or more. Preservation of power, critics would say, be-came more important than the process of change as the circle around Evo and Álvaro isolated themselves from the grass roots. This led to actions such as the ill-considered elimination of fuel subsidies that cost the MAS a good deal of their credibility.

At the same time, burgeoning income provided new opportunities that strengthened indigenous entrepreneurs, including owners of cooperative mines, land speculators, truckers, and traders of both contraband and legal goods. While focused on individual or family accumulation, these groups engaged indigenous family networks and notions of reciprocity to construct vertically integrated businesses that were accustomed to operating at the margins of the state and formal economy.[37] To a considerable extent, the ways they utilize their indigenous identities to build their businesses contradict the notions expressed by García Linera (see Chapter 5) of an indigenous communitarian economy.

While the 2003 and 2005 protests that brought down presidents promoted universal popular demands—nationalization of gas and control of natural resources, a new constitution and the reinvention of the state, and an end to impunity for government officials—the recent ones tend to focus on benefits for a few. It is as if the seeds of neoliberalism planted in the 1980s following the dismantling of the developmental state have flowered into the survival logic not only of the informal sector, but also of the broader social order, encouraging individual ambition rather than group loyalty.

While none of the blockades or strikes by themselves threaten the Morales administration, taken together, they undeniably debilitate the country and diminish its ability to move ahead, whether because eggs go bad before they reach the market; milk sours when pickups are delayed; or hundreds of thousands of people lose one, two, or five days of work or school due to the actions of a few. Summed across the population, not only do the protests impose significant costs that are far greater than the benefits that any individual group could attain, but they also restrict the ability of the government to implement basic policies. Ultimately, the protests reinforce Bolivia's economic dependence on natural resource extraction, because oil and gas producers, for example, can weather moments of instability far better than smaller firms.

Of course, the indigenous Americas are not only shaped by the short memory of neoliberalism but also by the long memory of five hundred years of colonialism. What we see in Bolivia is that the old is not destroyed but is simultaneously incorporated into and held apart from the new, which harks back to the concept of *ch'ixi*—the combining of two contrasting elements to create a third that simultaneously is both "of" and "not of"—that Silvia Rivera discusses.[38] The white thread of colonialism combined with the black thread of the nineteenth-century liberal revolution to create the republican state in 1825, and together they are woven into the fabric of the nation along with the liberal revolution and indigenous uprising of 1899, the Chaco War, the revolution of 1952, the rise (and fall) of the neoliberal state between 1985 and 2005, and now Evo's government.

The social movements that, working together, brought Morales to power, if divided can slowly strangle their own process of change. Morales has always sought to govern in the name of these movements while strengthening the MAS, even as the imperative to maintain political power for its own sake gains force. As our interviewees constantly told us, profound change is realized by people working together, not by any government, no matter how progressive.

The Way Forward

Bolivia cannot compete in industrial production with countries with better institutions, more efficient states, stronger educational systems, lower costs of capital, and access to the sea. The current constellation of markets within the logic of neoliberal globalization suggests that the country has little option but to come to terms with its role as a low-cost provider of raw materials, whether mineral, vegetable, or human.

The new Bolivia has yet to veer from the path commonly taken among poor countries in addressing what to do with its surplus labor. One strategy is to reduce overall labor costs and increase productivity, but even if labor costs were to fall to zero, the combined transportation and regulatory costs often make products too expensive to compete in a highly disciplined global market. A second approach is to export labor, something that the Philippines has incorporated into its development policy. For Bolivians, emigration has served as an individual solution for decades and has, through the remittances of the migrants, contributed almost as much as the natural gas boom to relatively fast growth. Just as Los Angeles is considered the second-largest Salvadoran city, Buenos Aires might be one of Bolivia's biggest urban areas, with smaller, but still significant, populations in São Paulo, Madrid, and suburbs in New Jersey and Virginia.

Relentless demand for natural resources is reshaping Latin America and Bolivia as much as if not more than its left-oriented governments. In a context of historic dependency, Evo is trapped between demands to protect the environment and the rights of indigenous people on one side, and the need to "grow the economy" through resource extraction on the other in perhaps the most glaring example of the juggling act all the pink tide governments face.

However, despite the daunting and perhaps irreconcilable challenges, the contradictions between discourse and action have led to a national discussion about what alternative development models might exist. Even in communities such as the Chiquitano and Ayoreo, which are experiencing ongoing destruction due to extractive activities, people still express hope that this government will protect their lands. This faith stems from the recognition of the substantial gains in land titling, representation, and transfer payments Evo's government has brought them.[39]

Breaking with five hundred years of an extraction-based economy in under a decade is simply not feasible for any country. Political scientist Raúl Prada recognizes that "it is going to be difficult to transition from an extractive economy. We clearly can't close mines straightaway, but we can develop a model where this economy has less and less weight. It will need policies developed in participation with movements . . . and redirection of investment and policies toward different ecological models of development. . . . Our ecological and social crisis is not just a problem for Bolivia or Ecuador; it is a problem for all of us. We need to pull together peoples, researchers, and communities to develop real concrete alternatives so that the dominant systems of exploitation don't just continue by default. This is not an easy task, but I believe with international solidarity, we can and must succeed."[40]

Bolivia might decide it wants to play a different game entirely, which the Morales government has, discursively at least, begun through the concept of Vivir Bien. To embark forcefully on such a path, however, would require both political and ideological changes that reject the internalized neoliberal global citizen on the one hand and incorporate redoubled efforts to create jobs on the other. Such a transformation necessitates a process of ideological revision, which is well recognized by many within the MAS. As Gramsci explains, the common sense about how we organize daily life is not a universal constant but is instead constructed in civil society, including the media, schools, families, and religious institutions as well as through the daily barrage of messages that shape both our thoughts and actions.[41]

JULIA RAMOS, FORMER EXECUTIVE SECRETARY OF BARTOLINAS, MINISTER OF STATE, AND NATIONAL DEPUTY[42]

It still seems like a dream to me that I came from a small village in Tarija and, with a great deal of sacrifice by my family, became a leader first in my community and then at the departmental and national level. I never, ever thought this would be possible. I was convinced that success was reserved for rich and powerful people. I, and others along with me, have achieved this because of a process that we developed ourselves, of founding a political instrument that has allowed many women in *polleras*, braids, and *abarcas*[43] like me to enter the highest levels of government. First I was elected national deputy from Tarija and then became the Chamber of Deputy's first vice president.

We are building a communal and solidarity economy based on our own experience and cultures, gaining space for all of those who before were excluded and marginalized, particularly for indigenous women, who were always the most badly treated. We have initiated aggressive campaigns against corruption, contraband, and drug trafficking. Our emphasis on technical education will, we hope, provide us with a leap forward so that Bolivia can become industrialized. All these projects must be carried out in coordination with the social movements, utilizing concepts of social control to strengthen community democracy. We want a healthy, educated population, which has stable work, so that we can be independent and not subject to being tricked by anyone, as has happened so often in the past.

The principal difficulty that blocks our road is a lack of consciousness. We have passed some very important laws, but it is really difficult to change people's way of thinking. Some want to keep hold of their entrenched privileges, and others feel that the time has come for them to benefit. We need to work even harder to organize in communities at the same time as we strengthen the capacities of government institutions and constantly clarify our objectives. More immediately, we need to organize to win the 2014 elections so that we can keep this process alive and form new leaders who will do even better than we have at advancing changes.

Everything I have done has come from my heart and values, focused on a better future for my sisters and brothers in the countryside. I have tried to be an example to indigenous women to encourage them to participate and to value themselves. I want to see us build a life with dignity, in harmony with our mother earth, caring for each other. We must solidify laws on the environment, not just nationally, but internationally, because we need to change the mentality in the industrialized countries.

Vivir Bien is the only option for the poor, the only thing that will change the state and allow us a better future. Our goal is to eradicate poverty and create the conditions for equality. I am confident that we are on the right path and that Bolivia can show the world that there is a different way of running a government and of running organizations.

If, as James Dunkerley suggests, Bolivia's imagined community resides around collective ownership,[44] then the government could support communitarian values not just as an argument to increase production levels but also to improve quality of life. However, while communal and collective values are closer to the surface in indigenous communities, these are still deeply shaped by the lived experience of capitalism, neoliberal or otherwise. In today's Bolivia, the individual and the collective can exist simultaneously, often jockeying against each other from one minute to the next.

Efforts, both small and large, to draw on this reality to forge different kinds of economic and social relationships are critical in developing alternatives to the current extractive economic model. The government, for example, could promote an agricultural policy framed by the concept of Vivir Bien that substituted 100 ecologically sustainable holdings of 100 acres for every 10,000 acres currently dedicated to soy or cattle. Around the world, small farms absorb more labor, use fewer hydrocarbons, and produce more per unit of energy than state-of-the-art chemical-dependent agro-industrial operations.[45] To achieve these ends, however, the MAS would have to embrace a more radical development path than the current model. And at this juncture, it seems unlikely that they either have the administrative capacity or could muster the political support to carry out any program of truly innovative restructuring.

To be successful, transformative policies that are focused on Vivir Bien also have to be vertically integrated and find a productive place for the now urban, often impoverished majority, who identify as indigenous but speak only Spanish, and who dream of decolonization even as they participate in global popular culture. This might entail embracing more fully the concept of *ch'ixi* and recognizing that rather than play according to the rules defined by neoliberal globalization, Bolivia and countries like it need to create a new game.

Is this possible? Not over the short run, but even the limited gains from the sustained efforts of social movements that put the chaotic and often contradictory Morales administration in power are preferable to the reality offered by a return to business as usual under global neoliberalism.

Notes

Chapter One

1. Van Cott 2001, 30.
2. Dangl 2007, 95.
3. Gordon and Ledebur 2005. The five previous countries are: Venezuela in 1998 (Hugo Chávez), Chile in 1999 (Ricardo Lagos), Brazil in 2002 (Luiz Inácio Lula da Silva), Argentina in 2003 (Néstor Kirchner), and Uruguay in 2004 (Tabaré Vázquez). Morales's 2005 victory was followed by Rafael Correa in Ecuador, Manuel Zelaya in Honduras, Michelle Bachelet in Chile, and Daniel Ortega in Nicaragua, all during 2006; Cristina Fernández in Argentina and Álvaro Colom in Guatemala during 2007; Fernando Lugo in Paraguay in 2008; El Salvador's Carlos Mauricio Funes in 2009; and Ollanta Humala in Peru during 2011.
4. "Another world is possible" is a popular slogan of globally oriented social movements. Its origins are often attributed to the phrase "to divine another possible world" in Eduardo Galeano's 2000 book, *Upside Down: A Primer for the Looking-glass World*. The slogan quickly became the rallying cry at the World Social Forum, headquartered in Porto Alegre, Brazil.
5. Lievesley and Ludlam 2009. What constitutes left is, of course, elastic and debatable but can broadly be described as political parties and social movements with historical roots in communist and socialist principles that focus on economic redistribution and social justice for disadvantaged populations (adapted from Cleary 2006). Here, we use "left" or "left-wing" or "pink tide" or "left oriented" interchangeably to designate all the governments that use these terms to describe themselves.
6. Latin America had two successful leftist armed struggles that overthrew dictators—Fulgencio Batista in Cuba in 1959 and Anastasio Somoza in Nicaragua in 1979. The largest remaining proponent of armed struggle is Colombia's FARC (Revolutionary Armed Forces of Colombia), which has been fighting since 1964. In late 2012, it entered into a new round of negotiations with the Colombian government.
7. Prevost, Oliva Campos, and Vanden 2012.

8. Fortes 2009; Weyland 2010.

9. Beasley-Murray, Cameron, and Hershberg 2010, 3; Levitsky and Roberts 2011; Weyland 2010, 8.

10. Petkoff 2005; Webber and Carr 2012.

11. Buxton 2009, 58.

12. Arditi 2008.

13. Flores-Macías 2012.

14. Kohl and Farthing 2012; Weyland 2010. See Bunker 1985 on extractive economies.

15. Interview by Linda Farthing, La Paz, October 19, 2007. Courtesy of KMF Productions. All interviews originally in Spanish are our translations unless otherwise noted.

16. Movimiento al Socialismo.

17. GOB 2007.

18. Forero 2012. Bolivia is one of the ten most biologically diverse countries on earth.

19. *Guinness World Records* cited in Dunkerley (2007a, 5).

20. Rivera Cusicanqui 2010.

21. Author interview, Tiquipaya, Cochabamba, July 15, 2008.

22. Panizza 2009.

23. Prevost, Oliva Campos, and Vanden 2012. Between 1990 and 2005, eleven Latin American governments were overthrown, not by the traditional U.S.-supported military coup but by popular uprisings (Lievesley and Ludlam 2009, 9).

24. In countries without such powerful movements, such as Venezuela and Chile, the government has more room to maneuver (Luna 2010).

25. Federación de Juntas Vecinales, often just called *juntas vecinales*, or neighborhood organizations.

26. *La Jornada* 2011.

27. Central Obrera Boliviana. See Dunkerley 1984 for a history of the labor struggle through the return to civilian rule in 1982.

28. Federación Sindical de Trabajadores Mineros de Bolivia.

29. Alexander and Parker 2005; John 2009. What Ecuador's president Rafael Correa has named "the long neoliberal night" led to a massive reduction of the public sector workforce and growth of informal jobs throughout Latin America (Lievesley and Ludlam 2009; Reygados and Filguiera 2010, 18).

30. *Campesino*—literally a person who lives in the country; in the Bolivian context, it refers to indigenous peasants. This term for rural indigenous people was introduced after the 1952 revolution because *indio* (Indian) was widely used as a derogatory term. *Campesino* reflected the modernist aspirations of the 1952 revolutionary project.

31. Confederación Sindical Única de Trabajadores Campesinos de Bolivia.

32. In honor of indigenous heroine Bartolina Sisa, wife of Tupac Katari, who led Bolivia's most celebrated indigenous uprising in 1781.

33. Healy 2001; Lucero 2008.

34. Confederación de Pueblos Indígenas de Bolivia.

35. Confederación Sindical de Comunidades Interculturales de Bolivia.

36. Bloque Oriente; Garcés 2011.

37. Banzer was military dictator from 1971 to 1978. His 1997 win was achieved through political pacts, as he only had 22 percent of the vote. Political scientist Terry Lynn Karl (1987) coined the term "pacted democracy" to describe elected governments held together through agreements between elite groups. The most notorious was Venezuela's Punto Fijo Pact, which alternated power between 1958 and 1998.

Rent-seeking refers to attempts by public or private actors to take advantage of their position for financial gain or profit beyond what is accepted in their society as fair compensation or normal profit. It encompasses activities that include but are not limited to taking or paying bribes and using influence to shape regulations or avoid oversight.

38. Farthing and Kohl 2001.

39. The altiplano is a high, flat, mostly treeless plateau that lies between a split in the Andean mountain range. Most of it is higher than 12,000 feet above sea level.

40. Kohl 2003a.

41. Panizza 2009.

42. *Ayllu* is the preconquest Andean social organization that combines both kinship and territorial ties. Persisting in more remote parts of the Andes, *ayllus* are characterized by rotating leadership, participatory decision making, and leveling mechanisms to ensure a relatively equitable distribution of resources. See Orta 2013 for a summarized discussion.

43. Consejo Nacional de Ayllus y Markas del Qullasuyu. Komadina Rimassa 2011; Lucero 2008.

44. The pact originally comprised CONAMAQ, CIDOB, CSUTCB, CSCIB, and smaller groups ranging from the Afro-Bolivian Cultural Association and the National Association of Irrigators and Community Water Systems to the Coordinator of Ethnic Groups of Santa Cruz.

45. Farthing, Arbona, and Kohl 2006.

46. Arbona 2008.

47. Federación de Juntas Escolares and Federación de Padres de Familias respectively.

48. Lazar 2008.

49. This was far from the first time protesters used La Paz's limited outlets to the altiplano to lay siege to the city: the most famous was the six-month siege in 1781 under the leadership of Aymara rebels Tupac Katari and Bartolina Sisa (Thomson 2002).

50. Spronk 2012.

51. Van Cott 2003.

52. Molina 2009.

53. Dunkerley 1984; Kohl and Farthing 2012; Molina 2009.

54. Coordinadora Nacional de la Recuperación y Defensa del Gas.

55. Assies 2004; Gómez 2004.

56. Adapted from Kohl, Farthing, and Muruchi 2011, 204.

57. Author interview, La Paz, May 8, 2012.

58. Assies 2004. After Goni fled, following constitutional procedure, Vice President Carlos Mesa assumed the presidency.

59. Webber 2011.
60. Gascó and Cúneo 2011; Rivera Cusicanqui 2003.
61. Zuazo 2009.
62. Anria 2010; Stefanoni 2010.
63. Do Alto 2011.
64. Anria 2010; Kohl and Farthing 2006, 84–102; Oviedo Obarrio 2010.
65. Do Alto 2011; Harten 2011; Zegada, Torrez, and Cámara 2008.
66. Interview courtesy of Jessica Robinson, Tiquipaya, Cochabamba, May 23, 2012.
67. Gotkowitz 2008.
68. Anria 2010; Postero 2010.
69. Komadina Rimassa 2008.
70. Laserna 2007; Mayorga 2005; Torranza Roca 2008.
71. Stefanoni 2003.
72. Author interview, Cochabamba, July 10, 2008.
73. García Linera, 2007, 165; our translation.
74. In Spanish, *mandar obedeciendo*.
75. Harten 2011; Stefanoni 2010.
76. Evo skillfully defeated Cochabamba peasant leader Alejandro Véliz in a late-1998 confrontation and successfully marginalized MAS cofounder Román Loayza in their 2009 split.
77. Panizza 2005.
78. Miguel Centeno and Fernando López-Alves (2001, 5–6), cited in French 2010, 47.
79. Reid 2007. Luna (2010) notes that Chile's more gradual process emerged from well-established political parties.
80. Weyland 2010.
81. Panizza 2009, 192–194.
82. Arditi 2008.
83. Consciencia de Patria; Unidad Cívica Solidaridad.
84. Zuazo 2009.
85. Anria 2010; Do Alto 2011.
86. Calderón 2007.
87. Farthing 2007; Monasterios, Stefanoni, and Do Alto 2007.
88. Excerpt from Kohl, Farthing, and Muruchi 2011, xxi–xxii.
89. A *bastón de mando* is a wood-and-silver scepter used to indicate authority and the passing of power from one leader to the next.
90. Howard 2010.

Chapter Two

1. WWF 2012.
2. Brie 2008.
3. Klein 1992.
4. According to the 2001 census.
5. Known as *reducciones*. Intricately carved Chiquitano-built churches, the only

ones to survive the Jesuit expulsion in 1767, still dot towns such as Concepción and San Javier.

6. Webber 2010.

7. Gustafson 2009a.

8. Groesbeck 2008.

9. World Economic Forum 2011.

10. Weisbrot, Ray, and Johnston 2009.

11. Kolata 1993.

12. Janusek 2008.

13. See McEwan 2006, 93–96, for a discussion.

14. Orta 2013; Platt 1982.

15. Known as *chacha warmi* in Aymara.

16. Lehman 1982.

17. Kohl, Farthing, and Muruchi 2011, 21–24.

18. The tensions between the collective and individual and between western and Aymara worldviews are brilliantly portrayed in Jorge Sanjinés's 1989 Spanish- and Aymara-language film *La nación clandestina*.

19. Arnold et al. 2009.

20. Canessa 2008.

21. Klein 1998.

22. Ibid.

23. Spaulding 1984, 134. Other scholars (Mann 2005) put the estimates at over 90 percent.

24. Camacho Nassa 2010; *Página Siete* 2013.

25. Kirshner 2012.

26. Malloy 1970.

27. Movimiento Nacionalista Revolucionario.

28. Dunkerley 1984.

29. Spronk 2012.

30. Kohl, Farthing, and Muruchi 2011.

31. Conaghan and Malloy 1994.

32. Sachs 1987.

33. Crabtree, Duff, and Pearce 1987.

34. Spronk 2012. The Central Única dos Trabalhadores (CUT) was founded in 1983 and has since become Brazil's principal union, Latin America's largest, and the world's fifth-largest, confederation. Mexico's Unión Nacional de Trabajadores (UNT) formed in 1997 and has emerged as an important force for progressive social change in Mexico (La Botz 2005).

35. Norberto García (2007), cited in Spronk 2012, 81. Some 55 percent of new jobs in the rest of Latin America are estimated to originate in informal sectors.

36. Farthing 1991.

37. Federación Nacional de Cooperativas Mineras de Bolivia.

38. Absi 2010.

39. Kohl 2003b, 319.

40. Kohl and Farthing 2006.

41. Albro 2005; Olivera and Lewis 2004.

42. Kirshner 2012.

43. Ibid.
44. Albó 2011.
45. Albó 2011.
46. Farthing, Arbona, and Kohl 2006.
47. City Population Data 2013; Goldstein 2004, 230.
48. Goldstein 2012.
49. Kohl and Farthing 2012.
50. Business Wire 2007; Weisbrot and Sandoval 2006.
51. Burron 2012; Rice 2011, 9–10. These were the Movimiento Nacionalista Revolucionario (MNR; National Revolutionary Movement), which had led the 1952 revolution; Banzer's right-wing Acción Democrática Nacionalista (ADN; Democratic Nationalist Action) party, based in Santa Cruz; and a former left-wing party, Movimiento de la Izquierda Revolucionaria (MIR; Revolutionary Left Movement).

Chapter Three

1. The *wiphala* is the Pan-Andean indigenous flag with forty-nine squares of seven different colors that represent the different regions once incorporated into the Inka Empire.
2. The MNR is the centrist political party that dominated Bolivian politics from the 1952 revolution until Evo was elected.
3. The Presidential or Executive Decree, called Decreto Supremo in Bolivia, is used throughout the world to enact change when congressional approval is unattainable. As a result, it lacks the same weight as a law.
4. The largely symbolic move infuriated high-ranking public employees, as none can earn more than the president. It proved particularly problematic when few of the essential hydrocarbons engineers would work for this salary. Deteriorating salaries also persuaded many judges to resign, facilitating replacement of these former government appointees with judges more sympathetic to the MAS (BBC News 2006).
5. The conflict had its roots in the 1985 state mine closures when unemployed miners grouped into "cooperatives," steadily encroached on shrinking unionized areas. With the commodity boom that began around 2005, those who control the cooperatives, who have supported Evo in elections, have emerged as a powerful political force.

In Huanuni, by 2006, only one thousand unionized state miners were left, while the cooperative sector had swollen to four thousand. The combination of complex unfulfilled commitments with a bankrupt British mining firm (Allied Deals); unionized miners desperate to protect their hard-won wages and benefits; and a rapidly expanding, ambitious group of cooperative miners motivated by the rapidly rising price of tin created an explosive situation.
6. Howard and Dangl 2009.
7. Corporación Minera de Bolivia. Möeller 2007. Working conditions, as in most of Bolivia's mines, have not improved, and miners still face short, hard lives. See King 2009.

8. Stein 2010.

9. The forty-year concession granted in 1997 to a consortium led by one of the world's largest urban water companies, French firm Suez-Lyonnaise des Eaux (now Ondeo), permitted the company to limit its service commitments. Unsurprisingly, it avoided extending water lines to poorer, more marginal, and, therefore, less profitable areas. Tired of high connection fees, thousands of Alteños took to the streets in January 2005 to pressure for public control. Echoing the Cochabamba Water War, they shouted, "The water is ours, dammit!" as their neighborhood organizations (FEJUVE) mounted a paralyzing three-day general strike that forced President Carlos Mesa to rescind the contract.

10. Empresa Pública Social de Agua y Saneamiento.

11. Tapia 2013.

12. Adapted from Farthing 2007.

13. Radio Fides 2011.

14. Gustafson 2011; Perreault 2008.

15. Econoticias 2006.

16. World Public Opinion 2006.

17. Yacimientos Petrolíferos Fiscales Bolivianos.

18. Forero 2006; Kohl 2004; Luoma and Gordon 2006. By 2005, YPFB only supplied 7 percent of government income. A two-tier royalty payment system designed to encourage new exploration charged "existing" natural gas wells 50 percent royalties, while "new" wells paid only 18 percent. Multinational owners were able to categorize most wells as "new," which created a windfall that generated extremely profitable returns.

19. Haslam 2010. Petrobras and Repsol, the largest foreign players in South America, control 74 percent of reserves. Bolivia's gas supplies about 50 percent of Brazil's needs, particularly for São Paulo's industrial corridor, followed in importance by Argentina.

20. Webber 2011, 81.

21. Bolpress 2011.

22. Liptak 2012.

23. Cameron and Sharpe 2010.

24. Latin America holds world records in constitution writing, with the Dominican Republic having produced thirty-two documents and Venezuela twenty-six since independence.

25. Tiro 1958, 59.

26. Garcés 2011.

27. Bedregal Gutiérrez 1994, 4.

28. According to Hale (2005), neoliberal multiculturalism provides for a limited recognition of cultural rights without redistribution of power or resources.

29. *La Razón* 2006.

30. *Polleras* are a wide, pleated women's skirts, worn over petticoats. Variations of it have been worn by highland indigenous women since it was introduced by the Spanish.

31. Interview courtesy of Anne Catherine Bajard, Concepción, Santa Cruz, October 6, 2012.

32. Holston 2009.

33. Author interview, La Paz, March 27, 2012.
34. Mayorga Ugarte 2006.
35. Assies 2010.
36. Author interview, La Paz, March 27, 2012.
37. Democracy Center 2008.
38. Garcés 2011.
39. Oscar Vega presentation, Latin American Studies Association meetings, San Francisco, May 27, 2012.
40. Crabtree 2009.
41. Becker 2011; Wilpert 2003.
42. Albro 2010, 72.
43. Assies 2010.
44. Buxton 2008.
45. Garcés 2011, 50–58.
46. Becker 2007.
47. Assies 2010; Fabricant and Gustafson 2011.
48. Buxton 2008.
49. CLAD 2009.
50. Comités de Vigilancia.
51. Dunkerley 1984.
52. *La Razón* 2013a.
53. Buxton 2008.
54. Author interview, La Paz, March 27, 2012.
55. Becker 2011.
56. Cameron and Sharpe 2010, 75.
57. Interview courtesy of Anne Catherine Bajard, Concepción, Santa Cruz, October 6, 2012.
58. Sivak 2011.
59. Gordon 2009; Tapper 2012.
60. Author interview, La Paz, May 8, 2012.
61. AIN 2011.
62. *La Jornada* 2011.
63. Bolivia Transition Project 2009.
64. Five rebellions against central authority demanding a federalist system have erupted since 1876, three of them in Santa Cruz (Farthing 2007).
65. Soruco, Plata, and Medeiros 2008.
66. Fabricant 2012; Rice 2011, 5.
67. A similar discourse is used by Italy's northern league to disparage southern Italians.
68. AIN 2010.
69. Eaton 2007.
70. Although Bolivia established the region's first Truth Commission in 1982, it never really got off the ground. The MAS government adopted a National Action Plan on Human Rights 2009–2013, but human rights groups and families of those disappeared during dictatorships complain that it has done very little. They point to far more aggressive actions elsewhere, such as the pressure the Chilean judiciary brought against Pinochet and the fifty-year sentence handed down in 2012

for former dictator General Vidalia in Argentina. Bolivian survivors of the dictatorships have held a vigil since March 2012 outside the Justice Ministry in downtown La Paz demanding compensation, the release of military documents, and an end to impunity (Robinson 2012).

71. Sivak 2010, 196. Armed forces' response to this challenge varied. The faction identified with the populist military tradition that Venezuela's Hugo Chávez represents embraced the new government 100 percent. A more mainstream group worried that after the attempt to extradite Chile's General Pinochet for human rights abuses from the United Kingdom in 2000, their impunity had been threatened, and so they tend to be increasingly supportive of democratically elected governments, including Evo's. The most reactionary bloc, centered on a retired military officers' organization, grumbled but have remained largely quiescent as Evo has striven to ensure their loyalty through increasingly generous budget allocations and maintaining their privileged position (Lemoine 2006).

72. Author interview, La Paz, April 2, 2012.

73. Author interview, Santa Cruz, July 15, 2008.

74. Author interview, Santa Cruz, July 15, 2008.

75. In 2009, with the adoption of the new constitution, the title of prefect was changed to governor.

76. Hodges 2008.

77. Kathryn Ledebur, e-mail communication, June 20, 2008.

78. Fabricant 2011.

79. Author interview, María Julia Gutiérrez, Santa Cruz, July 16, 2008. The Pro–Santa Cruz Civic Committee has represented local elite interests since the 1950s.

80. AIN 2008.

81. People from Cochabamba.

82. Alem Rojo and Rocha Monroy 2008.

83. Personal communication, Cochabamba, July 20, 2008.

84. Cited in Gotkowitz 2011, 1.

85. Personal communication, Santa Cruz, April 22, 2012.

86. Brie 2008.

87. Centellas and Buitrago 2009. According to Soruco Sologuren (2011, 74), land is to Santa Cruz elites what mines once were to the Andean upper class.

88. Romero 2008; Unión Juvenil Cruceñista.

89. Gustafson 2008.

90. Author interview, Santa Cruz, July 14, 2008.

91. Author interview, La Paz, August 8, 2008.

92. Evo Morales speech in Plaza Murillo, La Paz, August 8, 2008.

93. Impuesto Directo a los Hidrocarburos (IDH).

94. Humphreys Bebbington 2008.

95. Hertzler 2010.

96. Chávez 2009.

97. Goldberg was following in the maladroit footsteps of his colleague Manuel Rocha, whose 2002 public warning to Bolivians not to vote for Evo backfired. Evo joked that he wanted to hire Rocha as his campaign manager.

98. Declassified documents later obtained under the U.S. Freedom of Informa-

---

tion Act provide proof of U.S. financing to "democracy" programs that aimed to contain MAS influence, another example of enduring U.S. intervention in Latin America (Burron 2012; the documents are available at Bolivia Matters: http://boliviamatters.wordpress.com/).

99. Fabricant 2011.

100. Vaca 2008.

101. Comunica Bolivia 2008.

102. Human Rights Watch 2009.

103. Gustafson 2009a. Bordering on Brazil, the tropical frontier region still suffers debt peonage and atrocious working conditions, particularly in the seasonal Brazil-nut industry. Wealth and power are concentrated among old-fashioned political bosses accustomed to relying on violence to enforce their will. The flow of cocaine and contraband gold across the borders only bolsters the atmosphere of illegality and impunity. Groups fighting for peasant and indigenous rights suffer constant attacks in this semifeudal, lawless state within a state.

104. Kohl and Bresnahan 2010.

105. Gustafson 2009a.

106. Adapted from Farthing 2009b.

107. Carroll and Schipani 2009, n.p.

108. Hatheway 2009.

109. Medeiros 2001; Rice 2011.

110. Movimiento Sin Miedo (MSM) is a center-left political party originally organized in 1991 to win mayoral elections in La Paz for its leader Juan del Granado, a progressive attorney, who is generally considered to have done an excellent job as the city's mayor.

111. Webber 2010. Although peace was restored, it is unclear, for example, if fulfilling Potosí's demand for an international airport will pay off in terms of increased tourism or economic development.

112. *La Jornada* 2012b.

113. BIF 2011b.

114. Author interview, La Paz, September 26, 2011.

115. People from La Paz.

116. Created as a national park in 1965, the TIPNIS was designated a combined indigenous territory and national park in 1990 following the March for Territory and Dignity on La Paz. The Isiboro-Sécure has a unique flora and fauna, including eleven endangered animals. It is also the last place where the Mojene people can live in relative isolation.

117. García Linera 2012.

118. Painter 1994.

119. UNODC 2011.

120. Author interview, Santa Cruz, April 18, 2012.

121. Achtenberg 2012.

122. Author interview, La Paz, October 12, 2011.

123. Achtenberg 2013b.

124. Walsh 2012.

125. Johnson, Mendelson, and Bliss 2012. Some 60 percent of Bolivian business leaders think their police are dishonest.

126. Goldstein (2012, 32) argues that rather than an absence of the law in marginal neighborhoods, in fact it imposes certain kinds of regulation while ignoring others, creating what he calls a "phantom state" that haunts the margins of the city.

127. Johnson, Mendelson, and Bliss 2012.

128. Pearson (2011) reports that crime in Caracas reportedly declined by 53 percent a year later.

Chapter Four

1. Tapia 2007, 59.

2. Dunkerley 2007b.

3. Prevost, Oliva Campos, and Vanden 2012. In Argentina, Néstor Kirchner and Cristina Fernández drew on their Peronist background to perpetuate social movement co-optation, while in Venezuela under Chávez, deeply entrenched corporatism shifted to some degree to community organizations (Wilpert 2006). In Chile, over twenty years, Concertación governments increasingly sought to extend their co-optation of social movements. Ecuador's Rafael Correa has the region's most contentious relationship with social movements, as he has struggled to keep their demands at bay. It should be noted that some degree of co-optation is inevitable, as it brings movements immediate benefits at the same time that it grants a government greater stability.

4. Tapia 2007.

5. Author interview, Montréal, September 6, 2007.

6. Do Alto and Poupeau 2008.

7. Becerra R. 2011.

8. Aguilar Agramont 2012a.

9. Aguilar Agramont 2012b.

10. Galindo 2013.

11. Ibarnegaray Ortiz 2011.

12. Author interviews, La Paz, March 2012. For an accessible discussion of the evolution of decolonization theories, see Kohn and McBride 2011.

13. Ibarnegaray Ortiz 2011.

14. Author interview, Santa Cruz, April 17, 2012.

15. Kohl 2010.

16. Interview courtesy of Freddy Condo, La Paz, November 13, 2012.

17. Author interview, June 15, 2009.

18. Fondo Nacional de Desarrollo Alternativo (FONADAL).

19. Author interview, La Paz, January 24, 2012.

20. BIF 2012.

21. Author interview, Cochabamba, April 24, 2012.

22. Author interview, La Paz, February 7, 2012.

23. Personal communication, La Paz, March 20, 2008.

24. Author interview, La Paz, February 7, 2012.

25. According to Olivera (2012, 15), to "rule by obeying" requires a profound cultural and personal change designed to bring subordination, dependency, au-

thoritarianism, and violence to an end. It deploys authority not as an action of the powerful but as part of a collective mandate informed by new ethical principles. See also "Seven Principles of Ruling by Obeying": http://www.zapatismo.flory canto.net/docs/zapatistasevenprinciplesgoodgovernment.pdf.

26. Stefanoni 2011, 36.
27. Zegada et al. 2011.
28. Author interview, La Paz, February 10, 2012.
29. Farthing 1992.
30. Kohl 2010, 114.
31. Author interview, La Paz, January 19, 2011.
32. Author interview, La Paz, February 10, 2012.
33. *The Economist* 2005; 2011.
34. In 2011, Transparency International ranked Bolivia 118 of 183 countries, in the 64th percentile, compared to 2004, when it was ranked 122 of 146, or in the 84th percentile. Debate exists about the validity and accuracy of the ranking system used by TI, as corruption is so difficult to measure (Wilpert 2006).
35. Author interview, La Paz, July 20, 2009.
36. Zegada et al. 2011; Albro 2007; Do Alto 2009. *Le Monde diplomatique* 11 (February 2009): 6–9.
37. Personal communication, Kathryn Ledebur, April 20, 2008.
38. Miller Llana and Barnes 2011.
39. Ley de Lucha Contra la Corrupción, Enriquecimiento Ilícito e Investigación de Fortunas "Marcelo Quiroga Santa Cruz." This provision was overturned in late 2012 as contravening international agreements.
40. *Los Tiempos*, April 3, 2010.
41. Rice 2011.
42. Author interview, Betanzos, Potosí, April 14, 2012.
43. *La Razón* 2011b.
44. *La Prensa* 2010; Federación de Juntas Vecinales.
45. Do Alto 2011.
46. Loayza Bueno 2012, 8.
47. Agrawal et al. 2012.
48. Author interview, Santa Cruz, April 17, 2012.
49. Albó 2008b; Becker 2011.
50. Interview courtesy of Felix Muruchi, Wila Apacheta, April 7, 2012.
51. This provision caused an uproar among the media, which denounced its vague wording as encouraging censorship.
52. Htun 2002.
53. Author interview, La Paz, June 6, 2009. Nonetheless, the Vice Ministry of Decolonization, housed within the Ministry of Culture, was renamed the Vice Ministry of Decolonization and Dismantling of Patriarchy, although references to patriarchy have been scarce in the vice ministry's publications.
54. "Women present in history: never again without us" campaign (*Mujeres presentes en la historia: nunca más sin nosotras*).
55. Villaroel 2011.
56. Butters 2012.
57. Bolpress 2012a. The countries with the highest gender equity index in the

region are Panama, followed by Argentina, Costa Rica, Uruguay, and Nicaragua. The lowest are El Salvador, Honduras, Colombia, Venezuela, and Mexico.

58. Villaroel 2011.

59. Author interview, Montréal, September 6, 2007.

60. FM Bolivia 2012.

61. Alemán, forthcoming.

62. The Peronist political movement has dominated Argentinean politics since it was founded by former Argentinean president Juan Perón and Eva Perón. Peron served three terms between 1946 and 1975. The Partido Revolucionario Institucional (PRI) dominated Mexico from 1920 to 2000, regaining power in 2012.

63. The decline spurred the formation of new oppositional, anticorporatist labor confederations, notably the CUT in Brazil and the CTA in Argentina. See the brief description of the Central Única dos Trabalhadores (CUT; Unified Workers Central) in Chapter 2. The Central de Trabajadores de Argentina (CTA; Argentina Workers Central), formed in 1991 as a breakaway from the corporatist Confederación General de Trabajo (CGT; General Confederation of Labor), is now the country's third-largest union configuration.

64. Spronk 2012.

65. Alemán, forthcoming.

66. Anner 2011.

67. Atzeni, Durán-Palma, and Ghiglian (2011), cited in Alemán (forthcoming, 21).

68. However, unlike in most countries in the world, labor did not lose members in Brazil over the last ten years. Personal communication, Mark Anner, director, Global Center for Worker Rights, April 3, 2013. http://lser.la.psu.edu/gwr.

69. Escobar de Pabón and Rojas Callejas 2009.

70. Author calculation based on UN (2011) inflation figures.

71. *Revista ¡OH!* 2013.

72. Personal communication, Mark Anner, March 24, 2013.

73. *La Razón* 2010.

74. Venezolana de Televisión 2013.

75. Corrales and Combs 2013.

76. Mollman 2013.

77. Farthing 1993.

78. Farthing 2005.

79. Paredes 2012.

80. Cummins 2011.

81. In April 2013, U.S. secretary of state John Kerry caused an uproar when he referred to Latin America as the United States's backyard.

82. Peñaranda U. 2011.

83. Dunkerley 2011; Farthing and Kohl 2010.

84. BIF 2009.

85. Kohl and Farthing 2009.

86. Trading Economics 2013.

87. Sánchez 2007.

88. Author interview, La Paz, April 2, 2012.

89. Koenig 2005.

90. Minería de Bolivia 2012.

91. A bloody struggle broke out shortly after at Colquiri Mine between cooperative miners and state miners over who would have access to the mine.

92. ALBA comprises Antigua and Barbados, Bolivia, Cuba, Dominica, Ecuador, Nicaragua, Saint Vincent and the Grenadines, and Venezuela. Surinam and Saint Lucia joined in 2012 as guest countries.

93. Another regional integration initiative, the twelve-country Union of South American Nations (UNASUR), formed in 2004, is less explicitly anti-neoliberal and anti-imperialist than ALBA. It seeks to incorporate the region as a bloc into world markets and promote a better integrated regional infrastructure.

94. Interview courtesy of Freddy Condo, La Paz, November 13, 2012.

95. Rosenthal 2009.

96. Hunzicker 2012.

97. Author interview, La Paz, April 1, 2012.

98. French proverb: "The more things change, the more they stay the same."

99. Tapia 2011, 161.

100. Author interview, Cochabamba, April 24, 2012.

Chapter Five

1. Author interview, La Paz, March 28, 2012.

2. Author interview, La Paz, May 1, 2012.

3. Goldstein 2012.

4. Gudynas 2010.

5. Gross Domestic Product refers to the value of all goods and services produced in a country during the course of a year.

6. World Bank 2012b.

7. See Nash (1979) and Kohl, Farthing, and Muruchi (2011) for compelling accounts of life in the mines.

8. Scott 2009.

9. Sachs and Warner (1997) suggest the lower figure, although in cases of "tropical" countries they add another 0.085 percent. Mackellar, Wörgötter, and Wörz (2002) use the higher figure.

10. It is important to note that as an isolated figure, GDP reveals nothing about economic composition, distribution, or sustainability.

11. Jenkins and Barbosa 2012.

12. Bebbington 2009.

13. As a consequence, local conflicts over resource extraction have grown exponentially. Bolivia is no exception. See Bebbington 2012; Observatory of Mining Conflicts transparency. globalvoicesonline.org.

14. MercoPress 2012; U.S. Energy Administration Information 2012.

15. Bebbington and Bebbington 2010.

16. Luoma and Gordon 2009.

17. U.S. Energy Administration Information 2012.

18. Monge 2013.

19. Kohl and Farthing 2012, 231.

20. Author interview, La Paz, April 5, 2012.

21. After the 1952 revolution, laws were passed so that state mines could never be privatized.

22. Catacora 2007, 249.

23. Cited in Molina 2013, 14.

24. Often mistaken for a grain, quinoa is actually a chenopod (the same family as spinach and beets).

25. Friedman-Rudovsky 2012b; Laguna 2013.

26. Auty 1993; Karl 1997.

27. Karl 1997; Kaup 2010.

28. Lay, Thiele, and Wiebelt 2008.

29. McPhail 2009.

30. Eifert, Gelb, and Tallroth 2003.

31. Kaup 2010.

32. Personal communication, Cochabamba, July 2003.

33. McGuigan 2007.

34. Banco Central de Bolivia 2013.

35. Personal communication, La Paz, January 25, 2012.

36. Arce 2011, 8.

37. Achtenberg 2013c; *La Razón* 2013a.

38. Achtenberg 2013c.

39. Author interview, La Paz, April 4, 2012.

40. Ellner 2010.

41. Morales 2011; Laserna 2011b; Arce 2011.

42. *Revista Jubileo* 2010.

43. Gray Molina 2010.

44. UNCTAD 2011, 344; Webber 2012, 4. Just as in the rest of the region, most was for extractive industries.

45. Mendonça Cunha and Gonçalves 2010.

46. Webber and Carr 2012, 9.

47. Author interview, La Paz, June 20, 2009.

48. Patzi 2011. A principal goal is to increase technical capacity and capital to microenterprises and the campesino economy, a strategy not dissimilar to that promoted by conservative president Hugo Banzer in the late 1990s.

49. Stefanoni 2007, 35.

50. Achtenberg 2013c. Critics argue that this simply heralds a return to the economic model in vogue from the 1950s to the mid 1980s. García Linera disagrees, pointing out that while this earlier era conceived of a homogeneous, modernized, and Spanish-speaking economy of salaried workers, the new model encompasses the diversity of economic production from the modern industrial economy to the urban labor-intensive microenterprise and the rural peasant economy. See García Linera 2007, 162.

51. García Linera 2011, 77.

52. Valdez 2012.

53. Ibid.

54. Boliviana de Aviación.

55. Pimentel Castillo 2013.

56. Laserna 2011b.
57. Author interview, Cochabamba, April 22, 2012.
58. Arias 2012.
59. Coolidge and Rose-Ackerman 1999.
60. Jindal Steel Bolivia 2009.
61. Osorio M. 2011.
62. Quispe 2012.
63. Garzón 2013.
64. Jindal Steel Bolivia 2009.
65. Hite 2004, 53. For a detailed account of Ciudad Guyana, see Peattie 1987.
66. LIDEMA 2010.
67. Author interview, La Paz, June 28, 2009.
68. Author interview, La Paz, June 28, 2009.
69. Smith 2013.
70. Author interview, La Paz, June 30, 2009.
71. Author interview, La Paz, June 28, 2009.
72. Asamblea del Pueblo Guaraní. BolPress 2008.
73. Vásquez 2012b.
74. Cited in Hindery 2013, 177.
75. Forero 2012.
76. A Latin America–wide illegal wood trafficking ring was broken up by Interpol in early 2013.
77. Friedman-Rudovsky 2011.
78. Non-governmental organization.
79. Pacheco 2005.
80. Author interview, La Paz, June 28, 2009.
81. Bolpress 2013b.
82. Condori 2013.
83. Bolpress 2013a.
84. Author interview, Sucre, June 24, 2009.
85. Popper 2012.
86. Farthing 2009a; Sachs and Warner 1999.
87. Seligson 2008, 1–2.
88. Latin America is characterized by low overall labor productivity, insufficient investment, and high economic volatility. CEPAL 2012.
89. Adding to the insecurity, the government has announced that it plans to renegotiate all treaties that fail to conform to the new constitution (*La Razón* 2011, 30 November; Soria O., 2012, 20 October).
90. *La Razón* 2012b.
91. Antelo López 2008.
92. Whitesell 2009.
93. Jemio and Pacheco 2010, 24.
94. Author interview, Cochabamba, April 22, 2012.
95. While the concept of the informal sector is ill defined—see Castells and Portes (1989) for an introductory discussion—it does provide a useful framework for understanding some of the problems facing job creation in Bolivia.

96. Author interview, La Paz, April 28, 2012. In 2013, Banco Unión became a state bank.

97. Gray Molina 2010; Wanderley 2008.

Chapter Six

1. Evo accomplishes. The US$480 million program, largely financed by Venezuela, has funded some 3,900 small and quickly executed infrastructure projects across the country (Molina 2013).

2. Central Cooperativo Sueco, Cochabamba. http://www.sccportal.org/.

3. Personal communication, Cochabamba, January 25, 2012.

4. Personal communication, Santa Cruz, April 18, 2012.

5. Interview courtesy of Felix Muruchi, Wila Apacheta, March 12, 2012.

6. Author interview, Santa Cruz, April 18, 2012.

7. Author interview, Santa Cruz, April 19, 2012.

8. McLeod and Lustig 2011.

9. More information on MUSOL is available at http://www.bolivia-online.net /de/potosi/132/musol.

10. Author interview, Potosí, April 14, 2012.

11. Author interview, Sucre, April 13, 2012. Blossoming trade with China has undercut local production while making a new generation of globe-trotting Aymara traders wealthy (Tassi et al. 2012). China's manufacturing sector is highly mechanized and produces on a massive scale, its cheap labor is poorly protected, and its currency is undervalued against the dollar. In contrast, countries like Bolivia produce on a small, largely artisanal scale. Used clothing imports, mostly from the United States, have damaged Bolivia's domestic textile production, costing an estimated 160,000 jobs between 2000 and 2008. The Morales government raised tariffs in 2009, but it has had little impact (Valdez 2012).

12. *América Economía* 2011. Damian and Boltvinick (2006) remind us that using these figures—the only ones available—provide a partial view of poverty, and a skewed one at that.

13. Roberts 2012.

14. Inter-American Dialogue 2009.

15. Some argue that a more accurate translation is Convivir Bien, or Living Together Well (Albó 2008a). Personal communication, Felix Muruchi, La Paz, June 12, 2013.

16. Téllez 2012.

17. Mandepora 2011.

18. Huanacuni Mamani 2010.

19. Medina 2008.

20. Calestani 2009.

21. Lennon 2013.

22. Author interview, La Paz, October 19, 2007. Social policy initiatives have benefited from substantial bilateral aid from both Venezuela and Cuba, in addition to more traditional and multilateral sources such as the European Union, the

United States, Japan, the United Nations, and the Inter-American Development Bank, and foreign nongovernmental organizations as diverse as Oxfam UK and World Vision.

23. McLeod and Lustig 2011, 6. Inequality declined in thirteen out of seventeen countries during the 2000s, while it climbed in the rest of the world (López-Calva and Lustig 2012). Key contributors to this reduction are economic growth, better income distribution, and drops in birth rate (CEPAL 2010).

24. *América Economía* 2011; Hunter and Martorano 2012.

25. Lievesley and Ludlam 2009, 16.

26. López-Calva and Lustig 2012.

27. Perla, Mojica, and Bibler 2012.

28. Bunting 2010.

29. Roberts 2012.

30. Dignity Payment.

31. Laserna 2011b.

32. Personal communication, La Paz, March 19, 2012.

33. HelpAge International 2004.

34. Author interview, Cochabamba, June 12, 2009.

35. Mesa-Lago 2006.

36. Weisbrot and Sandoval 2006. Aside from Argentina, 1990s privatization, based on the Chilean model, was adopted by Peru, El Salvador, and Uruguay (Brooks 2005).

37. Kritzer, Kay, and Sinha 2011.

38. Valdez 2010.

39. Juancito Pinto Stipend. Juancito Pinto was a twelve-year-old drummer who died in combat in the 1880s war against Chile.

40. Observatorio Social de Políticas Educativas de Bolivia 2011.

41. Worth US$258 in 2008.

42. The woven cloth that many indigenous people use for carrying.

43. Author interview, Shinahota, Chapare, May 27, 2009.

44. *La Jornada* 2012a.

45. Hoey and Pelletier 2011; Morales, Pando, and Johannsen 2010.

46. *La Razón* 2011a.

47. *Página Siete* 2011. In fact, the percentage of the extreme poverty decline attributable to the transfers amounts to only about 2 percent of the total (UDAPE 2011, 28).

48. McLeod and Lustig 2011, 27; Silva 2010b. In Nicaragua, concerns have been raised that the drop is due to uncontrolled expansion of the agricultural frontier.

49. García Linera 2011, 102–103. Despite the gradual improvements, however, Bolivia still ranks among the most unequal societies in the world.

50. BIF 2011a. Income inequality figures are notoriously unreliable.

51. Catholic News Agency 2006.

52. Klein 1992, 227.

53. Anaya 1996, 4.

54. Serrano Torrico 1995, 19.

55. Luykx 1999.

56. This is an imperfect method of assessing education, but the one most commonly used.

57. Zoido 2009.

58. *The Economist* 2009a.

59. Levy 2010; Pearson 2010.

60. Damé 2010.

61. Mills 2012.

62. Anaya 1996; Arispe 1996; Hale 2005.

63. According to the 2001 census.

64. Several innovative leaders and programs, operated outside the state, such as Eduardo Leandro Nina Quispe and the Sociedad de Educación Indigenal Kollasuyo. Personal communication, Karen Marie Lennon, March 29, 2013.

65. Steele 2008.

66. World Bank 2013.

67. Author interview, Cochabamba, October 14, 2007.

68. Another reason for stagnating neoliberal reforms was, for example, parental opposition to bilingualism in some rural regions, because it was perceived as an impediment to children entering the hegemonic Spanish-speaking market economy. Rural teachers had a variety of objections, including the fact that many couldn't speak an indigenous language themselves. They opposed the pedagogical approach on philosophical or political grounds, or they resented higher paid consultants "telling them how to teach." Personal communication, Karen Marie Lennon, March 29, 2013.

69. Anaya 2009.

70. Luykx 1999; author interview, La Paz, 1997.

71. These school committees emerged as the second most important organizational grouping in El Alto, playing a critical role in the 2003 Gas War.

72. The influential urban unions encompass all school personnel, from teachers to porters, and date back to around 1910, with separate rural unions not forming until the late 1940s. Although roughly equal in size, the two confederations display significant political differences. The urban union was often openly racist against their rural counterparts, who serve an almost exclusively indigenous population. Union participation is obligatory, and fines are levied against those who don't participate, leading to the entrenchment of a corporatist, often corrupt structure. With considerable Trotskyist influence, urban unions have often advanced unattainable demands, such as insisting on a 1,000 percent salary increase in 2002. (They ultimately accepted 5 percent.) Anaya 2009.

73. Ibid.

74. Personal communication, La Paz, April 28, 2012.

75. Quoted in Strom 2011.

76. Alpert 2012.

77. The groundbreaking school, in the northern altiplano, was founded in 1931 and played an important role in advancing indigenous and popular education throughout Latin America.

78. Strom 2011.

79. TeleSUR 2010.

80. Author interview, La Paz, March 16, 2012.

81. *Khipus* are a collection of colored knotted strings used to keep records. The knot's shape denoted a number, and its placement indicated units based on multiples of ten. A *khipu* could have as many as two thousand strings.

82. CEBIAE 2012.

83. Ibid.

84. UNIBOL—Universidad Indígena de Bolivia (Bolivian Indigenous University).

85. The first Latin American initiative was the founding of an indigenous-oriented institution in Sinaloa, Mexico, in 1999. Similar projects took off in the 1960s in the United States and Canada. In 2010, Venezuela inaugurated an indigenous university in southeast Tauca, and Peru approved an indigenous study center near southern Puno. Even when universities are not specifically indigenous oriented, improving low-income students' access to universities has been fundamental to pink tide education policy in both Brazil and Venezuela.

86. Author interview, Warisata, May 9, 2012.

87. Mandepora 2011.

88. Ibid.

89. Prosalus 2009.

90. Missoni and Solimano 2010.

91. Tockman 2009.

92. Salud Familiar Comunitaria Intercultural (Community Intercultural Family Health).

93. World Health Organization and United Nations Children Fund.

94. Johnson 2010.

95. Shand 2012.

96. Ecuador began a similar program in May 2012.

97. In reality, everything is still fluid and in flux. In some areas, the western doctors coordinate well with the traditional ones, but in other areas, they're at each other's throats. Personal communication, Brian Johnson, March 31, 2013.

98. Personal communication, Brian Johnson, October 30, 2012.

99. FM Bolivia 2011; Tockman 2009.

100. Author telephone interview, May 5, 2012.

101. Johnson 2010. A modest degree of plant-based interventions are included in the Cuban system, semiformally or otherwise.

102. *Los Tiempos* 2012.

103. Author interview, La Paz, May 1, 2012.

104. *Cambio* 2011b; Ministerio de Salud y Deportes 2009.

105. Author interview, La Paz, June 6, 2009.

106. MEFP 2012.

Chapter Seven

1. *El Deber* 2009. Transported as slaves for the seventeenth-century silver mines, Africans proved ill suited to the cold high altitude and were shifted to coca and coffee plantations in the Yungas. There they gradually mixed and integrated

to such a degree with local Aymaras that, three centuries later, many had no idea of their origins. For the first time in the 2012 census, they were recognized as a separate ethnicity. See Léons (1978) and "We of the Saya," http://www.nosotros losdelasaya.com/.

2. Author interview, Chinchipe Yariza, North Yungas, May 25, 2009.

3. Hacienda owner.

4. *El Deber* 2009.

5. Binswanger-Mkhize, Bourguignon, and Van den Brink 2009; Lipton 2009; Pacheco et al. 2008.

6. Binswanger-Mkhize, Bourguignon, and Van den Brink 2009.

7. Gotkowitz 2008, 19.

8. Wiener Bravo 2011, 8.

9. Particularly in Central America, from the end of the nineteenth century to the middle of the twentieth, U.S. agricultural corporations, most infamously United Fruit (now Chiquita Brands), controlled enormous estates principally dedicated to banana production. That's why Honduras and Guatemala became known as the Banana Republics.

10. Pacheco et al. 2008.

11. de Janvry and Sadoulet 2002. Nicaragua provides a telling example. Despite sweeping 1980s reform, the smallholders who account for 75 percent of all landowners have only increased their land share from 12 percent to 20 percent (Pacheco et al. 2008, 2).

12. MercoPress 2012b.

13. Movimiento Sin Tierra (Landless Movement).

14. Author interview, La Paz, May 1, 2012.

15. Urioste 2009.

16. Dangl 2012.

17. Movimento dos Trabalhadores Sem Terra (Movement of Landless Workers). The Brazilian MST is Latin America's largest social movement, with over a million members. Half the cultivable land in Brazil is owned by 1 percent of the population (Prevost, Oliva Campos, and Vanden 2012, 46).

18. Binswanger-Mkhize, Bourguignon, and Van den Brink 2009, 69, 278; Thomas 2012.

19. Hellinger 2012.

20. Romero 2007a.

21. Burke 1971, 302. Although Crown land grants (*encomiendas*) established haciendas, some indigenous peoples successfully escaped to more remote, less fertile areas, particularly in the northern highlands and valleys surrounding Cochabamba and Sucre. By the mid-nineteenth century, the insatiable appetite of the criollo upper class for land and the government's need for cash led to the Law of Separation, a thinly disguised device to seize more indigenous land. "My great-grandparents narrowly escaped a massacre outside Oruro and fled to a cold, dry, isolated place about 13,700 feet above sea level," recounts ex-miner and activist Felix Muruchi. "It had such limited productive possibilities that it was of no interest to the criollos who had stolen all the land at lower altitudes" (Kohl, Farthing, and Muruchi 2011, 7).

22. Patch 1961.
23. Pacheco et al. 2008.
24. Gotkowitz 2008; Patch 1961.
25. Urioste 2004.
26. Patch 1961; Rance 1991; Silva 2010b.
27. Goutsmit 2008.
28. Clark 1967.
29. Ibid.
30. Index Mundi 2008.
31. Pacheco et al. 2008; Urioste 2004. In northeastern Beni, the government provided highland migrants both abandoned and virgin lands to farm.
32. Moore 2005; Pacheco et al. 2008.
33. Author interview, Santa Cruz, April 19, 2012.
34. About half of Santa Cruz's rural population are now from the highlands (Fabricant 2012).
35. USAID 2010.
36. Amemiya 1996.
37. PNUD 2005.
38. Author interview, Santa Cruz, April 18, 2012.
39. Hecht 2005.
40. Assies 2006.
41. Tierras Comunitarias de Origen (TCOs); First Nations or "Original" Community Territories. With the 2009 Constitution, these became Indigenous Community Territories of Origin (Territorios Indígena Originario Campesinos; TIOCs) and through the autonomy process are slated to convert to Autonomía Indígena Originario Campesino; AIOC), a process that requires communities to first be designated TIOCs (Fundación Tierra 2011a).
42. Postero 2007.
43. Kohl and Farthing 2006.
44. Burbach 2006.
45. *El Mundo* 2006.
46. Read 2006.
47. Fondo para la Compra de Tierra con Equidad de Género; Silva 2010a.
48. This basic violation of human rights affected an estimated 30,000 workers as late as 2009. Inter-American Commission on Human Rights 2009, 7.
49. Hertzler 2009.
50. *The Economist* 2006.
51. Achtenberg 2013a.
52. Galindo and Chávez 2013; Rojas Calizaya 2011.
53. Fundación Tierra 2013.
54. Author interview, Santa Cruz, April 20, 2012.
55. E-mail communication, July 25, 2012.
56. BIF 2012; Hertzler 2009.
57. Achtenberg 2013a; *La Razón* 2012d.
58. Inter-American Commission on Human Rights 2010.
59. Ibid.

60. Van Schaick 2008.
61. Asamblea del Pueblo Guaraní.
62. Van Schaick 2008.
63. *El Diario* 2011; Fundación Tierra 2010.
64. Fabricant 2012.
65. CIDOB 2009.
66. PIEB 2012.
67. Van Cott 2001.
68. Hale 2005; Lehm 2009; Postero 2007.
69. As of early 2013, only applications from municipalities were accepted.
70. Banks 2012.
71. Tockman and Cameron 2012.
72. Fundación Tierra 2012b, 18.
73. Orta 2013.
74. Cameron 2012.
75. Fundación Tierra 2011a.
76. Ibid.
77. Author interview, Santa Cruz, April 19, 2012.
78. Fundación Tierra 2012b.
79. Land Foundation.
80. Both Freddy Condo, adviser to the Unity Pact, and Adalberto Kopp, who worked at the Ministry of Rural Development and Land, reported that this is a common view.
81. Shahriari 2011.
82. Author interview, Santa Cruz, April 17, 2012.
83. Author interview, Santa Cruz, April 19, 2012.
84. *Prensa Latina* 2013; The MST continues to lose militants to assassination. Friends of the MST 2013.
85. Achtenberg 2013a.

Chapter Eight

1. Ledebur 2005.
2. UNODC 2011.
3. Allen 1988; Nicolás, Fernández, and Flores 2007, 280–281.
4. Farthing and Kohl 2005.
5. Romero 2010.
6. Spedding Pallet 2004.
7. Farthing 2008; Harten 2011. Different dynamics in Peru—from land tenure to government policy to a history of armed insurgency and early drug cartel involvement—have left grower organizations less cohesive, lacking the party organization and strong leadership evident in Bolivia. For more, see Rojas (2005) and Felbab-Brown (2006).
8. Conzelman 2007; Kohl and Farthing 2008.
9. Harten 2011; Recasens 1996.

10. Painter 1994, 46–48.

11. Gootenberg 2009. In Peru, the military role in the drug trade was most pronounced during the 1990s under Fujimori.

12. The younger Roberto was then awaiting trial for cocaine smuggling in the United States. Healy 1988; *Los Angeles Times* 2000.

13. Laserna 2011a; Rojas 2005. In Peru, as repression destroyed Colombian cartels, their Mexican counterparts stepped in.

14. Just a couple of recent examples demonstrate this long-standing phenomenon. In 2009, UN drug czar Antonio María Costa presented evidence that drug money had prevented financial meltdown in world banks (Syal 2009). And in 2012, the Obama administration fined global HSBC bank for laundering vast sums of Mexican and Colombian cartel drug profits (Taibbi 2012).

15. Ledebur 2005; Ramírez Lemus et al. 2005; Rojas 2005.

16. Sivak 2011.

17. For more on the Peruvian legislation, see van Dunn (2009, 72).

18. Demonstrating how arbitrary the coca quantity deemed "legal" is, the 1978 Peruvian law mandated exactly the same amount of coca for traditional consumption as Bolivia (Rojas 2005, 216).

19. Unidad Móvil de Patrullaje Rural; Kohl and Farthing 2001. A police unit with the same functions—and exactly the same name—was established under the 1978 Peruvian law.

20. Farthing and Kohl 2005.

21. Bustillos Zamorano 2012.

22. Harten 2011.

23. Plan Dignidad.

24. This U.S.-driven insistence on militarized eradication was also applied in Peru during the 1990s and Colombia after 2000.

25. Farthing and Ledebur 2004.

26. Peru did not undergo a similar decentralization process, despite neoliberal reforms (Bartholdson, Rudqvist, and Widmark 2002).

27. Kohl and Farthing 2008, 80.

28. Conzelman 2007.

29. FAO 2007.

30. Given differential yields, the *cato* comprises 1,600 square meters in the Chapare, and when it was adopted in the Yungas under Morales, 2,500 square meters, as soils there are less productive.

31. Author interview, Villa Tunari, July 31, 2007.

32. *La Razón* 2012c.

33. Cárdenas 2011.

34. Author interview, La Paz, June 5, 2009. (All May–June 2009 interviews were conducted for the film *Cocaine Unwrapped*. https://distrify.com/films/290 ?widget_id=238.)

35. Author interview, Coroico, June 7, 2009.

36. Adapted from Melendres 2012.

37. See discussion about social control in the new constitution in Chapter 3.

38. Author interview, Kathryn Ledebur, Cochabamba, April 24, 2012.

39. Farthing and Kohl 2012.

40. Programa de Apoyo al Control Social de la Producción de la Hoja de Coca; PACS (Support Program for Social Control of Coca Leaf Production).

41. Author interview, La Paz, May 20, 2009.

42. Author interview, Villa Tunari, May 30, 2009.

43. PACS 2011, 20.

44. Author interview, Villa Tunari, May 30, 2009.

45. PACS 2008.

46. However, the government exercises only limited control over the principal legal markets in Sacaba, Cochabamba, and even less over the one in Villa Fátima, La Paz.

47. Author interview, Shinahota, May 29, 2009.

48. Author interview, Villa Tunari, May 30, 2009.

49. Author interview, Villa Tunari, May 23, 2009.

50. PACS 2009, 124.

51. Author interview, Cochabamba, January 28, 2012.

52. Personal communication, Kathryn Ledebur, Cochabamba, June 5, 2013.

53. *La Prensa* 2008.

54. Friedman-Rudovsky 2008.

55. Author interview, social control program director Reynaldo Molina, La Paz, January 24, 2012.

56. Palacios 2011.

57. Author interview, Cochabamba, January 30, 2012.

58. Cusicanqui 2011.

59. Palacios 2011.

60. Personal communication, Kathryn Ledebur, April 2, 2013.

61. Brocchetto 2012.

62. Friedman-Rudovsky 2012a; personal communication, Kathryn Ledebur, March 28, 2013.

63. UNODC 2012. U.S. figures almost coincide with UN ones, since coca monitoring has improved so much that political manipulation of the figures is less feasible. Personal communication, Kathryn Ledebur, April 2, 2013.

64. Author interview, Cochabamba, April 27, 2012. In a moment of journalistic hyperbole, Reinicke was hailed the "Indiana Jones" of the Chapare (Rotella 1999). He currently directs Punte Enlace e Investigación (Network and Investigation Center), which focuses on coca/cocaine issues. http://www.piebolivia.org.bo/.

65. UNODC 2009, 8.

66. Calizaya 2011.

67. Fuerza Especial de la Lucha contra el Narcotráfico (FELCN). The UMO-PAR is its rural arm. Author interview, La Paz, June 6, 2009.

68. Author interview, near Bulo Bulo, Chapare, May 28, 2009.

69. Ibid.

70. Author interview, Villa Tunari, May 23, 2009.

71. Ledebur 2005.

72. Author interview, La Paz, June 6, 2009.

73. Personal communication, Diego Giocaman, March 2012.

74. Author interview, Chimoré, Chapare, May 28, 2009.

75. EFE 2012b.

76. Author interview, Cochabamba, April 24, 2012.

77. *eju!* 2012.

78. Calizaya 2013.

79. Calizaya 2012.

80. Personal communication, Joe Loney, attorney and Maryknoll lay missioner, Cochabamba, April 26, 2012; Giacoman 2010. The minister of justice, Cecilia Aillón, estimated in September 2011 that it would take another ten to fifteen years to reform the judicial system.

81. Author interview, Cochabamba, April 27, 2012.

82. Davis 2010.

83. Not her real name. Author interview, Cochabamba, April 26, 2012.

84. Seligson 2008.

85. Ramsey 2011.

86. Schipani 2010.

87. Farthing and Kohl 2012; Ledebur and Youngers 2012.

88. BBC News 2012.

89. ANF-Agencia 2011.

90. Author interview, La Paz, May 20, 2009.

91. Author interview, La Paz, March 12, 2012.

Chapter Nine

1. UNDP 2010.

2. *La Razón* 2012a.

3. Author interview, La Paz, March 10, 2012.

4. Author interview, La Paz, April 2, 2012.

5. Interview courtesy of Jessica Robinson, Tiquipaya, Cochabamba, May 23, 2012.

6. Ayala et al. 2009.

7. Canessa, 2012.

8. Cameron 2012.

9. Author interview, Cochabamba, April 22, 2012.

10. Author interview, Cochabamba, July 20, 2008. A founder of the Housewives Committee of Siglo XX mines, Domitila Barrios de Chungara became famous when she told her life story in *Let Me Speak!* (Monthly Review Press, 1978). She was best known for her role with three other women in leading a 1977 hunger strike that brought down the Banzer dictatorship. When she died on March 13, 2012, three days of national mourning were decreed to honor her.

11. Webber and Carr 2012, 23.

12. Cited in Earle 2011.

13. Spronk 2012.

14. Author interview, Cochabamba, April 25, 2012.

15. See Bebbington 2012.

16. Perreault 2012.

17. Wright 2010.

18. Mulvany and Kaskey 2012.

19. Garcés 2011, 64; Gustafson 2011.

20. Author interview, La Paz, March 10, 2012.

21. Excerpted from interview with Gonzalo Lema, Movimiento Sin Miedo, La Paz, March 2011.

22. Motta 2009, 76.

23. Partido dos Trabalhadores.

24. Buxton 2009.

25. Do Alto and Poupeau 2008.

26. Do Alto 2009.

27. Further confusion revolves around issues such as communal administration of justice and the meaning of individual and collective citizenship in a plurinational state.

28. Svampa and Stefanoni 2007, 29.

29. Paredes 2013.

30. Author interview, La Paz, February 29, 2012.

31. Notwithstanding the rhetoric of social control, in practice, there has been a tendency to transfer decision making from the grass roots to the state (Rice 2011, 266).

32. Dunkerley 2011, 179, 182.

33. In March 2013, Aymara leader Felipe Quispe called for forming a broad alliance to challenge the MAS in the 2014 elections.

34. Paredes 2012.

35. Zegada et al. 2011, 196.

36. Ovideo Obarrio 2010; Zandivliet 2010.

37. Tassi 2012.

38. Rivera Cusicanqui 2010.

39. Hindery 2013.

40. Cited in Buxton 2011.

41. Gramsci 1971.

42. Interview courtesy of Freddy Condo, La Paz, November 13, 2012.

43. *Abarcas* are sandals made of used tires and in particular are worn by rural people.

44. Dunkerley 2011, 197.

45. Chappell and LaValle 2011.

References

Absi, Pascale. 2010. "La parte ideal de la crisis: Los mineros cooperativistas de Bolivia frente a la recesión." *Cuadernos de Antropología Social* 31 (1): 33–54.

Achtenberg, Emily. 2012. "Bolivia: TIPNIS Marchers Return Home, Pledge to Resist Government Consulta." *North American Congress on Latin America* (hereafter *NACLA*). Accessed July 16, 2012. http://nacla.org/blog/2012/7/13/bolivia-tipnis-marchers-return-home-pledge-resist-government-consulta.

———. 2013a. "Bolivia: The Unfinished Business of Land Reform." *NACLA*, April 1. Accessed June 25, 2013. https://nacla.org/blog/2013/3/31/bolivia-unfinished-business-land-reform.

———. 2013b. "Contested Development: The Geopolitics of Bolivia's TIPNIS Conflict." *NACLA Report on the Americas* 46 (2): 6–11.

———. 2013c. "Economic Growth with More Equality: Learning from Bolivia." *NACLA*, February 15, 2013. Accessed 3/13/2013. https://nacla.org/blog/2013/2/15/economic-growth-more-equality-learning-bolivia.

Agrawal, Nina, Richard André, Ryan Berger, and Wilda Escarfuller. 2012. "Political Representation, Policy and Inclusion." *Americas Quarterly*, May 9. Accessed September 17, 2012. http://americasquarterly.org/political-representation.

Aguilar Agramont, Ricardo. 2012a. "La descolonización aún se encuentra en el plano discursivo." *La Razón*, August 26. Accessed November 5, 2012. http://www.la-razon.com/suplementos/animal_politico/descolonizacion-encuentra-plano-discursivo_0_1675632467.html.

———. 2012b. "Viceministerio perfila ley para erradicar la exclusión social." *Cambio*, October 12. Accessed October 24, 2012. http://www.cambio.bo/politica/20121012/viceministerio_perfila_ley_para_erradicar_la_exclusion_social_81228.htm.

Albó, Xavier. 2008a. "Bien Vivir = Convivir Bien." February 17. Accessed June 25, 2013. http://www.cipca.org.bo/index.php?option=com_content&view=article&catid=78&id=248.

———. 2008b. *Movimientos y poder indígena en Bolivia, Ecuador y Perú*. Vol. 71 of Cuadernos de Investigación. La Paz: CIPCA.

———. 2011. "El Alto in Flux: Crossroads between La Paz and the Altiplano in Bolivia: Revolutions and Beyond." *ReVista: Harvard Review of Latin America* (Fall). David Rockefeller Center for Latin American Studies, Harvard University. Accessed September 11, 2012. http://www.drclas.harvard.edu /publications/revistaonline/fall-2011/el-alto-flux.

Albro, Robert. 2005. "The Water Is Ours, Carajo!: Deep Citizenship in Bolivia's Water War." In *Social Movements: An Anthropological Reader*, ed. June Nash, 249–271. Oxford and Cambridge, MA: Basil Blackwell.

———. 2007. "Indigenous Politics in Bolivia's Evo Era: Clientelism, Llunkerío, and the Problem of Stigma." *Urban Anthropology* 36 (3): 281–320.

———. 2010. "Confounding Cultural Citizenship and Constitutional Reform in Bolivia." *Latin America Perspectives* 37 (3): 71–90.

Alemán, José A. Forthcoming. "The Left Turn in Latin America: Consequences for Employment Relations." In *Oxford Handbook of Employment Relations: Comparative Employment Systems*. Oxford: Oxford University Press.

Alem Rojo, Roberto, and Ricardo Rocha Monroy. 2008. *¡Nunca más!: A un año del 11 de enero*. Santa Cruz de la Sierra, Bolivia: Editorial El País.

Alexander, Robert J. 2005. *A History of Organized Labor in Bolivia*. Westport, CT: Praeger.

Allen, Catherine J. 1988. *The Hold Life Has: Coca and Cultural Identity in an Andean Community*. Washington, DC: Smithsonian Institute Press.

Alpert, Emily. 2012. "Bolivian President's School Reforms Facing Resistance." *PRI's The World*. Accessed November 3, 2012. http://www.theworld.org/2012/01/bo livian-president-evo-morales-school-reforms-facing-resistance/.

Amemiya, Kozy K. 1996. "The Bolivian Connection: U.S. Bases and Okinawan Emigration." *Japan Policy Research Institute*, Working Paper No. 25. Accessed April 12, 2013. http://www.jpri.org/publications/workingpapers/wp25.html.

América Economía. 2011. "Cepal: Indice de pobreza en Bolivia bajó hasta el 54%." *América Economía*, November 30. Accessed November 2, 2011. www.america economia.com/economia-mercados/finanzas/cepal-indice-de-pobreza-en -bolivia-bajo-hasta-el-54.

Anaya, Amalia. 1996. *Proceso de formulación de la Reforma Educativa*. Working Document No. 01/95, Universidad Católica Boliviana-Harvard Institute for International Development.

———. 2009. *Sindicatos docentes y reformas educativas en América Latina*. La Paz: Konrad Adenauer Stiftung.

Andean Information Network (cited as AIN). 2006. "Bolivian Congress Passes Agrarian Reform Legislation in Spite of Heightened Regional Tensions." Andean Information Network, December 1. Accessed October 30, 2012. http:// ain-bolivia.org/2006/12/bolivian-congress-passes-agrarian-reform/.

———. 2008. "Illegal Autonomy Referendum Deepens Division in Bolivia." Accessed November 15, 2012. http://ain-bolivia.org/2008/04/illegal-autonomy -referendum-deepens-division-in-bolivia/.

———. 2010. "Does Morales's 'Socialist' Agenda Pose a Threat to American Values?" Accessed July 22, 2012. http://ain-bolivia.org/2010/02/does-moraless -socialist-agenda-pose-a-threat-to-american-values/.

———. 2011. "Black October Verdict: All Officials Guilty." Accessed July 16, 2012. http://ain-bolivia.org/2011/08/verdict-nears-in-%E2%80%9Cblackoctober%E2%80%9D-trial-could-set-important-precedent-for-bolivian-human-rights-cases/.

———. 2012. "Mallku Khota Mining Mess." Accessed September 19, 2012. http://ain-bolivia.org/2012/07/mallku-khota-mining-mess-analysis.

ANF-Agencia. 2011. "Morales: Narcotraficantes están mejor equipados que el Gobierno." *Los Tiempos*, December 13. Accessed March 12, 2012. http://www.lostiempos.com/diario/actualidad/nacional/20111213/evo-narcotraficantes-estan-mejor-equipados-que-el_153174_318453.html.

Anner, Mark. 2011. *Solidarity Transformed: Labor Responses to Globalization and Crisis in Latin America*. Ithaca: ILR Press, an imprint of Cornell University Press.

Anria, Santiago. 2010. "Bolivia's MAS: Between Party and Movement." In *Latin America's Left Turns: Politics, Policies, and Trajectories of Change*, ed. Maxwell Cameron and Eric Herschberg, 101–126. Boulder, CO: Lynne Rienner.

Antelo López, Ernesto. 2008. "Migrantes bolivianos: '2,5 millones de héroes y heroínas.'" *Bolivia: Migración, Remesas y Desempleo* 16 (159): 2. Accessed August 15, 2012. http://ibce.org.bo/publicaciones-descarga.php?id=11&opcion=#.U boJF5zXuSo.

Arbona, Juan M. 2008. "Histories and Memories in the Organisation and Struggles of the Santiago II Neighbourhood of El Alto, Bolivia." *Bulletin of Latin American Research* 27 (1): 24–42.

Arce, Luis. 2011. "El nuevo modelo económico, social, comunitario y productivo." *Economía Plural* 1 (1). Accessed November 2, 2012. http://medios.economiayfinanzas.gob.bo/MH/documentos/Materiales_UCS/Revistas/Revista_01.pdf.

Arditi, Benjamin. 2008. "Arguments about the Left Turns in Latin America: A Post-Liberal Politics?" *Latin American Research Review* 43 (3): 59–81.

Arias, Sandra. 2012. "Corrupción y baja ejecución debilitan gestión pública." *Los Tiempos*, April 8. Accessed September 19, 2012. http://www.lostiempos.com/diario/actualidad/economia/20120805/corrupcion-y-baja-ejecucion-debilitan-gestion_180970_382784.html.

Arispe, Valentín. 1996. "El proceso de configuración de una escuela campesina: la experiencia de la comunidad de Rumi Muqu, 1989–1993." Unpublished *licenciado* thesis, Universidad Mayor de San Simón, Cochabamba, Bolivia.

Arnold, Denise, Rossana Barragán, Pamela Calla Ortega, Alison Spedding, and Juan de Dios Yapita, eds. 2009. *¿Indígenas u obreros? La construcción política de las identidades en el Altiplano boliviano*. La Paz: Fundación UNIR.

Assies, Willem. 2004. "Bolivia: A Gasified Democracy." *Revista Europea de Estudios Latinoamericanos y del Caribe* 76 (April): 25–43.

———. 2006. "Land Tenure Legalization, Pluriculturalism and Multiethnicity in Bolivia." Paper presented at the Colloque international "Les frontières de la question foncière/At the Frontier of Land Issues," Montpellier, France.

———. 2010. "Bolivia's New Constitution and Its Implications." In *Evo Morales and the Movimiento al Socialismo in Bolivia*, ed. A. Pearce, 93–116. London: Bolivia Information Forum/Institute for the Study of the Americas.

Auty, Richard M. 1993. *Sustaining Development in Mineral Economies: The Resource Curse Thesis*. London: Routledge.

Ayala, Rodrigo, Gustavo Fernández, Jorge Lazarte, and Fernando Mayorga. 2009. *Conflictos: Una mirada hacia el futuro.* La Paz: Fundación Boliviana para la Democracia Multipartidaria—FBDM; Fundación Friedrich Ebert—FES; Instituto Latinoamericano de Investigaciones Sociales—ILDIS.

Banco Central de Bolivia. 2013. "Reservas de Bolivia llegan a $14.069 miliones." February 3. Accessed March 12, 2013. http://www.bcb.gob.bo/webdocs/Febrero2009/semanalesentero20-3.pdf.

Banks, Emma. 2012. "Indigenous Autonomies in Bolivia; Part I: Legal Guidelines and Gaps." Andean Information Network. Accessed March 3, 2012. http://ain-bolivia.org/2012/02/indigenous-autonomies-in-bolivia-part-i-legal-guidelines-and-gaps/.

Barnes de Marschall, Katherine. 1970. *Revolution and Land Reform in the Bolivian Yungas of La Paz.* La Paz: Servicio Nacional de Reforma Agraria, Sección Investigaciones.

Barrionuevo, Alexei. 2009. "Brazil Aims to Prevent Land Grabs in Amazon." *New York Times,* December 27. Accessed March 15, 2012. http://www.nytimes.com/2009/12/27/world/americas/27brazil.html?pagewanted=all.

Barrios de Chungara, Domitila, and Moema Viezzer. 1978. *Let Me Speak!: Testimony of Domitila, a Woman of the Bolivian Mines.* New York: Monthly Review Press.

Bartholdson, Örjan, Anders Rudqvist, and Charlotta Widmark. 2002. "Popular Participation in Bolivia, Colombia and Peru: A Synthesis of Three Studies." Accessed October 2, 2012. http://www.kus.uu.se/SAdelstudie.pdf.

BBC News. 2006. "Bolivia Leader Halves His Own Pay." Accessed July 12, 2009. http://news.bbc.co.uk/2/hi/americas/4652940.stm.

———. 2008. "Chavez Acts over U.S.-Bolivia Row." Accessed March 25, 2010. http://news.bbc.co.uk/2/hi/americas/7611705.stm.

———. 2012. "Peru's Coca Cultivation Increases Again, Says UN Study." BBC News, September 26. Accessed February 4, 2013. http://www.bbc.co.uk/news/world-latin-america-19737984.

Beasley-Murray, John, Maxwell A. Cameron, and Eric Hershberg. 2010. "Latin America's Left Turns: A Tour d'horizon." In *Latin America's Left Turns: Politics, Policies and Trajectories,* ed. Maxwell A. Cameron and Eric Hershberg, 1–22. Boulder, CO: Lynne Rienner.

Bebbington, Anthony. 2009. "The New Extraction: Rewriting the Political Ecology of the Andes." *NACLA Report on the Americas* 42 (5): 12–20.

———, ed. 2012. *Social Conflict, Economic Development and Extractive Industry: Evidence from South America.* London: Routledge.

Bebbington, Denise Humphreys, and Anthony Bebbington. 2010. "Anatomy of a Regional Conflict: Tarija and Resource Grievances in Morales's Bolivia." *Latin American Perspectives* 37 (4): 140–160.

Becerra R., Mauricio. 2011. "Félix Cárdenas, Viceministro de Descolonización de Bolivia: 'Todos los Estados de este continente son coloniales.'" *El cuidadano,* April 14. Accessed November 4, 2012. http://www.elciudadano.cl/2011/04/14/34772/felix-cardenas-viceministro-de-descolonizacion-de-bolivia-%E2%80%9Ctodos-los-estados-de-este-continente-son-coloniales%E2%80%9D/.

Becker, Emily. 2007. "Bolivia's Constituent Assembly Approves Text, Referendums Pending." Accessed February 1, 2008. http://ain-bolivia.org/2007/12/bolivian-constitutional-assembly-approves-text-referendums-pending/.

Becker, Marc. 2011. "Correa, Indigenous Movements, and the Writing of a New Constitution in Ecuador." *Latin American Perspectives* 38 (1): 47–62.

Bedregal Gutiérrez, Guillermo. 1994. *Bolivia: Capitalización, participación popular y liberalismo en la mundialización económica.* Cochabamba, Bolivia: Editorial Los Amigos del Libro.

Binswanger-Mkhize, Hans P., Camile Bourguignon, and Rogerius J. E. van den Brink. 2009. *Agricultural Land Redistribution: Toward Greater Consensus.* Washington, DC: World Bank.

Boeglin, Nicolas. 2012. "Argentina: Towards a Possible New Withdrawal from ICSID?" *CADTM.* Accessed September 20, 2012. http://cadtm.org/Argentina-towards-a-possible-new.

Bolivia Information Forum (cited as BIF). 2009. "International Relations." Accessed April 6, 2012. http://www.boliviainfoforum.org.uk/inside-page.asp?section=3&page=33.

———. 2011a. "Development and Social Statistics." Accessed November 2, 2012. http://www.boliviainfoforum.org.uk/inside-page.asp?section=2&page=3.

———. 2011b. "To the Brink, and Back Again: Special Briefing." Accessed January 21, 2011. http://www.boliviainfoforum.org.uk/news-detail.asp?id=84.

———. 2012. Bolivia Information Forum No. 23 (September). Accessed March 24, 2013. http://www.boliviainfoforum.org.uk/documents/908907171_BIF%20Bulletin%2023.pdf.

Bolivia Transition Project. 2009. "Goni, Going, Gone?" Accessed July 14, 2012. http://boliviatransitionproject.blogspot.com/2009/11/goni-going-gone.html.

Bolpress (Electronic news service). 2008. "Pueblos indígenas, originarios y comunidades campesinas vigilarán a las petroleras." Accessed July 10, 2009. http://www.bolpress.com/art.php?Cod=2008071004.

———. 2011. "Agenda de octubre: Gobierno no cumplió compromisos con el pueblo." Accessed October 14, 2012. http://www.bolpress.com/art.php?Cod=2011101104.

———. 2012a. "Bolivia por debajo del promedio latinoamericano en equidad de género." March 7. Accessed July 15, 2012. http://www.bolpress.com/art.php?Cod=2012030703.

———. 2012b. "García Linera: Defender a Evo del 'colonialismo dominador.'" March 23. Accessed May 10, 2012. http://www.bolpress.com/art.php?Cod=2012032301.

———. 2013a. "El gobierno adjudica parques y reservas naturales a las petroleras." May 24. Accessed June 25, 2013. http://www.bolpress.com/art.php?Cod=2013052401.

———. 2013b. "El gobierno legitima desmontes ilegales y suspende la reversión de más de 5 millones de hectáreas." January 12. Accessed June 25, 2013. http://www.bolpress.com/art.php?Cod=2013011203.

Brie, César. 2008. "Humillados y ofendidos." Video. http://www.youtube.com/watch?v=27i9SsZOFT0.

Brocchetto, Maria. 2012. "Bolivia's Morales to UN: Legalize Coca-Leaf Chewing." CNN, March 13. Accessed June 15, 2013. http://www.bbc.co.uk/news/world-latin-america-20994392.

Brooks, Sara. 2005. "Interdependent and Domestic Foundations of Policy Change: The Diffusion of Pension Privatization around the World." *International Studies Quarterly* 49, 273–294.

Bunker, Stephen G. 1985. *Underdeveloping the Amazon: Extraction, Unequal Exchange, and the Failure of the Modern State*. Chicago: University of Chicago Press.

Bunting, Madeline. 2010. "Brazil's Cash Transfer Scheme Is Improving the Lives of the Poorest." *The Guardian*. Accessed July 24, 2012. http://www.guardian.co.uk/global-development/poverty-matters/2010/nov/19/brazil-cash-transfer-scheme.

Burbach, Roger. 2006. "Confrontation in Bolivia over Agrarian Reform." *NACLA Report on the Americas*, November 23. Accessed June 10, 2007. www.nacla.org.

Burke, Melvin. 1971. "Land Reform in the Lake Titicaca Region." In *Beyond the Revolution: Bolivia since 1952*, ed. J. Malloy and R. Thorn, 301–340. Pittsburgh, PA: University of Pittsburgh Press.

Burron, Neil. 2012. "Unpacking U.S. Democracy Promotion in Bolivia: From Soft Tactics to Regime Change." *Latin American Perspectives* 39 (1): 115–132.

Business Wire. 2007. "Fitch Revises Bolivia's Outlook to Stable; Affirms IDR at 'B-'." 27_July_27/ai_n19393641. Accessed December 10, 2007. http://findarticles.com/p/articles/mi_m0EIN/is_2007.

Bustillos Zamorano, I. 2012. "Evo se salvará sólo si erradica toda la coca del trópico." *La Razón*. Accessed February 15, 2012. http://www.la-razon.com/suplementos/animal_politico/Evo-salvara-erradica-coca-tropico_0_1534046617.html.

Butters, Rossana. 2012. "Political Femicide." *Bolivian Express* 20 (August): 16–17.

Buxton, Julia. 2009. "Venezuela: The Political Evolution of Bolivarianism." In *Reclaiming Latin America: Experiments in Radical Social Democracy*, ed. Geraldine Lievesley and Steve Ludlam, 57–74. London: Zed Books.

Buxton, Nick. 2008. "Constituting Change in a Divided Bolivia." Accessed February 20, 2008. http://www.tni.org/detail_page.phtml?act_id=17834&menu=11 f.

———. 2011. "The law of Mother Earth: Behind Bolivia's historic bill." *Yes! Magazine*, April. Accessed June 25, 2013. www.yesmagazine.org/planet/the-law-of-mother-eart-behind-bolivias-historic-bill.

Cabitza, Mattia. 2011. "Bolivia Bids to Turn Coca into Compost Not Cocaine." BBC News, La Paz. Accessed February 3, 2012. http://www.bbc.co.uk/news/world-latin-america-14987479.

Calderón, Fernando. 2007. "Oportunidad histórica: Cambio político y nuevo orden sociocultural." *Nueva Sociedad* 209 (May–June): 32–45.

Calestani, M. 2009. "An Anthropology of 'The Good Life' in the Bolivian Plateau." *Social Indicators Research* 90 (1): 141–153.

Calizaya, Ernesto. 2011. "Del 60% al 80% de la cocaína boliviana es enviada a Brasil." *La Razón*, December 13. Accessed March 20, 2012. http://www.la-razon.com/ciudades/seguridad_ciudadana/cocaina-boliviana-enviada-Brasil_0_1522047840.html.

———. 2012. "Romero plantea 'nacionalizar' la lucha contra el narcotráfico."

La Razón, January 31. Accessed March 12, 2012. http://www.la-razon.com/na
cional/Romero-plantea-nacionalizar-lucha-narcotrafico_0_1551444898.html.

———. 2013. "Incautación de cocaína creció en 234% sin participación de la
DEA." *La Razón*, January 20. Accessed February 14, 2013. http://www.la-razon
.com/nacional/seguridad_nacional/Incautacion-cocaina-crecio-participacion
-DEA_0_1763823702.htm.

Camacho Nassa, Carlos. 2010. *Entre el etnocidio y la extinción: Pueblos indígenas
aislados, en contacto inicial e intermitente en las tierras bajas de Bolivia*. Informe
IWGIA 6. Accessed March 12, 2012. http://www.iwgia.org/iwgia_files_publi
cations_files/0276_Bolivia_-_Entre_El_Ethnicido_-_Informe_6.pdf.

Cambio. 2011a. "Erradicación de coca llega a 10.051 hectáreas y se bate otro ré-
cord." *Cambio*, February 12, 2011. Accessed March 12, 2012. http://www.cam
bio.bo/noticia.php?fecha=2011-12-02&idn=59566.

———. 2011b. "Municipios se fortalecen con 60 postas de salud." *Cambio*,
March 6, 2011. Accessed April 1, 2012. http://www.cambio.bo/noticia.php?fe
cha=2011-06-03&idn=46726.

Cameron, John. 2012. "Bolivia's Contentious Politics of 'Normas y Procedimien-
tos Propios' Paper." Paper presented at the 30th Congress of the Latin American Studies Association. http://lasa.international.pitt.edu/members/congress
-papers/lasa2012/files/7416.pdf.

Cameron, Maxwell A., and Eric Hershberg, eds. 2010. *Latin America's Left Turns:
Politics, Policies, and Trajectories of Change*. Boulder, CO: Lynne Rienner.

Cameron, Maxwell A., and Kenneth Sharpe. 2010. "Andean Left Turns: Constituent Power and Constitution Making." In *Latin America's Left Turns*, ed. Maxwell A. Cameron and Eric Hershberg, 61–78. Boulder, CO: Lynne Rienner.

Canessa, Andrew. 2008. "The Past Is Not Another Country: Exploring Indigenous Histories in Bolivia." *History and Anthropology* 19 (4): 353–369.

———. 2012. "Conflict, Claim and Contradiction in the New Indigenous State
of Bolivia." DesiguALdades.net. Accessed June 25, 2013. http://www.desigual
dades.net/bilder/Working_Paper/22_WP_Canessa_online.pdf.

Cárdenas, José Arturo. 2011. "Bolivia Bid to Decriminalize Coca Leaf Chewing." Agence France-Presse, January 19. Accessed January 25, 2012. http://www
.amigosdeboliviayperu.org/NewsStories2011/B505BoliviaBid.html.

Carroll, Rory, and Andres Schipani. 2009. "Evo Morales Wins Landslide Victory in Bolivian Presidential Elections." *The Guardian*, December 7. Accessed
March 27, 2012. http://www.guardian.co.uk/world/2009/dec/07/morales-pres
idential-victory.

Castells, Manuel, and Alejandro Portes. 1989. "World Underneath: The Origins,
Dynamics and Effects of the Informal Economy." In *The Informal Economy:
Studies in Advanced and Less Developed Countries*, ed. Alejandro Portes, Manuel
Castells, and Lauren A. Benton, 11–37. Baltimore: Johns Hopkins University
Press.

Catacora, Georgina. 2007. "Soya en Bolivia: Producción de oleaginosas y depen-
dencia." In *Repúblicas Unidas de la Soja: Radiografía de un modelo violento*, ed.
Javiera Rulli, 235–251. Asunción: Grupo de Reflexión Rural.

Catholic News Agency. 2006. "Bolivian President, Education Minister Slam Bish-
ops." La Paz, July 26.

CEBIAE (Centro Boliviano de Investigación y Acción Educativas). 2012. "Nuevas palabras para una nueva educación." *La Razón*, April 7, Sección Especial.

Centellas, Miguel, and Miguel A. Buitrago. 2009. "The Political Economy of Bolivia's New Regionalism: Electoral Patterns in Santa Cruz, Tarija, and Chuquisaca." Paper presented at the Midwest Political Science Association, April, Chicago.

Centeno, Miguel Angel, and Fernando López-Alves, eds. 2001. *The Other Mirror: Grand Theory through the Lens of Latin America*. Princeton: Princeton University Press.

CEPAL (Comisión Económica para América Latina y el Caribe). 2010. "El progreso de América Latina y el Caribe hacia los objetivos de desarrollo del milenio: Desafíos para lograrlos con igualdad." Accessed July 24, 2012. http://www .eclac.org/publicaciones/xml/1/39991/2010-622-ODM-ESPANOL_CapII .pdf.

———. 2012. "La inversión en América Latina es insuficiente para alcanzar el desarrollo." CEPAL: Comunicados de prensa, January 24. Accessed November 2, 2012. http://www.eclac.cl/cgi-bin/getProd.asp?xml=/prensa/noticias/comuni cados/8/45758/P45758.xml&.

Chappell, Michael J., and Liliana A. LaValle. 2011. "Food Security and Biodiversity: Can We Have Both? An Agroecological Analysis." *Agriculture and Human Values* 28 (1): 3–26.

Chávez, Marxa. 2009. "Weaving the Rebellion: Plan 3000, Center of Resistance in Eastern Bolivia." *Socialism and Democracy* 23 (3): 101–116.

CIA (Central Intelligence Agency). 2011. *The World Factbook*. Accessed September 29, 1011. https://www.cia.gov/library/publications/the-world-factbook/ge os/bl.html.

CIDOB (Confederación de Pueblos Indígenas de Bolivia). 2009. "Rodolfo López, cacique mayor de la OICH: 'La prioridad es consolidar nuestros gobiernos autónomos.'" CIDOB, April 4. Accessed October 30, 2012. http://www .cidob-bo.org/index.php?option=com_content&view=article&id=235:ro dolfo-lopez-cacique-mayor-de-la-oich-qla-prioridad-es-consolidar-nuestros -gobiernos-autonomosq&catid=82:noticias&Itemid=2.

City Population Data. 2013. Accessed June 3, 2013. http://www.citypopulation .de/Bolivia.html.

CLAD (Centro Latinoamericano de Administración para el Desarrollo). 2009. "Bolivia: Garantizada la ética, la transparencia y el control social en la nueva Constitución Política de Bolivia." Accessed January 12, 2012. www.clad.org /noticias/bolivia-garantizada-la-etica-la-transparencia-y-el-control-social -en-la-nueva-constitucion-politica-de-bolivia.

Clark, Ronald J. 1967. "Problems and Conflicts over Land Ownership in Bolivia." *Inter-American Economic Affairs* 22 (4): 3–18.

Cleary, Matthew R. 2006. "A 'Left Turn' in Latin America? Explaining the Left's Resurgence." *Journal of Democracy* 17 (4): 35–49.

Comunica Bolivia. 2008. "Masacre en Pando." Video. http://www.youtube.com /watch?v=-J-eBCmkYn0.

Conaghan, Catherine M., and James M. Malloy. 1994. *Unsettling Statecraft:*

Democracy and Neoliberalism in the Central Andes. Pittsburgh, PA: University of Pittsburgh Press.

Condori, Iván. 2013. "Agro proyecta ampliar frontera agrícola hasta 15 millones de ha." *La Razón,* January 12. Accessed March 30, 2013. http://www.la-razon.com /economia/Agro-proyecta-frontera-agricola-millones_0_1759624072.html.

Conzelman, Caroline S. 2007. "Coca Leaf and *Sindicato* Democracy in the Bolivian Yungas: The Andeanization of Western Political Models and the Rise of the New Left." PhD diss., University of Colorado, Boulder.

Coolidge, Jacqueline, and Susan Rose-Ackerman. 1999. "High-Level Rent-Seeking and Corruption in African Regimes: Theory and Cases." Accessed October 26, 2012. http://siteresources.worldbank.org/INTWBIGOVANTCOR/Re sources/wps1780.pdf.

Corrales, Javier, and Cameron Combs. 2013. "5 LGBT Trends to Watch for in the Americas in 2013." *Huffington Post,* January 10. Accessed March 21, 2013. http://www.huffingtonpost.com/javier-corrales/5-lgbt-trends-to-watch-for-in -the-americas-in-2013_b_2441863.html.

Crabtree, John. 2005. *Patterns of Protest: Politics and Social Movements in Bolivia.* London: Latin America Bureau.

———. 2009. "Bolivia: New Constitution, New Definition." openDemocracy, January 22. Accessed July 9, 2012. http://www.opendemocracy.net/article /bolivia-new-constitution-new-definition.

Crabtree, John, Gavan Duff, and Jenny Pearce. 1987. *The Great Tin Crash: Bolivia and the World Tin Market.* London: Latin American Bureau.

Cummins, J. 2011. "Global Development Voices: Living with Disabilities." *The Guardian,* December 15. Accessed March 22, 2013. http://www.guardian.co.uk /global-development/2011/dec/15/disability-voices-development#F.

Cusicanqui, Juan. 2011. "Celin afirma que 8000 ha de coca bastan para el consumo." *La Razón,* November 25, A8.

Damé, Luiza. 2010. "In Brazil, Lula Boasts of His Education Policy and Credits Teachers' Strikes for Advances." *O Globo.* Accessed July 24, 2012. http://lo-de -alla.org/2010/04/in-brazil-lula-boasts-of-his-education-policy-and-credits -teachers%E2%80%99-strikes-for-advances/.

———. 2011. "Baja en 58% tasa de mortalidad infantil." *El Día.* Accessed July 23, 2012. http://www.eldia.com.bo/index.php?cat=362&pla=3&id_articulo=51819.

Damian, Areceli, and Julio Boltvinik. 2006. "A Table to Eat On: The Meaning and Measurement of Poverty in Latin America." In *Latin America after Neoliberalism: Turning the Tide in the 21st Century?,* ed. Eric Hershberg and Fred Rosen, 144–170. New York: New Press.

Dangl, Benjamin. 2007. *The Price of Fire: Resource Wars and Social Movements in Bolivia.* Edinburgh, UK; Oakland, CA: AK Press.

———. 2012. "A Coup over Land: The Resource War behind Paraguay's Crisis." *Toward Freedom,* July 16. Accessed July 18, 2012. http://www.towardfreedom .com/home/americas/2898-a-coup-over-land-the-resource-war-behind-para guays-crisis.

Davis, Charles. 2010. "Bolivia Breaks with U.S. Policy, But Not the War on Drugs." Change.org, October 5. Accessed March 12, 2012. http://news.change .org/stories/bolivia-breaks-with-u-s-policy-but-not-the-war-on-drugs.

de Janvry, Alain, and Elisabeth Sadoulet. 2002. "Land Reforms in Latin America: Ten Lessons toward a Contemporary Agenda." Paper presented at the World Bank's Latin American Land Policy Workshop. Accessed June 12, 2012. http://are.berkeley.edu/~sadoulet/papers/Land_Reform_in_LA_10_lesson.pdf.

Democracy Center. 2008. "Bolivia's Struggle for a New Constitution." *Jallalla* 2 (January): 4–6.

Do Alto, Hervé. 2009. "'More of the Same'? Or a Break with 'Traditions'? The MAS: A Paradoxical Case of Democratisation." *Alternatives International*, March 17. Accessed March 24, 2012. http://www.alterinter.org/article3079.html ?lang=fr.

———. 2011. "Un partido campesino en el poder: Una mirada sociológica del MAS boliviano." *Nueva Sociedad* 234 (July–August). Accessed December 12, 2011. http://www.nuso.org/revista.php?n=234.

Do Alto, Hervé, and Franck Poupeau. 2008. "Bolivia: Morales Is Checked." *Counterpunch*, March 8–10. Accessed October 20, 2011. http://www.counterpunch.org/alto03082008.html.

Dobyns, Henry F. 1966. "An Appraisal of Techniques with a New Hemispheric Estimate." *Current Anthropology* 7 (4): 395–416.

Dominguez, Francisco, Geraldine Lievesley, and Steve Ludlam, eds. 2011. *Right-wing Politics in the New Latin America: Reaction and Revolt*. London: Zed Books.

Dunkerley, James. 1984. *Rebellion in the Veins: Political Struggle in Bolivia, 1952–1982*. London: Verso.

———. 2007a. *Bolivia: Revolution and the Power of History in the Present*. London: Institute for the Study of the Americas.

———. 2007b. "Evo Morales, the 'Two Bolivias' and the Third Bolivian Revolution." *Journal of Latin American Studies* 39 (1): 133–166.

———. 2011. "Pachakuti in Bolivia: A Personal Diary." In *Evo Morales and the Movimiento al Socialismo*, ed. Adrian J. Pearce, 175–212. London: Bolivia Information Forum/Institute for the Study of the Americas.

Earle, Ethan. 2011. "Bolivia and the Changing Shape of U.S. Power." *NACLA* 45 (4): 12–15. Accessed June 25, 2013. https://nacla.org/article/bolivia-and-changing-shape-us-power.

Eaton, Kent. 2007. "Backlash in Bolivia: Regional Autonomy as a Reaction against Indigenous Mobilization." *Politics & Society* 35 (1): 71–102.

The Economist. 2005. "Fall from Grace in Lulaland: A Popular President Is Left Politically Wounded." July 14. Accessed September 17, 2012. http://www.economist.com/node/4174235.

———. 2006. "Land Battles: Evo Morales Collides with the Commercial Farmers." September 23. Accessed March 24, 2012. http://www.economist.com/node/7945821.

———. 2009a. "Correa's Curriculum: The President Seeks to Improve Ailing Schools and Universities." August 20. Accessed July 24, 2012. http://www.economist.com/node/14258942.

———. 2009b. "Not Yet the Promised Land." Accessed October 30, 2012. www.economist.com/node/15176507.

———. 2011a. "Fuel on the Fire." June 16. Accessed March 22, 2012. http://www.economist.com/node/17851429?story_id=17851429.

————. 2011b. "Health Care in Brazil: An Injection of Reality." Accessed September 12, 2012. http://www.economist.com/node/21524879.

————. 2011c. "The Mother of All Scandals?" Accessed September 17, 2012. http://www.economist.com/node/18836612.

Econoticias. 2006. "Evo da 180 días para que las petroleras firmen nuevos contratos." Accessed March 22, 2012. http://old.kaosenlared.net/noticia/nacionaliza cion-hidrocarburos-bolivia-evo-da-180-dias-para-petroleras-.

EFE. 2012. "La última agencia antidroga de EEUU en Bolivia se queda pero con menos presupuesto." EFE, July 8. Accessed January 15, 2013. http://actualidad .rt.com/actualidad/view/48731-La-%C3%BAltima-agencia-antidroga-de -EE.UU.-en-Bolivia-se-queda-pero-con-menos-presupuesto.

Eifert, Benn, Alan Gelb, and Nils Borje Tallroth. 2003. "Managing Oil Wealth." *Finance and Development* 40 (1): 40–45. Accessed December 15, 2010. http:// www.imf.org/external/pubs/ft/fandd/2003/03/eife.htm#author.

eju! 2012. "Con menos financiamiento se está consiguiendo los resultados requeridos." February 28. Accessed March 10, 2012. http://eju.tv/2012/02/narco trfico-camuflaban-droga-en-madera-inicia-querella-al-ser-confundido-con -el-narcoamauta/.

El Comercio. 2012. "Humala aseguró que erradicación de cultivos ilegales de coca mejorará." Accessed October 3, 2012. http://elcomercio.pe/politica/1135891/no ticia-humala-aseguro-que-erradicacion-cultivos-ilegales-coca-mejorara.

El Deber. 2009. "El Presidente entregó tierra revertida a Goni en Yungas." May 24. Accessed July 20, 2012. http://www.ftierra.org/ft/index.php?option=com_con tent&view=article&id=1094:rair&catid=98:noticias&Itemid=243.

El Diario. 2011. "Productores de Alto Parapetí duplicaron producción de maíz." July 11. Accessed July 20, 2012. http://www.eldiario.net/noticias/2011/2011_07 /ntl10711/3_04ecn.php.

Ellner, Steve. 2010. "Hugo Chávez's First Decade in Office: Breakthroughs and Shortcomings." *Latin American Perspectives* 37 (1): 77–96.

El Mundo. 2006. "Productores crean Comité de defensa de sus tierras." Accessed October 30, 2012. http://www.elmundo.com.bo/Secundarianew.asp?edicion =31/05/2006&Tipo=Economia&Cod=5037.

Embassy La Paz. 2008. *Bolivia: Morales Declares Ambassador Persona Non Grata,* 08LAPAZ1942. Accessed June 24, 2012. http://wikileaks.org/cable/2008/09 /08LAPAZ1942.html.

Escobar de Pabón, Silvia, and Bruno Rojas Callejas. 2009. *¡No hay derecho! Situación de los derechos laborales en Bolivia.* La Paz: CEDLA.

————. 2012. "Más asalariados, menos salario: La realidad detrás del mito del país de independientes—Situación de los derechos laborales en Bolivia." *Boletín Alerta Laboral* 65 (May). Accessed March 12, 2013. http://www.cedla.org/sites /default/files/situacion_ddll_2012.pdf.

European Union (cited as EU). 2007. "Peru: Country Strategy Paper 2007–2013." Accessed October 2, 2012. http://eeas.europa.eu/peru/csp/07_13_en.pdf.

Fabricant, Nicole. 2010. "Between the Romance of Collectivism and the Reality of Individualism: Ayllu Rhetoric in the Landless Peasant Movement (MST-Bolivia)." *Latin American Perspectives* 37 (4): 88–107.

————. 2011. "A Realigned Bolivian Right: New 'Democratic' Destabilizations."

NACLA Report on the Americas 44: 30–31. Accessed July 27, 2012. https://nacla
.org/news/realigned-bolivian-right-new-%E2%80%98democratic%E2
%80%99-destabilizations.

———. 2012. *Mobilizing Bolivia's Displaced: Indigenous Politics and the Struggle Over
Land.* Chapel Hill: University of North Carolina Press.

FAO (Food and Agriculture Organization). 2007. "Mainstreaming in Bolivia: an
overview." FAO. Accessed November 7, 2009. http:///dwms.fao.org/narcotics
/data/asspps/CountryPapers/PaperDraft1DrugsMainstreamingPeruNov07
.doc.

Farthing, Linda. 1992. "Carrots and Coke." *This Magazine* 26 (October): 29–31.

———. 1993. "¿Gays? ¿en Cochabamba?" *Los Tiempos*, A9.

———. 2005. "La Familia Galán and Queer Groups vs. John Roberts." *This Way
Out*, July 25. Accessed March 20, 2013. http://www.radio4all.net/index.php
/program/13415.

———. 2007. "Everything Is Up for Discussion: A Fortieth Anniversary Conversation with Silvia Rivera Cusicanqui." *NACLA Report on the Americas* 40
(4): 4–9.

———. 2008. "Coca and the Search for Alternatives." In *Dignity and Defiance:
Stories from Bolivia's Challenge to Globalization*, ed. Jim Shultz and Melissa C.
Draper, 202–210. Berkeley: University of California Press.

———. 2009a. "Bolivia's Dilemma: Development Confronts the Legacy of Extraction." *NACLA Report on the Americas* 42 (5): 25–29.

———. 2009b. "Thinking Left in Bolivia: An Interview with Vice President
Álvaro García Linera." *The Nation.* Accessed November 11, 2012. http://www
.thenation.com/article/thinking-left-bolivia.

Farthing, Linda, Juan Manuel Arbona, and Benjamin Kohl. 2006. "The Cities
That Neoliberalism Built: Exploring Urbanization in La Paz–El Alto." *Harvard International Review.* Accessed November 25, 2011. http://hir.harvard.edu
/the-cities-that-neo-liberalism-built.

Farthing, Linda, and Benjamin Kohl. 2001. "Bolivia's New Wave of Protest."
NACLA Report on the Americas 34 (5): 8–11.

———. 2005. "Conflicting Agendas: The Politics of Development Aid in Drug-
Producing Areas." *Development Policy Review* 23 (2): 183–198.

———. 2010. "Social Control: Bolivia's New Approach to Coca Reduction."
Latin American Perspectives 37 (4): 197–213.

———. 2012. "Supply-Side Harm Reduction Strategies: Bolivia's Experiment
with Social Control." *The International Journal on Drug Policy* 23 (6): 488–494.

Farthing, Linda, and Kathryn Ledebur. 2004. "The Beat Goes On: The US War
on Coca." *NACLA Report on the Americas* 38 (3): 34–39.

Felbab-Brown, Vanda. 2006. "Trouble Ahead: The Cocaleros of Peru." *Current
History* 105 (688): 79–83. Accessed October 2, 2012. http://live.belfercenter
.org/files/felbab-brown.pdf.

Flores-Macías, Gustavo. A. 2012. *After Neoliberalism? The Left and Economic Reforms in Latin America.* Oxford: Oxford University Press.

FM Bolivia. 2011. "Alcanza la operación milagro en Bolivia más de 600,000
operaciones de la vista." Accessed July 23, 2012. http://www.fmbolivia.net

/noticia34104-alcanza-la-operacin-milagro-en-bolivia-mas-de-600–000
-operaciones-de-la-vista.html.

———. 2012. "Feministas denuncian coplas ante Viceministerio de Descolonización." Accessed November 29, 2012. http://www.fmbolivia.com.bo/noticia775
32-feministas-denuncian-coplas-ante-viceministerio-de-descolonizacion
.html.

Forero, Juan. 2006. "Now the Hard Part: Bolivia Faces Pitfalls of Gas Takeover."
New York Times, May 8.

———. 2012. "Guess Who's Chopping Down the Amazon Now?" Accessed September 12, 2012. http://www.npr.org/2012/09/06/160171565/guess-whos-chop
ping-down-the-amazon-now.

Fortes, Alexandre. 2009. "In Search of a Post-Neoliberal Paradigm: The Brazilian Left and Lula's Government." *International Labor and Working-Class History* 75 (1): 109–125.

French, John D. 2010. "Many Lefts, One Path? Chávez and Lula." In *Latin
America's Left Turns: Policies, Politics and Trajectories of Change*, ed. Maxwell
Cameron and Eric Hershberg, 41–60. Boulder, CO: Lynne Rienner.

Friedman-Rudovsky, Jean. 2008. "Bolivia's Surprising Anti-Drug Success." *Time*,
August 15. Accessed September 20, 2009. http://www.time.com/time/world
/article/0,8599,1829782,00.html.

———. 2011. "Can Bolivia Harvest Its Forests Sustainably?" *Time*, May 16. Accessed
March 31, 2013. http://www.time.com/time/world/article/0,8599,2071694,00
.html.

———. 2012a. "Bolivian Buzz: Coca Farmers Switch to Coffee Beans." *Time*, February 29. Accessed April 5, 2013. http://www.time.com/time/world/article
/0,8599,2107750,00.html.

———. 2012b. "Quinoa: The Dark Side of an Andean Superfood." *Time*,
April 3. Accessed April 4, 2012. http://www.time.com/time/world/article
/0,8599,2110890,00.html.

Friends of MST (Movimento Sem Terra). 2013. "Campaign against Impunity."
Accessed March 14, 2013. http://www.mstbrazil.org/.

Fundación Tierra. 2010. "INRA tiene en la mira a más haciendas en Alto Parapetí." December 9. Accessed June 15, 2013. http://www.ftierra.org/ft/index
.php?option=com_content&view=article&id=4221:inra-tiene-en-la-mira-a
-mas-haciendas-en-alto-parapeti&catid=170:tierra&Itemid=243.

———. 2011a. "La autonomía indígena originaria campesina en Bolivia: ¿Crónica
de una muerte anunciada?" *Fundación Tierra*, December 20. Accessed February
22, 2012. http://www.ftierra.org/ft/index.php?option=com_content&view=ar
ticle&id=8158:rair&catid=177:autonomias-indigenas&Itemid=243.

———. 2011b. *Territorios indígena originario campesinos entre la Loma Santa y la
Pachamama*. La Paz: Fundación Tierra.

———. 2012a. "Diversos obstáculos impiden el avance de las autonomías indígenas en Bolivia." *Nuestra Tierra* 3 (9): 2. Accessed March 16, 2012. http://
www.ftierra.org/ft/index.php?option=com_wrapper&view=wrapper&Item
id=216.

———. 2012b. "'Entendemos que el proceso autonómico es lento': Entrevista con

Evo's Bolivia

204 Evo's Bolivia

Ministra de Autonomías Claudia Peña." *Nuestra Tierra* 3 (9): 18. Accessed June 20, 2013. http://www.ftierra.org/9/nt4a.html.

———. 2013. "Los datos sobre tierras en discurso presidencial." Accessed March 14, 2013. http://www.ftierra.org/ft/index.php?option=com_content&view=articl e&id=13584:rair&catid=164:fundacion-tierra-en-los-medios&Itemid=242.

Galeano, Eduardo. 2000. *Upside Down: A Primer for the Looking-Glass World.* Translated by Mark Fried. New York: Picador USA/Henry Holt.

Galindo, C., and M. Chávez. 2013. "El INRA revirtió de empresarios 35 MM de hectáreas de tierra." *La Razón*, March 18. Accessed June 15, 2013. http:// www.la-razon.com/sociedad/INRA-revirtio-empresarios-MM-hectareas _0_1798620150.html.

Galindo, María. 2013. *No se puede descolonizar, sin despatriarcalizar.* La Paz: Mujeres Creando.

Garcés, F. 2011. "The Domestication of Indigenous Autonomies in Bolivia." In *Remapping Bolivia: Resources, Territory and Indigeneity in a Plurinational State*, ed. Nicole Fabricant and Bret Gustafson, 46–67. Santa Fe, NM: School for Advanced Research Press.

García Linera, Álvaro. 2007. "Las reformas pactadas: Entrevista de José Natanson." *Nueva Sociedad* 209 (May–June): 160–172.

———. 2011. "Vicepresidente: Las empresas estatales son rentables y el pilar de la economía de los bolivianos." *Sala de Prensa de la Vicepresidencia del Estado Plurinacional*, November 7, 2011. Accessed December 2, 2011. http://www.vicepresi dencia.gob.bo/Vicepresidente-Las-empresas.

———. 2012. "Geopolitics of the Amazon." Accessed June 10, 2013. http://boli viarising.blogspot.com.au/2012/12/alvaro-garcia-linera-geopolitics-of.html.

Garzón, Dionisio. 2013. "Mutún 2013." *La Razón*, March 22. Accessed April 24, 2013. www.la-razon.com/opinion/columnistas/Mutun_0_1801019894.html.

Gascó, Emma, and Martín Cúneo. 2011. "Entrevista a la socióloga Silvia Rivera Cusicanqui: 'Evo Morales se ha visto con su límite; se acabó la luna de miel.'" *Horizonte Sur.* Accessed March 15, 2012. http://horizontesur.com.ar/radio /index.php/cartas/409-entrevista-a-la-sociologa-silvia-rivera-cusicanqui-evo -morales-se-ha-visto-con-su-limite-se-acabo-la-luna-de-miel-emma-gasco-y -martin-cuneo-.html.

Giacoman, Diego. 2010. "Drug Policy and the Prison Situation in Bolivia." In *Systems Overload: Drug Laws and Prisons in Latin America*, ed. Pien Metaal and Coletta Youngers, 21–29. Washington, DC: Transnational Institute, Washington Office on Latin America (WOLA). Accessed June 15, 2013. http://reform drugpolicy.com/wp-content/uploads/2011/09/Systems-Overload.pdf.

GOB (Gobierno de Bolivia). 2007. *Decreto Supremo N° 29117.* La Paz: Gobierno de Bolivia.

Goldstein, Daniel M. 2004. *The Spectacular City: Violence and Performance in Urban Bolivia.* Durham, NC: Duke University Press.

———. 2012. *Outlawed: Between Security and Rights in a Bolivian City.* Durham, NC: Duke University Press.

Gómez, Luis A. 2004. *El Alto de pie: Una insurrección aymara en Bolivia.* La Paz: HdP, Comuna, Indymedia.

Gootenberg, Paul. 2009. *Andean Cocaine: The Making of a Global Drug*. Chapel Hill: University of North Carolina Press.

Gordon, Gretchen. 2009. "The Trial of Gonzalo Sánchez de Lozada." Accessed July 16, 2012. http://democracyctr.org/blog/2009/05/trial-of-gonzalo-sanchez-de-lozada.html.

Gordon, Gretchen, and Kathryn Ledebur. 2005. "US Interests and Bolivian Elections: Demonizing Morales, Jeopardizing Stability." Accessed March 15, 2012. http://venezuelanalysis.com/analysis/1477.

Gotkowitz, Laura. 2008. *A Revolution for Our Rights: Indigenous Struggles for Land and Justice in Bolivia, 1880–1952*. Durham, NC: Duke University Press.

———, ed. 2011. *Histories of Race and Racism: The Andes and Mesoamerica from Colonial Times to the Present*. Durham, NC, and London: Duke University Press.

Goutsmit, A. 2008. "Exploiting the 1953 Agrarian Reform: Landlord Persistence in Northern Potosí, Bolivia." *The Journal of Latin American and Caribbean Anthropology* 13 (2): 361–386.

Gramsci, Antonio. 1971. *Selections from Prison Notebooks*. New York: International Publishers.

Gray Molina, George. 2010. "The Challenge of Progressive Change under Evo Morales." In *Leftist Governments in Latin America: Successes and Shortcomings*, ed. Kurt Weyland, Raúl L. Madrid, and Wendy Hunter, 57–76. Cambridge: Cambridge University Press.

Groesbeck, G. 2008. "Almost a Utopia: A Brief History of the Jesuit Missions of Chiquitos." Accessed March 1, 2012. http://www.colonialvoyage.com/eng/america/bolivia/jesuit_missions.html.

Gudynas, Eduardo. 2010. "The New Extractivism of the 21st Century: Ten Urgent Theses about Extractivism in Relation to Current South American Progressivism." In *Americas Program Report: Center for International Policy*. Accessed April 5, 2013. http://www.iadb.org/intal/intalcdi/PE/2010/04716.pdf.

Gustafson, Bret. 2008. "By Means Legal and Otherwise: The Bolivian Right Regroups." *NACLA Report on the Americas* 41 (1): 20–25.

———. 2009a. "Bolivia 9/11: Bodies and Power on a Feudal Frontier." *Caterwaul Quarterly*. Accessed June 15, 2013. http://upsidedownworld.org/main/content/view/1987/.

———. 2009b. *New Languages of the State: Indigenous Resurgence and the Politics of Knowledge in Bolivia*. Durham, NC: Duke University Press.

———. 2011. "Flashpoints of Sovereignty: Territorial Conflict and Natural Gas in Bolivia." In *Crude Domination: The Anthropology of Oil*, ed. Andrea Behrends, Stephen Rayna, and Günther Schlee, 220–240. Oxford, UK: Berghahn Books.

Gustafson, Bret, and Nicole Fabricant. 2011. "Introduction: New Cartographies of Knowledge and Struggle." In *Remapping Bolivia: Resources, Territory, and Indigeneity in a Plurinational State*, ed. Nicole Fabricant and Bret Gustafson, 1–25. Santa Fe, NM: School for Advanced Research Press.

Hale, Charles. 2005. "Neoliberal Multiculturalism: The Remaking of Cultural Rights and Racial Dominance in Central America." *PoLAR: Political and Legal Anthropology Review* 28 (1): 10–28.

Harten, Alan. 2009. "Repsol Spends Big on Bolivian Gas Production." *Spanish*

News. Accessed July 12, 2012. http://www.spanishnews.es/20090919-repsol
-spend-big-on-bolivian-gas-production/id=20091026/.

Harten, Sven. 2011. *The Rise of Evo Morales and the MAS*. London: Zed Books.

Haslam, Paul Alexander. 2010. "Foreign Investors Over a Barrel: Nationalizations
and Investment Policies." In *Latin America's Left Turns: Politics, Policies, and
Trajectories of Change*, ed. Maxwell Cameron and Eric Herschberg, 209–230.
Boulder, CO: Lynne Rienner.

Hatheway, Erin. 2009. "Who's Who in the Bolivian Presidential Elections: Anyone New Opposing Morales?" Accessed March 26, 2012. ain-bolivia.org/2009
/08/who%E2%80%99s-who-in-the-bolivian-presidential-elections-anyone-
new-opposing-morales/.

Healy, Kevin. 1979. "Power, Class and Rural Development in Southern Bolivia."
PhD diss., Cornell University, Ithaca.

———. 1991. "The Political Ascent of Bolivia's Coca Leaf Producers." *Journal of
Interamerican Studies and World Affairs* 33 (1): 87–121.

———. 2001. *Llamas, Weavings, and Organic Chocolate: Multicultural Grassroots Development in the Andes and Amazon of Bolivia*. Notre Dame: University of Notre
Dame Press.

Hecht, Susanna B. 2005. "Soybeans, Development and Conservation on the Amazon Frontier." *Development and Change* 36 (2): 375–404.

Hellinger, Daniel. 2012. "Venezuela: Movements for Rent?" In *Social Movements
and Leftist Governments in Latin America: Confrontation or Co-option?*, ed. Gary
Prevost, Carlos Oliva Campos, and Harry E. Vanden, 138–169. London: Zed
Books.

HelpAge International. 2004. *Age and Social Security: How Social Pensions Can Deliver Effective Aid to Poor Older People and Their Families*. International Policy
Report. London: HelpAge International.

Hertzler, Doug. 2009. "The United States Should Support Land Reform in
Bolivia." Andean Information Network. Accessed January 23, 2009. http://ain
-bolivia.org/2009/01/us-support-land-reform/.

———. 2010. "Debunking Myths Part II: Bolivia's Autonomy Initiatives." Accessed June 7, 2013. http://ain-bolivia.org/2010/02/debunking-myths-part-ii
-bolivia%E2%80%99s-autonomy-initiatives/.

Hindery, Derrick. 2013. *From Enron to Evo: Pipeline Politics, Global Environmen-
talism, and Indigenous Rights in Bolivia*. Tucson: University of Arizona Press.

Hite, Amy B. 2004. "Natural Resource Growth Poles and Frontier Urbanization in Latin America." *Studies in Comparative International Development* 34 (3):
50–75.

Hodges, Tina. 2008. "Bolivia's Gas Nationalization: Opportunity and Challenges
(3)." Andean Information Network, January 16. Accessed March 21, 2012.
http://ain-bolivia.org/2008/01/opportunity-and-challenges-3/.

Hoey, Lesli, and David L. Pelletier. 2011. "Bolivia's Multisectoral Zero Malnutrition Program: Insights on Commitment, Collaboration, and Capacities." *Food
and Nutrition Bulletin* 32 (Supplement, June 2): 70S–81S.

Holston, James. 2009. "Insurgent Citizenship in an Era of Global Urban Periph-
eries." *City and Society* 1 (2): 245–267.

Howard, April, and Benjamin Dangl. 2009. "Tin War in Bolivia: Conflict Between Miners Leaves 17 Dead." Accessed March 23, 2012. http://www.to wardfreedom.com/americas/900-tin-war-in-bolivia-conflict-between-miners -leaves-17-dead.

Howard, Rosalind. 2010. "Language and the Performance of Power: The Discursive Production of Decolonization in the Bolivia of Evo Morales." *Latin American Perspectives* 37 (3): 176–194.

Htun, Mala N. 2002. "Mujeres y poder político en Latinoamérica." In *International IDEA, Mujeres en el Parlamento: Más allá de los números*, 19–44. Stockholm: IDEA.

Huanacuni Mamani, Fernando. 2010. *Vivir Bien/Buen Vivir: Filosofía, políticas, estrategias y experiencias regionales*. La Paz: Coordinadora Andina de Organizaciones Indígenas (CAOI).

Huber, Evelyn, and John D. Stephens. 2012. *Democracy and the Left: Social Policy and Inequality in Latin America*. Chicago: University of Chicago Press.

Human Rights Watch. 2009. "Bolivia: Unequivocally Condemn Mob Violence." Accessed February 22, 2012. http://www.hrw.org/news/2009/03/12/bolivia-un equivocally-condemn-mob-violence.

Humphreys Bebbington, Denise. 2008. "Letter from Tarija: To the Brink and Back Again." Bolivia Information Forum 11: 7–8. Accessed June 14, 2013. http://www.boliviainfoforum.org.uk/documents/791414829_BIF%20Bulletin %20No%2011.pdf.

Hunter, Wendy, and Natasha B. S. Martorano. 2012. "Conditional Cash Transfer Programs: Assessing Their Achievements and Probing Their Promise." *LASA Forum* 43 (3): 9–10.

Hunzicker, Robert. 2012. "Bolivia: Life at the Extreme Edge of Climate Change." *Counterpunch*. Accessed October 29, 2012. http://www.counterpunch.org/2012 /10/22/bolivia-life-at-the-extreme-edge-of-climate-change/.

Ibarnegaray Ortiz, Jenny. 2011. "Descolonización y despatriarcalización en debate." *PNUD*. Accessed November 4, 2012. http://www.gobernabilidad.org.bo /documentos/democracia2011/Ponencia.Ybernegaray.06.12.11.pdf.

Index Mundi. 2008. "Bolivia—Poverty Headcount Ratio." Accessed October 30, 2012. http://www.indexmundi.com/facts/bolivia/poverty-headcount-ratio.

Inter-American Commission on Human Rights. 2009. *Captive Communities: Situation of the Guaraní Indigenous People and Contemporary Forms of Slavery in the Bolivian Chaco*. Accessed October 30, 2012. http://www.cidh.org/countryrep /ComunidadesCautivas.eng/Chap.IV.htm.

Inter-American Dialogue. 2009. "Pobreza y desigualdad en America Latina." Accessed July 24, 2012. http://www.thedialogue.org/PublicationFiles/Politica %20Social%20Sintesis%20No%201%20Pobreza%20y%20Desigualdad%20 en%20America%20Latina.pdf.

Itriago, Deborah. 2012. "Taxation in Paraguay: Marginalization of Small-Scale Farming." Accessed November 9, 2012. http://www.oxfam.org/sites/www.ox fam.org/files/dp-creating-fair-tax-system-paraguay-farmers-24052012-en .pdf.

Janusek, John Wayne. 2008. *Ancient Tiwanaku*. Cambridge: Cambridge University Press.

Jaskula, B. W. 2011. "Mineral Commodity Summaries." Accessed October 7, 2011. http://minerals.usgs.gov/minerals/pubs/commodity/lithium/mcs-2011-lithi .pdf.

Jelsma, Martin. 2011. "Lifting the Ban on Coca Chewing: Bolivia's Proposal to Amend the 1961 Single Convention." Series on Legislative Reform of Drug Policies 11. Accessed March 12, 2012. http://www.tni.org/sites/www.tni.org /files/download/dlr11.pdf.

Jemio, Luis C., and Mario N. Pacheco. 2010. "Bolivia: Migración y remesas." In *Globalización, migración y remesas*, ed. Luis C. Jemio, Roberto Laserna, Mario Napoleón Pacheco, and Saúl Roberto Quispe A., 11–48. La Paz: Fundación Milenio.

Jenkins, Rhys, and Alexandre de Freitas Barbosa. 2012. "Fear for Manufacturing? China and the Future of Industry in Brazil and Latin America." *The China Quarterly* 209 (1): 59–81.

Jindal Steel Bolivia. 2009. "Jindal Steel Bolivia." Accesssed October 5, 2011. http:// www.jindalsteelpower.com/business/jindal-steel-bolivia.aspx.

John, S. Sándor. 2009. *Bolivia's Radical Tradition: Permanent Revolution in the Andes*. Tucson: University of Arizona Press.

Johnson, Brian B. 2010. "The Paradoxes of Decolonization: The (Re)envisioning of Health in Bolivia." *Latin American Perspectives* 37 (3): 139–159.

Johnson, Stephen, Johanna Mendelson, and Sandra Bliss. 2012. "Police Reform in Latin America." Center for Strategic and International Studies. Accessed June 17, 2013. http://www.scribd.com/doc/100832543/Police-reform-in-Latin -America-Implications-for-US-policy.

"Just the Facts." 2012. Accessed June 16, 2013. http://justf.org/All_Grants_Country.

Karl, Terry L. 1987. "Petroleum and Political Pacts: The Transition to Democracy in Venezuela." *Latin American Research Review* 22 (1): 63–94.

———. 1997. *The Paradox of Plenty: Oil Booms in Petro-States*. Berkeley: University of California Press.

Kaup, Brent. 2010. "A Neoliberal Nationalization? The Constraints on Natural Gas–Led Development in Bolivia." *Latin American Perspectives* 37 (3): 123–138.

Kay, Cristóbal, and Manuel Urioste. 2007. "Bolivia's Unfinished Agrarian Reform: Rural Poverty and Development Lessons." In *Land, Poverty and Livelihood in an Era of Globalization: Perspectives from Developing and Transition Countries*, ed. A. Haroon Akram-Lodhi, Saturnino M. Borras Jr., and Cristóbal Kay, 41–79. London and New York: Routledge.

Kelley, Jonathan, and Herbert Klein. 1981. *Revolution and the Rebirth of Inequality: A Theory Applied to the National Revolution in Bolivia*. Berkeley: University of California Press.

King, Peadar. 2009. "Bolivia: Partners not Masters." Video. *What in the World*, Series 3 (Television program). Dublin: KMF Productions.

Kirshner, Joshua. 2012. "City Profile: Santa Cruz de la Sierra." *Cities* 31: 544–552.

Klein, Herbert S. 1992. *Bolivia: The Evolution of a Multi-ethnic Society*. New York: Oxford University Press.

———. 1998. *The American Finances of the Spanish Empire: Royal Income and Expenditures in Colonial Mexico, Peru, and Bolivia, 1680–1809*. Albuquerque: University of New Mexico Press.

Koenig, Peter. 2005. "Secretive Swiss Trader Links City to Iraq Oil Scam." *Sunday Times*, September 25. Accessed June 15, 2013. http://www.thesundaytimes.co.uk/sto/business/article149517.ece.

Kohl, Benjamin. 2003a. "Democratizing Decentralization in Bolivia: The Law of Popular Participation." *Journal of Planning Education and Research* 23: 153–164.

———. 2003b. "Nongovernmental Organizations and Decentralization in Bolivia." *Environment and Planning C: Governance and Planning* 23 (2): 317–331.

———. 2004. "Privatization Bolivian Style: A Cautionary Tale." *International Journal of Urban and Regional Research* 28 (4): 893–908.

———. 2010. "Bolivia under Morales: A Work in Progress." *Latin American Perspectives* 37 (3): 107–122.

Kohl, Benjamin, and Rosalind Bresnahan. 2010. "Introduction Bolivia under Morales (Part 2): National Agenda, Regional Challenges, and the Struggle for Hegemony." *Latin American Perspectives* 37 (4): 5–20.

Kohl, Benjamin, and Linda Farthing. 2001. "The Price of Success: Bolivia's War Against Drugs and the Poor." *NACLA Report on the Americas* 35 (1): 35–41.

———. 2006. *Impasse in Bolivia: Neoliberal Hegemony and Popular Resistance*. London: Zed Books.

———. 2008. "New Spaces New Contests: Appropriating Decentralization for Political Change in Bolivia." In *Planning and Decentralization: Contested Spaces for Public Action in the Global South*, ed. Victoria Beard, Faranak Miraftab, and Christopher Silver, 69–86. London and New York: Routledge.

———. 2009. "'Less Than Fully Satisfactory Development Outcomes': International Financial Institutions and Social Unrest in Bolivia." *Latin American Perspectives* 36 (3): 59–78.

———. 2012. "Material Constraints to Popular Imaginaries: The Extractive Economy and Resource Nationalism in Bolivia." *Political Geography* 31 (4): 225–235.

Kohl, Benjamin, and Linda Farthing, with Felix Muruchi. 2011. *From the Mines to the Streets: A Bolivian Activist's Life*. Austin: University of Texas Press.

Kohn, Margaret, and Keally McBride. 2011. *Political Theories of Decolonization: Postcolonialism and the Problem of Foundations*. Oxford: Oxford University Press.

Kolata, Alan. 1993. *The Tiwanaku: Portrait of an Andean Civilization*. Cambridge, MA: Blackwell.

Komadina Rimassa, Jorge. 2008. "The Symbolic Strategy of the Movimiento al Socialismo." *T'inkazos* 11. Accessed February 11, 2011. http://socialsciences.scielo.org/scielo.php?pid=S1990-74512008000100001&script=sci_arttext.

———. 2011. *El debate sobre el control social*. Cochabamba, Bolivia: CEASDEC.

Kritzer, Barbara, Stephen Kay, and Tapen Sinha. 2011. "Next Generation of Individual Account Pension Reforms in Latin America." *Social Security Bulletin* 71. Accessed October 29, 2012. www.ssa.gov/policy/docs/ssb/v71n1/v71n1p35.pdf.

La Botz, Dan. 2005. "Mexico's Labor Movement in Transition." *Monthly Review Press* 57 (2): 62–72.

Laguna, Pablo. 2013. "Desmarañando el embrollo: ¿Es la mercantilización de la quinua real tan negativa como nos lo cuentan?" Presentation at Universidad Mayor de San Andrés, April, La Paz.

La Jornada. 2011. "FEJUVE El Alto: 'Agenda de Octubre' no va a ser cerrada,

sino reforzada." September 19. Accessed June 12, 2012. http://www.jornadanet
.com/n.php?a=69347-1.

————. 2012a. "Bono Juana Azurduy reduce en 3 años mortalidad infantil y
materna en Bolivia." May 28. Accessed July 20, 2012. http://www.jornadanet
.com/n.php?a=77506-1.

————. 2012b. "El Gobierno destinará $us. 1.060 millones en subvención de los
hidrocarburos." November 7. Accessed June 15, 2013. http://www.jornadanet
.com/n.php?a=83476-1.

La Prensa. 2008. "Cocaleros del Chapare hacen tres sugerencias al Gobierno." *La
Prensa*, December 28. Accessed February 15, 2012. http://educamposv.lacoc
telera.net/post/2008/12/28/cocaleros-del-chapare-hacen-tres-sugerencias-al
-gobierno.

————. 2010. "Fejuve alteña hace críticas al Gobierno de Evo Morales." *La Prensa*,
July 7. Accessed March 25, 2012. http://www.fmbolivia.com.bo/noticia31049
-fejuve-altena-hace-criticas-al-gobierno-de-evo-morales.html.

La Razón. 2006. "El MAS gana en el país con el 45,7%." *La Razón*, July 4, A1.

————. 2010. "Los criterios discriminatorios para dar empleo aún persisten." *La
Razón*, October 25. Accessed March 20, 2013. http://www.la-razon.com/socie
dad/criterios-discriminatorios-dar-empleo-persisten_0_1273672643.html.

————. 2011a. "FAO: La desnutrición crónica en Bolivia bajó de 27 a 20%." *La
Razón*, September 23. Accessed April 5, 2012. http://www.ftierra.org/ft/index
.php?option=com_content&view=article&id=7428:rair&catid=98:noticias
&Itemid=175.

————. 2011b. "Feliz Cumpleaños, País." *La Razón*, August 6. Accessed March
21, 2013. http://www.la-razon.com/nacional/FELIZ-CUMPLEANOS-PAIS
_0_1444655533.html.

————. (2011c). "Socios y no patrones." *La Razón*, November 30. Accessed
March 24, 2013. http://www.la-razon.com/opinion/editorial/Socios-patrones
_0_1514248645.html.

————. 2012a. "Destacan inclusión de indígenas en el país." *La Razón*, April 6, A4.

————. 2012b. "El gobierno propone destinar a un fondo el 10% de las reservas."
La Razón, February 14, A10.

————. 2012c. "Haremos campaña internacional por el acullico." *La Razón*,
January 16. Accessed February 21, 2012. http://www.la-razon.com/nacional
/Haremos-campana-internacional-acullico_0_1542445772.html.

————. 2012d. "Tenencia de la tierra." *La Razón*, December 16. Accessed March
30, 2013. http://www.la-razon.com/opinion/editorial/Tenencia-tierra_0_1743
425644.html.

————. 2013a. "Documento: Ley de Participación y Control Social." *La Razón*,
March 4. Accessed March 31, 2013. http://www.la-razon.com/nacional/DO
CUMENTO-LEY-PARTICIPACON-CONTROL-SOCIAL_0_17902210
24.html.

————. 2013b. "Se suspende temporalmente segunda emisión de bonos." *La
Razón*, June 24. Accessed June 25. http://www.la-razon.com/economia/Bolivia
-suspende-temporalmente-segunda-emision_0_1857414336.html.

Laserna, Roberto. 2007. "El caudillismo fragmentado." *Nueva Sociedad* 209 (May–
June): 100–117.

————. 2011a. *El fracaso del prohibicionismo: Estudios socioeconómicos para una historia de las políticas antidrogas en Bolivia*. La Paz: Fundación Vicente Pazos Kanki.

————. 2011b. "Falling in the Rentier Trap: Or How Evo Morales Is Missing an Opportunity." *ReVista: Harvard Review of Latin America* (Fall). David Rockefeller Center for Latin American Studies, Harvard University. Accessed November 2, 2012. http://www.drclas.harvard.edu/publications/revistaonline /fall-2011/falling-rentier-trap.

Lay, Jann, Ranier Thiele, and Manfred Wiebelt. 2008. "Resource Booms, Inequality and Poverty: The Case of Gas in Bolivia." *Review of Income and Wealth* 54: 407–437.

Lazar, Sian. 2008. *El Alto, Rebel City: Self and Citizenship in Andean Bolivia*. Durham, NC: Duke University Press.

Ledebur, Kathryn. 2005. "Bolivia: Clear Consequences." In *Drugs and Democracy in Latin America: The Impact of U.S. Policy*, ed. Coletta A. Youngers and Eileen Rosin, 143–184. Boulder, CO: Lynne Rienner.

Ledebur, Kathryn, and Coletta A. Youngers. 2012. "Bolivian Drug Control Efforts: Genuine Progress, Daunting Challenges." Washington Office on Latin America/Andean Information Network, December 20. Accessed January 12, 2013. http://ain-bolivia.org/2012/12/bolivian-drug-control-efforts-ge nuine-progress-daunting-challenges/.

Lehm, Zulema. 2009. "Tierras bajas: Gobernanza, recursos naturales y tierra." In *Bolivia Post-Constituyente: Tierra, Territorio y Autonomías Indígenas*, ed. Fundación Tierra, 67–70. La Paz: Fundación Tierra.

Lehman, David, ed. 1982. *Ecology and Exchange in the Andes*. Cambridge: Cambridge University Press.

Lema, Gonzalo. 2011. *Transformación y democracia: Entrevista con Juan del Granado*. La Paz: Movimiento Sin Miedo.

Lemoine, Maurice. 2006. "Bolivia: The Military Plan and Wait." *Le Monde diplomatique*, February 8. Accessed February 15, 2012. http://mondediplo.com/2006 /02/08bolivia.

Lennon, Karen Marie. 2013. "The Pathways and Unresolved Contradictions of Vivir Bien in Bolivia." Paper presented at the 31st International Congress of the Latin American Studies Association, May, Washington, DC.

Léons, M. B. 1978. "Race, Ethnicity, and Political Mobilization in the Andes." *American Ethnologist* 5 (3): 484–494.

Levitsky, Stephen, and Kenneth Roberts. 2011. "Introduction." In *The Resurgence of the Latin American Left*, ed. Stephen Levitsky and Kenneth Roberts, 1–28. Baltimore: Johns Hopkins Press.

Levy, Daniel. 2010. "Hugo Chavez Transforms Venezuelan Higher Education." *Inside Higher Education*, September 13. Accessed July 24, 2012. http://www.in sidehighered.com/blogs/the_world_view/hugo_chavez_transforms_vene zuelan_higher_education#ixzz21Zwf0AqZ.

Lievesley, Geraldine, and Steve Ludlam, eds. 2009. *Reclaiming Latin America: Experiments in Radical Social Democracy*. London: Zed.

Liga de Defensa del Medio Ambiente (cited as LIDEMA). 2010. "Estado ambiental en Bolivia." Accessed January 19, 2012. estadoambiental2010.pdf.

Liptak, Adam. 2012. "'We the People' Loses Appeal with People around the World." *New York Times*, February 6.

Lipton, Michael. 2009. *Land Reform in Developing Countries: Property Rights and Property Wrongs*. Abington, UK: Routledge.

Loayza Bueno, Rafael. 2012. *Political Representation & Social Inclusion: Bolivia Case Study*. Accessed June 17, 2013. http://www.as-coa.org/files/PPBoliviaFINAL .pdf.

López, María. 2009. "Sindicatos docentes y reformas educativas en América Latina." La Paz: Konrad Adenauer Stiftung. Accessed April 6, 2012. http:// www.kas.de/sopla/es/publications/16862/.

López-Calva, Luis F., and Nora Lustig. 2012. "The Decline in Inequality in Latin America: The Role of Markets and the State." *LASA Forum* 43 (3): 4–6.

Los Angeles Times. 2000. "Roberto Suárez Gómez, Bolivian Drug Trafficker." *Los Angeles Times*, Obituaries, July 24. Accessed June 23, 2013. http://articles.la times.com/2000/jul/24/local/me-58236.

Los Tiempos. 2010. "La 'Ley Guillotina' y el Reinado del Terror." *Los Tiempos*, April 3. Accessed June 25, 2013. http://www.lostiempos.com/diario/opiniones /editorial/20100403/la-ley-guillotina-y-el-reinado-del-terror_64391_117174 .html.

———. 2012. "Médicos acuerdan retomar medidas de presión desde el martes." *Los Tiempos*, July 4. accessed April 7, 2012. http://www.lostiempos.com/diario /actualidad/nacional/20120407/medicos-acuerdan-retomar-medidas-de -presion-desde-el_167011_350350.html.

Lucero, José Antonio. 2008. *Voices of Struggle, Struggles of Voice: Indigenous Representation in the Andes*. Pittsburgh, PA: University of Pittsburgh Press.

Luna, Juan P. 2010. "The Left Turns: Why They Happened and How They Compare." In *Latin America's Left Turns: Politics, Policies and Trajectories of Change*, ed. Maxwell Cameron and Eric Hershberg, 23–39. Boulder, CO: Lynne Rienner.

Luoma, Aaron, and Gretchen Gordon. 2006. "Will Evo Morales' Attempt at Renationalization Bring Real Change?" *Dollars and Sense* (November/December). Accessed October 9, 2011. http://www.dollarsandsense.org/archives/20 06/1106luomagordon.html.

———. 2009. "Oil and Gas: The Elusive Wealth beneath Their Feet." In *Dignity and Defiance: Stories from Bolivia's Challenge to Globalization*, ed. Jim Shultz and Melissa Crane Draper, 77–114. Berkeley: University of California Press.

Luykx, Aurolyn. 1999. *The Citizen Factory: Schooling and Cultural Production in Bolivia*. Albany: State University of New York Press.

Mackellar, L., A. Wörgötter, and J. Wörz. 2002. "Economic Growth of Landlocked Countries." In *Ökonomie in Theorie und Praxis*, ed. G. Chaloupek, A. Guger, E. Nowotny, and G. Schwödiauer, 213–226. Berlin: Springer.

Malloy, James M. 1970. *Bolivia: The Uncompleted Revolution*. Pittsburg, PA: University of Pittsburg Press.

Mandepora, Marcia. 2011. "Bolivia's Indigenous Universities." *ReVista: Harvard Review of Latin America* (Fall). David Rockefeller Center for Latin American Studies, Harvard University. Accessed November 2, 2012. http://www.drc las.harvard.edu/publications/revistaonline/fall-2011/bolivia%E2%80%99s -indigenous-universities.

Mann, Charles. 2005. *1491: New Revelations of the Americas Before Columbus*. New York: Knopf.

Mayorga, René A. 2005. "La crisis del sistema de partidos políticos y el experimento del gobierno sin partidos en Bolivia." *Revista Futuros* 3 (9). Accessed July 17, 2013. http://www.revistafuturos.info/futuros_9/pp_bolivia1.htm.

Mayorga Ugarte, Fernando. 2006. "Referéndum y asamblea constituyente: Autonomías departamentales en Bolivia." Accessed July 9, 2012. http://www.scielo.org.co/scielo.php?pid=S0121-56122006000200004&script=sci_arttext.

McElhinny, Vincent. 2009. "Global Crisis Is Good News for IFIs in Latin America." Americas Program, January 27. Accessed September 19, 2012. http://www.cipamericas.org/archives/author/mcelhinny.

McEwan, Gordon F. 2006. *The Incas: New Perspectives*. Santa Barbara, CA: ABC-CLIO.

McGuigan, Claire. 2007. *The Benefits of FDI: Is Foreign Investment in Bolivia's Oil and Gas Delivering?* La Paz: Christian Aid and CEDLA.

McLeod, Darryl, and Nora Lustig. 2011. "Inequality and Poverty under Latin America's New Left Regimes." Tulane Economics Working Paper Series. Working Paper 1117 (March). Accessed July 23, 2012. http://econ.tulane.edu/RePEc/pdf/tul1117.pdf.

McPhail, Karen. 2009. "The Challenge of Mineral Wealth: Using Resource Endowments to Foster Sustainable Development." In *Mining, Society, and a Sustainable World*, ed. Jeremy Richards, 61–74. New York: Springer.

Mealla, Luis. 2012. "Gobierno busca industrializar la coca a través de tres proyectos." *La Razón*, February 27. Accessed March 10, 2012. http://www.la-razon.com/nacional/Gobierno-busca-industrializar-traves-proyectos_0_1567643261.html.

Medeiros, Carmen. 2001. "Civilizing the Popular: The Law of Popular Participation and the Design of a New Civil Society in 1990s Bolivia." *Critique of Anthropology* 21, 401–425.

Medina, Javier. 2008. *Suma Qamaña: La comprensión indígena de la Buena Vida*. La Paz: PADEP/GTZ.

Melendres, Miguel A. 2012. "Haremos campaña internacional por el acullico." *La Razón*, January 16, A4–A5.

Mendonça Cunha, Filho, Clayton, and Rodrigo S. Gonçalves. 2010. "The National Development Plan as a Political Economic Strategy in Evo Morales's Bolivia: Accomplishments and Limitations." *Latin American Perspectives* 37 (4): 177–196.

MercoPress. 2010. "Morales Promises a Tighter State Control Economy for 'Post-colonial' Bolivia." January 23. Accessed October 30, 2012. http://en.mercopress.com/2010/01/23/morales-promises-a-tighter-state-control-economy-for-post-colonial-bolivia.

———. 2012a. "Brazil Ready to Live a Natural Gas Golden Era with Self-sufficiency in Five Years." April 30. Accessed April 14, 2013. http://en.mercopress.com/2012/04/30/brazil-ready-to-live-a-natural-gas-golden-era-with-self-sufficiency-in-five-years.

———. 2012b. "'Land Grabbing' and the Concentration Process in Mercosur

Members." April 26. Accessed July 19, 2012. http://en.mercopress.com/2012/04
/26/land-grabbing-and-the-concentration-process-in-mercosur-members.

Mesa-Lago, Carmelo. 2006. "Private and Public Pension Systems Compared: An Evaluation of the Latin American Experience." *Review of Political Economy* 18 (3): 317–334.

Miller Llana, Sara, and Taylor Barnes. 2011. "Brazil Takes on a Centuries-Old Foe: Corruption. *Christian Science Monitor*, December 25. Accessed November 17, 2012. http://www.csmonitor.com/World/Americas/2011/1225/Brazil-ta kes-on-a-centuries-old-foe-corruption.

Mills, Frederick B. 2012. "Education Reform Gets High Marks in El Salvador." Council on Hemispheric Affairs, March 5. Accessed July 26, 2012. http://www .coha.org/education-reform-gets-high-marks-in-el-salvador/.

Minería de Bolivia. 2012. "Proyecto de instalación del horno Ausmelt tiene un avance del 60 percent." Accessed March 28, 2012. http://boliviaminera.blog spot.com/2012/03/proyecto-de-instalacion-del-horno.html.

Ministerio de Economía y Finanzas Públicas (cited as MEFP). 2012. "El Presupuesto 2013 cuadruplica los recursos para Salud y Educación." November 27. Accessed March 14, 2013. http://www.economiayfinanzas.gob.bo/index.php?o pcion=com_prensa&ver=prensa&id=2689&categoria=5&seccion=306.

Ministerio de Salud y Deportes. 2009. "Logros 2006–2009 y Estrategias 2010." Accessed April 7, 2012. http://www.sns.gob.bo/index.php?ID=LogrosyEs trategias.

Missoni, Eduardo, and Giorgio Solimano. 2010. "Towards Universal Health Coverage: The Chilean Experience." *World Health Report* 97: 119–124. Accessed July 23, 2012. http://www.who.int/healthsystems/topics/financing/hea lthreport/4Chile.pdf.

Möeller, Hans. 2007. "Mineros cooperativistas y mineros asalariados, una veta conflictiva." Accessed March 23, 2012. http://www.scielo.org.bo/pdf/rbcst/v10 n22/v10n22a06.pdf.

Molina, Fernando. 2009. *El pensamiento boliviano sobre los recursos naturales*. La Paz: Pulso.

———. 2013. "¿Por qué Evo Morales sigue siendo popular? Las fortalezas del MAS en la construcción de un nuevo orden." *Nueva Sociedad* 245. Accessed July 7, 2013. http://nuso.org/upload/articulos/3937_1.pdf.

Mollman, M. 2013. "Violence Still Prevalent Despite Progress on LGBTI Rights in Latin America." *Huffington Post*, January 7. Accessed March 20, 2013. http:// www.huffingtonpost.com/marianne-mollmann/violence-still-prevalent -despite-progress-on-lgbti-rights-in-latin-america_b_2409660.html.

Monasterios, Karin, Pablo Stefanoni, and Hervé Do Alto, eds. 2007. *Reinventando la Nación en Bolivia*. La Paz: CLACSO/Plural.

Monge, Carlos. 2013. "Mining and Development in the Andes." Paper presented at Alternative Strategies for Mining-Based Economies, March, University of London, UK.

Moore, Michelle. 2005. *Disease, Development, and Defining Indigenous Identity: The Emergence of the Machupo Virus in Post-Revolutionary Bolivia*. Wilmington: University of North Carolina-Wilmington.

Morales, Juan Antonio. 2011. "Post-Neoliberal Policies and the Populist Tradition." *ReVista: Harvard Review of Latin America* (Fall). David Rockefeller Center for Latin American Studies, Harvard University. Accessed November 2, 2012. http://www.drclas.harvard.edu/publications/revistaonline/fall-2011/post -neoliberal-policies.

Morales, Natasha, Eduardo Pando, and Julia Johannsen. 2010. "Comprendiendo el programa Desnutrición Cero en Bolivia: Un análisis de redes y actores." Banco Interamericano de Desarrollo. Accessed April 5, 2012. http://idbdocs .iadb.org/wsdocs/getdocument.aspx?docnum=35176287.

Moreno Morales, Daniel E., Eduardo C. Eguívar, Vivian S. Blum, Mitchell A. Seligson, and Gonzalo V. Villazón. 2008. "The Political Culture of Democracy in Bolivia, 2008: The Impact of Governance." Accessed March 6, 2012. http://www.vanderbilt.edu/lapop/bolivia/2008-politicalculture.pdf.

Motta, Sara C. 2009. "Venezuela: Reinventing Social Democracy from Below?" In *Reclaiming Latin America: Experiments in Radical Social Democracy*, ed. Geraldine Lievesley and Steve Ludlam, 75–90. London: Zed.

Moye Rosendo, A., L. Humaday Muiba, M. Cuellar, J. Chávez, Florentino, and A. Temo. 2010. "Indígenas del TIPNIS objetan carretera Villa Tunari–San Ignacio de Moxos." Accessed October 14, 2011. http://www.bolpress.com/art .php?Cod=2010050613.

Mulvany, Lydia, and Jack Kaskey. 2012. "Lithium Boom Spurs Production from Brine: Commodities." *Bloomberg News*, September 21. Accessed November 20, 2012. http://www.bloomberg.com/news/2012-09-19/lithium-boom-spurs-pro duction-from-california-brine-commodities.html.

Nash, June. 1979. *We Eat the Mines and the Mines Eat Us: Dependency and Exploitation in Bolivian Tin Mines*. New York: Columbia University Press.

Nicolás, Vincent, Marcelo Fernández, and Elba Flores, eds. 2007. *Modos originarios de resolución de conflictos en pueblos indígenas en Bolivia*. La Paz: PIEB/UNIR.

OEP (Órgano Electoral Plurinacional). 2013. "Resultados Deparamentales—Beni." Accessed June 16, 2013. http://www.oep.org.bo/oep/archivos/eleccio nes2013/ComputoFinalBeni2013.pdf.

Olivera, Mercedes. 2012. "Sobre las profundidades de mandar obedeciendo." In *Chiapas: Mirada de Mujer*, ed. Gómez Olivera and Damian Palencia, 11–64. Sombrerería, Bilbao: PTM-mundubat.

Olivera, Oscar, and Tom Lewis. 2004. *Cochabamba! Water War in Bolivia*. Boston: South End Press.

Opinión. 2011. "Gobierno atribuye al narcotráfico incremento en precio de la coca." August 12. Accessed February 3, 2012. http://www.opinion.com.bo /opinion/articulos/2011/0812/noticias.php?id=21326.

Orta, Andrew. 2013. "Forged Communities and Vulgar Citizens: Autonomy and Its Límites in Semineoliberal Bolivia." *Journal of Latin American and Caribbean Anthropology* 18 (1): 108–133.

Osorio M., María J. 2011. "Clientes deben sacar hierro de El Mutún por su cuenta." *Los Tiempos*, June 3. Accessed October 8, 2011. http://www.lostiem pos.com/diario/actualidad/economia/20110306/clientes-deben-sacar-hierro -de-el-mutun-por-su_115923_229935.html.

OSPE-B (Observatorio Social de Políticas Educativas de Bolivia). 2011. *Bono*

"Juancito Pinto": Evaluación de Resultados. Accessed June 25, 2013. http://www
.dvv-international.org.bo/archivos/publicaciones/libro_juancito_pinto1.pdf.
Oviedo Obarrio, Fernando. 2010. "Evo Morales and the Altiplano: Notes for an
Electoral Geography of the Movimiento al Socialismo, 2002–2008." *Latin
American Perspectives* 37 (3): 91–106.
Pacheco, Pablo. 2005. "The Decentralization of Forest Management in Bolivia:
Who Benefits and Why?" In *The Politics of Decentralization: Forests, People
and Power*, ed. Carol Pierce Colfer and Doris Capistrano, 167–183. London:
Earthscan.
Pacheco, Pablo, Deborah Barry, Peter Cronkleton, Anne Larson, and Iliana
Monterroso. 2008. "From Agrarian to Forest Tenure Reforms in Latin
America: Assessing Their Impacts for Local People and Forests." Paper pre-
sented at the 12th Biennial Conference of the International Association for the
Study of the Commons (IASC). Accessed June 3, 2012. http://iasc2008.glos
.ac.uk/conference%20papers/papers/P/Pacheco_118301.pdf.
PACS (Programa de Apoyo al Control Social de la Producción de Hoja de Coca).
2008. "Boletín informativo: El control social en el Trópico."
———. 2009. "Diagnóstico a las Organizaciones Sociales de Productores de Hoja
de Coca del Departamento de La Paz." Accessed February 2, 2012. http://www
.controlsocial.bo/respaldos_2/Estudios/005_DIAGNOSTICO_OS_LP.pdf.
———. 2011. "Sondeo de opinión del PACS de la producción de la hoja de coca
en el Trópico de Cochabamba." Accessed February 2, 2012. http://www
.controlsocial.bo/respaldos_2/Estudios/008_SONDEO_DE_PERCEP
CION_PACS_TROPICO.pdf.
Página Siete. 2011. "El PNUD y la Cepal destacan reducción de la pobreza."
Página Siete, December 2. Accessed April 5, 2012. http://www.ftierra.org/ft/in
dex.php?option=com_content&view=article&id=7945:rair&catid=98:noti
cias&Itemid=175.
———. 2013. "Buscan proteger a 15 pueblos indígenas en peligro de extinción."
Página Siete, June 2, A2.
Painter, James. 1994. *Bolivia and Coca: A Study in Dependency.* Boulder, CO: Lynne
Rienner.
Palacios, Roberto. 2011. "El desarrollo de un nuevo camino: Los éxitos y fracasos
de industrialización de la coca en Bolivia." La Paz: School for International
Training.
Panizza, Francisco. 2005. *Populism and the Mirror of Democracy.* London: Verso.
———. 2009. *Contemporary Latin America: Development and Democracy beyond the
Washington Consensus.* London: Zed.
Paredes, Iván. 2012. "Organizaciones sociales exigen que los proyectos 'bajen
hasta las bases.'" *La Razón*, December 31. Accessed April 4, 2013. http://www
.la-razon.com/nacional/Organizaciones-sociales-exigen-proyectos-bases_0
_1752424776.html.
———. 2013. "García: En el MAS prima la idea de un centralismo democrá-
tico." *La Razón*, January 11. Accessed April 5, 2013. http://www.la-razon.com
/nacional/Garcia-prima-idea-centralismo-democratico_0_1759024124.html.
Paredes, Julieta. 2012. "De amores y luchas." *La Razón*, December 12. Accessed

March 22, 2013. http://www.la-razon.com/opinion/columnistas/amores-luch as_0_1734426629.html.

Patch, Richard. 1961. "Bolivia: The Restrained Revolution." *Annals of the American Academy of Political and Social Science* 334 (March): 123–132.

Patzi, Félix. 2011. "Communal Economy: An Alternative to Socialism and Capitalism." *ReVista: Harvard Review of Latin America* (Fall). David Rockefeller Center for Latin American Studies, Harvard University. Accessed June 16, 2012. http://www.drclas.harvard.edu/publications/revistaonline/fall-2011/co mmunal-economy.

Pearson, Tamara. 2010. "UNESCO: Education in Venezuela Has Greatly Improved." Accessed July 24, 2012. http://venezuelanalysis.com/news/5107.

———. 2011. "Crime Drops in Caracas, Venezuela." Accessed June 25, 2013. venezuelanalysis.com/tag/police-reform.

Peattie, Lisa. 1987. *Planning, Rethinking Guyana*. Ann Arbor: University of Michigan Press.

Peñaranda U., Raúl. 2011. "Evo Morales: Portrait of Change." *ReVista: Harvard Review of Latin America* (Fall). David Rockefeller Center for Latin American Studies, Harvard University. Accessed April 12, 2012. http://www.drclas.har vard.edu/publications/revistaonline/fall-2011/evo-morales.

Perla, Héctor, Marco Mojica, and Jared Bibler. 2012. "From Guerrillas to Government: The Continued Relevance of the Central American Left." In *The New Latin American Left: Cracks in the Empire*, ed. Jeffery R. Webber and Barry Carr, 327–356. Lanham, MD: Rowman and Littlefield.

Perreault, Thomas. 2008. *Natural Gas, Indigenous Mobilization and the Bolivian State*. Geneva: United Nations Research Institute for Social Development.

———. 2012. "Dispossession by Accumulation: Political Ecologies of Mining and Water in the Bolivian Altiplano." Paper presented at the Latin American Studies Association Conference, May, San Francisco.

Petkoff, Teodoro. 2005. "Las dos izquierdas." *Nueva Sociedad* 197: 114–128.

PIEB (Programa de Investigación Estratégica en Bolivia). 2012. "La autonomía indígena en Lomerío encuentra nueve obstáculos burocráticos." *Periódico Digital PIEB*, April 26. Accessed November 3, 2012. http://www.pieb.com.bo/sip ieb_notas.php?idn=6816.

Pimentel Castillo, José. 2013. "Moving towards Industrialisation in the Mining Sector." *Bolivia Information Forum Bulletin, Special Edition on Extractive Industries*, March 5–6. Accessed March 22, 2013. http://www.boliviainfoforum.org .uk/documents/512190548_BIF%20Bulletin%20Special%20Edition%20Ex tractive%20Industries,%20March%202013.pdf.

Platt, Tristan. 1982. "The Role of the Andean *Ayllu* in the Reproduction of the Petty Commodity Regime in Northern Potosi (Bolivia)." In *Ecology and Exchange in the Andes*, ed. D. Lehman, 27–69. Cambridge: Cambridge University Press.

PNUD (Programa de Naciones Unidas para el Desarrollo). 2005. *Informe sobre Desarrollo Humano del PNUD, 7 September 2005*. La Paz: PNUD.

Popper, Helen. 2012. "Bolivian Farmers Urge Rethink on Mother Earth Law." October 31. Accessed November 14, 2012. http://www.reuters.com/article /2012/10/31/us-bolivia-soy-gmo-idUSBRE89U0S620121031.

Postero, Nancy G. 2007. *Now We Are Citizens: Indigenous Politics in Postmulti-cultural Bolivia*. Stanford: Stanford University Press.

———. 2010. "Morales's MAS Government: Building Indigenous Popular Hege-mony in Bolivia." *Latin American Perspectives* 37 (3): 18–34.

Prensa Latina. 2013. "Presidenta Rousseff promete impulsar la reforma agraria en Brasil." March 6. Accessed March 14, 2013. http://www.prensa-latina.cu/index .php?option=com_content&task=view&idioma=1&id=1177011&Itemid=1.

Prevost, Gary, Carlos Oliva Campos, and Harry E. Vanden, eds. 2012. *Social Movements and Leftist Governments in Latin America: Confrontation or Co-option?* London: Zed Books.

Prosalus. 2009. "Bolivia: Situación del País: Análisis de la realidad." Accessed April 5, 2012. http://www.prosalus.es/gestor/imgsvr/publicaciones/doc/An %C3%A1lisis%20de%20la%20realidad%20Bolivia.pdf.

Quigley, John A. 2012. "Coca Crop Rises for Sixth Year amid Trafficker Ef-ficiency." *Bloomberg Business Week*, September 27. Accessed October 4, 2012. http://www.businessweek.com/news/2012-09-27/peru-coca-crop-rises-for-si xth-year-amid-trafficker-efficiency.

Quispe, Aline. 2012. "Fiscalía pide a Migración informe sobre salida de ejecutivos de JSB." *La Razón*, July 23. Accessed July 27, 2012. http://www.la-razon.com /economia/Fiscalia-Migracion-informe-ejecutivos-JSB_0_1655834424.html.

Quispe Jiménez, Luz. 2011. "We Want Public Education!" *ReVista: Harvard Re-view of Latin America* (Fall). David Rockefeller Center for Latin American Studies, Harvard University. Accessed April 5, 2012. http://www.drclas.har vard.edu/publications/revistaonline/fall-2011/we-want-public-education.

Radio Fides. 2011. "La agenda de octubre sigue viva." Accessed October 12, 2011. http://www.jornadanet.com/n.php?a=68926-1.

Ramírez Lemus, María Clemencia, Kimberly Stanton, and John Walsh. 2005. "Colombia: A Vicious Circle of Drugs and War." In *Drugs and Democracy in Latin America: The Impact of US Policy*, ed. Coletta A. Youngers and Eileen Rosin, 99–142. Boulder, CO: Lynne Rienner.

Ramsey, Geoffrey. 2011. "Bolivian Govt Does Battle with Police Corruption." Insight Crime: Organized Crime in the Americas, March 18. Accessed March 20, 2012. http://www.insightcrime.org/insight-latest-news/item/691-bolivian -government-attempts-to-battle-police-corruption#bolivia.

Rance, Susanna. 1991. "The Hand That Feeds Us." *NACLA Report on the Ameri-cas* 25 (1): 30–36.

Read, James. 2006. "Bolivia Head Starts Land Handout." BBC News, June 4. Ac-cessed November 2, 2012. http://news.bbc.co.uk/2/hi/americas/5045424.stm.

Recasens, V. A. 1996. "Causa chun coca, wañuchun gringos! Etnicidad e invención de tradiciones en el Chapare." Paper presented at the 7th Congreso de Antro-pología Social, September, Zaragoza.

Reid, Michael. 2007. *Latin America's Soul*. New Haven, CT: Yale University Press.

Reuters. 2012. "Clashes in Bolivia over Contraband." Accessed November 28, 2012. http://www.reuters.com/video/2012/11/14/clashes-in-bolivia-over-con traband-measu?videoId=239119376.

Revista Jubileo. 2010. "La nueva gestión empieza con varios desafíos claves." *Re-*

vista Jubileo 16. Accessed February 11, 2011. http://www.jubileobolivia.org.bo
/recursos/files/pdfs/Revista_Jubileo_16.pdf.

Revista ¡OH! 2013. "Frank Taquichiri y la nueva Ley del Trabajo en Bolivia." *Los Tiempos*, January 6. Accessed March 19, 2013. http://www.lostiempos.com/oh
/entrevista/entrevista/20130106/frank-taquichiri-y-la-nueva-ley-del-trabajo
-en_198046_422137.html.

Reygados, Luis, and Fernando Filguiera. 2010. "Inequality and the Incorporation Crisis: The Left's Social Policy Toolkit." In *Latin America's Left Turns: Politics, Policies, and Trajectories of Change*, ed. Maxwell Cameron and Eric Hershberg, 171–192. Boulder, CO: Lynne Rienner.

Ribera Arismendi, Marco Octavio. 2013. "La falacia de la restitución de los bosques en Bolivia." *Revista Pukara* 79 (March): 8–9. Accessed June 15, 2013. http://www.periodicopukara.com/archivos/pukara-79.pdf.

Rice, Roberta. 2011. "Regional Autonomy and Municipal Politics in Post-Neoliberal Bolivia." Paper presented at the American Political Science Association, September, Seattle. Accessed March 26, 2012. http://papers.ssrn.com
/sol3/papers.cfm?abstract_id=1901983##.

Rivera Cusicanqui, Silvia. 2003. *Las fronteras de la coca: Epistemologías coloniales y circuitos alternativos de la hoja de coca: el caso de la frontera boliviano-argentina*. La Paz, Bolivia: IDIS, UMSA, Ediciones Aruwiyiri.

———. 2010. *Ch'ixinakax utxiwa: Una reflexión sobre prácticas y discursos descolonizadores*. Buenos Aires: Tinta Limón.

Roberts, Kenneth M. 2012. "The Politics of Declining Inequality." *LASA Forum* 43 (3): 11–12.

Robinson, Jessica. 2012. "Photo Update: Victims of Bolivian Dictatorships Protest Impunity and Lack of Compensation." Andean Information Network, November 16. Accessed June 25, 2013. http://ain-bolivia.org/2012/11/victims
-of-bolivian-dictatorships-protest-impunity-and-lack-of-compensation.

Rojas Calizaya, Juan C. 2011. "Tierra, propiedad y poder." Accessed January 15, 2012. http://constituyentesoberana.org/3/docsanal/122011/201211_1.pdf.

Rojas, Isaías. 2005. "Peru: Drug Control Policy, Human Rights and Democracy." In *Drugs and Democracy in Latin America*, ed. Coletta A. Youngers and Eileen Roisin, 185–230. Boulder, CO: Lynne Rienner.

Rojas M., Julay. 2011. "Coca se dispara; Gobierno pide control urgente." *Los Tiempos*, June 12. Accessed February 7, 2012. http://www.lostiempos.com
/diario/actualidad/nacional/20110612/coca-se-dispara-gobierno-pide-control
-urgente_129591_261768.html.

Romero, Simon. 2007a. "Chávez Keeping His Promise to Redistribute Land Wednesday." *New York Times*, May 17. Accessed July 19, 2012. http://www.ny
times.com/2007/05/17/world/americas/17iht-17venezuela.5749093.html
?pagewanted=all.

———. 2007b. "Venezuela Rivals U.S. in Aid to Bolivia." *New York Times*, February 23.

———. 2008. "In Bolivia, a Croat and a Critic Is Cast in a Harsh Light." *New York Times*, September 27. Accessed March 21, 2012. http://www.nytimes
.com/2008/09/27/world/americas/27bolivia.html?pagewanted=all.

———. 2010. "Coca Production Makes a Comeback in Peru." *New York Times*,

June 14. Accessed October 1, 2012. http://www.nytimes.com/2010/06/14/world/americas/14peru.html.

Rosenthal, Elizabeth. 2009. "Bolivia, Water and Ice Tell of Climate Change." *New York Times*, December 13.

Rotella, Sebastian. 1999. "A New Breed of Justice Reshaping Latin America." *Los Angeles Times*, October 11. Accessed June 10, 2012. http://articles.latimes.com/1999/oct/11/news/mn-21124.

Sachs, Jeffrey. 1987. "The Bolivian Hyperinflation and Stabilization." *American Economic Review* 77 (2): 279–283.

Sachs, Jeffrey D., and Andrew M. Warner. 1997. "Sources of Slow Growth in African Economies." *Journal of African Economies* 6 (3): 335–376.

———. 1999. "The Big Push, Natural Resource Booms and Growth." *Journal of Development Economics* 59 (1): 43–76.

Salman, Ton. 2012. "Book Review: *From Rebellion to Reform in Bolivia: Class Struggle, Indigenous Liberation and the Politics of Evo Morales* by Jeffery R. Webber." *Journal of Agrarian Change* 12 (October): 628.

Sánchez, Marcela. 2007. A Changed World? *Washington Post*, November 2.

Schipani, Andres. 2010. "Cocaine Production Rise Spells Trouble for Bolivia." BBC News, June 16. Accessed March 1, 2012. http://www.bbc.co.uk/news/10231343.

Scott, James. 2009. *The Art of Not Being Governed: An Anarchist History of Upland Southeast Asia*. New Haven: Yale University Press.

SEDEM (Servicio de Desarrollo de las Empresas Públicas Productivas). 2012. "Una empresa china pondrá en marcha a la estatal Papelbol a principios de 2013." SEDEM, March 14. Accessed November 2, 2012. http://papelbol.sedem.gob.bo/.

Seligson, Mitchell A. 2008. "The Role of the Government in Job Creation." *AmericasBarometer Insights* 1: 1–5. Accessed February 11, 2011. http://www.vanderbilt.edu/lapop/insights/I0801en.pdf.

Serrano Torrico, Sevando, ed. 1995. *Reforma Educativa, Ley No. 1565, 7 de julio de 1994*. Cochabamba: Serrano.

Shahriari, Sara. 2011. "Bolivia Looks to Land Redistribution." *Indian Country Today*, April 5. Accessed November 2, 2012. http://indiancountrytodaymedianetwork.com/2011/04/05/bolivia-looks-to-land-redistribution-24503#ixzz1owPNh1Jl.

Shand, Alix. 2012. "An Exploratory Study on Perceptions of the Social Oversight Mechanism and the Results of the Efforts of the Community Representatives in Health Network N° 1, the Municipality of La Paz, Bolivia." Master's thesis, Universidad Autónoma de Tomás Frías, La Paz.

Silva, José Adán. 2010a. "La tierra produce liberación para campesinas de Nicaragua." *IPS*. Accessed July 24, 2012. http://ipsnoticias.net/nota.asp?idnews=95484.

———. 2010b. "Pobreza extrema cae pero con críticas al cómo." Accessed July 24, 2012. http://ipsnoticias.net/nota.asp?idnews=96351.

Sivak, Martin. 2010. *Evo Morales: The Extraordinary Rise of the First Indigenous President of Bolivia*. New York: Palgrave MacMillan.

———. 2011. "Evo Morales through the Prism of Wikileaks." *ReVista: Harvard Review of Latin America* (Fall). David Rockefeller Center for Latin American Studies, Harvard University. Accessed July 20, 2012. http://www.drclas.har

vard.edu/publications/revistaonline/fall-2011/evo-morales-through-prism
-wikileaks.

Smith, M. 2013. "Deadly Thirst: South America's Water Wars." *Bloomberg Markets* 22 (3): 80–90.

Solyom, Catherine. 2013. "Canadian 'Invasion' of Guatemala's Mines Causing Conflicts." *Montreal Gazette*, March 22. Accessed April 7, 2013. http://www
.montrealgazette.com/new.s/Canadian+invasion+Guatemala+mines+caus
ing+conflicts/8140281/story.html#ixzz2PpQq07Lj.

Soria O., Hans. 2012. "Recomiendan aprobar ley de inversiones para crear empleo seguro." *Los Tiempos*, October 21. Accessed October 26, 2012. http://www
.lostiempos.com/diario/actualidad/economia/20121021/recomiendan-aprobar
-ley-de-inversiones-para-crear-empleo_189521_402881.html.

Soruco Sologuren, Ximena. 2011. "*El Porvenir*, the Future That Is No Longer Possible: Conquest and Autonomy in the Bolivian Oriente." In *Remapping Bolivia: Resources, Territory and Indigeneity in a Plurinational State*, ed. Nicole Fabricant and Bret Gustafson, 68–90. Santa Fe, NM: School for Advanced Research Press.

Soruco Sologuren, Ximena, Wilfredo Plata, and Gustavo Medeiros. 2008. *Los barones del Oriente: El poder en Santa Cruz ayer y hoy*. Santa Cruz de la Sierra, Bolivia: Fundación Tierra.

Spaulding, Karen. 1984. *Huarochirí: An Andean Society under Inca and Spanish Rule*. Stanford: Stanford University Press.

Spedding Pallet, Alison. 2004. *Kawsachun coca: Economía campesina cocalera en los Yungas y el Chapare*. La Paz: PIEB/EDOBOL.

Spronk, Susan. 2012. "Neoliberal Class Formations: The Informal Proletariat and 'New' Workers' Organizations in Latin America." In *The New Latin American Left: Cracks in the Empire*, ed. Jeffery Webber and Barry Carr, 75–93. Lanham, MD: Rowman and Littlefield.

Stadius, Eric. 2012. "Land Reform Issues Intensify as Paraguay Enters into a Political Crisis." Council on Hemispheric Affairs. Accessed July 19, 2012. http://www.coha
.org/land-reform-issues-intensify-as-paraguay-enters-into-a-political-crisis/.

Stefanoni, Pablo. 2003. "MAS-IPSP: La emergencia del nacionalismo plebeyo." *Observatorio Social de América Latina* 4. Accessed February 2, 2012. http://bib
liotecavirtual.clacso.org.ar/ar/libros/osal/osal12/d1stefanoni.pdf.

———. 2007. "Bolivia, bajo el signo del nacionalismo indígena: Seis preguntas y seis respuestas sobre el gobierno de Evo Morales." In *Reinventando la nación en Bolivia*, ed. Karin Monasterios, Pablo Stefanoni, and Hervé Do Alto, 11–46. La Paz: Clacso/Plural.

———. 2010. "Bolivia: Behind the 'MAS Crisis.'" Green Left Australia. Accessed February 11, 2011. http://www.greenleft.org.au/node/45296.

———. 2011. "Bolivia Hoy: Rupturas, inercias y desafíos." *Bolivian Studies Journal/Revista de Estudios Bolivianos* 18 (November): 23–48.

Stein, Felix. 2010. "Bolivian Tin Miners Reconciled." *Americas Quarterly*. Accessed March 23, 2012. http://americasquarterly.org/node/1922.

Strom, Helen. 2011. "The New Bolivian Education Law." *ReVista: Harvard Review of Latin America* (Fall). David Rockefeller Center for Latin American Studies,

Harvard University. Accessed April 16, 2012. http://www.drclas.harvard.edu /publications/revistaonline/fall-2011/new-bolivian-education-law.

Svampa, Martisella, and Pablo Stefanoni. 2007. "Entrevista a Álvaro García Linera: 'Evo simboliza el quiebre de un imaginario restringido a la subalternidad de los indígenas.'" In *Reinventando la nación en Bolivia*, Karin Monasterios, Pablo Stefanoni, and Hervé Do Alto, 147–172. La Paz: Clacso-Plural.

Syal, Rajeev. 2009. "Drug Money Saved Banks in Global Crisis, Claims UN Advisor." *The Observer*, December 12. Accessed June 25, 2013. http://www.guardian .co.uk/global/2009/dec/13/drug-money-banks-saved-un-cfief-claims.

Taibbi, Matt. 2012. "Outrageous HSBC Settlement Proves the Drug War Is a Joke." *Rolling Stone*, December 13. Accessed April 5, 2013. http://www.rolling stone.com/politics/blogs/taibblog/outrageous-hsbc-settlement-proves-the -drug-war-is-a-joke-20121213.

Tapia, Guadalupe. 2013. "AAPS interviene EPSAS y se da 6 meses para crear nueva empresa." *La Razón*, April 2. Accessed June 15, 2013. http://www.la-razon.com /ciudades/AAPS-interviene-EPSAS-nueva-empresa_0_1807619253.html.

Tapia, Luis. 2007. "El triple descentramiento: Igualdad y cogobierno en Bolivia." In *Reinventando la nación en Bolivia*, ed. Karin Monasterios, Pablo Stefanoni, and Hervé Do Alto, 47–70. La Paz: Clacso/Plural.

———. 2011. *El estado de derecho como tiranía*. La Paz: CIDES/UMSA.

Tapia Mealla, Luis, Álvaro García Linera, and Raúl Prada Alcoreza, eds. 2004. *Memorias de Octubre*. La Paz: Muela del Diablo.

Tapper, Jake. 2012. "Why Did the Obama Administration Deny Bolivia's Extradition Request?" ABC News. Accessed October 5, 2012. abcnews.go.com /blogs/politics/2012/09/why-did-the-obama-administration-deny-bolivias -extradition-request/.

Tassi, Nico. 2012. *La otra cara del mercado: Economías populares en la arena global*. La Paz: Ti'ko and Teko.

Tassi, Nico, Juan M. Arbona, Giovanna Ferrufino, and Antonio Rodríguez-Carmona. 2012. "El desborde económico popular en Bolivia: Comerciantes aymaras en el mundo global." *Nueva Sociedad* 241, 93–105. Accessed December 2, 2012. http://library.fes.de/pdf-files/nuso/nuso-241.pdf.

TeleSUR. 2010. "Morales: Soñamos con una educación descolonizadora." Video. Accessed April 6, 2012. http://www.youtube.com/watch?v=-yj1CZvlVIc.

Téllez, Juan. 2012. "Itinerario del desarrollo y el Vivir Bien en Bolivia." Zacatecas, Mexico: Universidad Autónoma de Zacatecas.

Thomas, Angeline. 2012. "Killing Two Birds with One Stone: Implementing Land Reform and Combating Climate Change in Brazil's Amazon under Law 11.952.09." *Seattle Journal for Social Justice* 9 (2): 15.

Thomson, Sinclair. 2002. *We Alone Will Rule: Native Andean Politics in the Age of Insurgency*. Madison: University of Wisconsin.

Tiro, Félix. 1958. *Las Constituciones de Bolivia*. Madrid: Instituto de Estudios Políticos.

Tockman, Jason. 2009. "Bolivia Prescribes Solidarity: Health Care Reform under Evo Morales." *NACLA*, August 16. Accessed April 7, 2012. https://nacla.org /node/6070.

Tockman, Jason, and John Cameron. 2012. "Indigenous Autonomy and the

Contradictions of Plurinationalism in Bolivia." Paper presented at the Canadian Association of Latin American and Caribbean Studies (CALACS), May, Kelowna, BC.

Torranza Roca, Carlos. 2008. "Bolivia, Nacionalismo Populista." Paper presented at "Latin America's Left Turns," Simon Fraser University, April, Vancouver, BC.

Trading Economics. 2013. "Bolivia Government Debt to GDP." Accessed June 15, 2013. http://www.tradingeconomics.com/bolivia/government-debt-to-gdp.

UDAPE (Unidad de Análisis de Políticas Sociales y Económicas). 2011. "Programas de transferencias condicionadas en Bolivia: Bono Juancito Pinto—Bono Juana Azurduy." Paper presented at a conference, May 29–30, Santiago, Chile. Accessed April 9, 2011. http://www.rlc.fao.org/es/prioridades/seguridad/ingreso6/documentos/Presentaciones/Pa%C3%ADses/BOLIVIA.pdf.

UNCTAD (United Nations Conference on Trade and Development). 2011. "Foreign Direct Investment (FDI) Overview." Accessed March 13, 2012. http://www.unctad.org/sections/dite_dir/docs/wir11_fs_bo_en.pdf.

UNDP (United Nations Development Program). 2010. *Los cambios detrás del cambio: Informe de Desarrollo Humano en Bolivia*. La Paz: United Nations Development Program.

United Nations. 2012. "Per capita GDP at current prices." Accessed July 15, 2012. http://data.un.org/Data.aspx?d=SNAAMA&f=grID%3A101%3BcurrID%3AUSD%3BpcFlag%3A1.

UNODC (United Nations Office on Drugs and Crime). 2009. "Resumen ejecutivo del informe mundial sobre las drogas 2009 de la oficina de las Naciones Unidas contra las drogas y el crimen." Accessed June 22, 2013. http://www.unodc.org/documents/wdr/WDR_2009/Executive_summary_Spanish.pdf.

———. 2012. "Coca Crop Cultivation Falls Significantly in Bolivia." Accessed October 23, 2012. http://www.unodc.org/unodc/en/press/releases/2012/September/coca-crop-cultivation-falls-significantly-in-bolivia-according-to-2011-coca-monitoring-survey.html.

UNODC and Estado Plurinacional de Bolivia. 2011. "Monitoreo de coca 2010." Accessed February 5, 2012. http://cd1.eju.tv/index_files/1/monitoreo_coca_2010_unodc.pdf.pdf.

Urioste, Miguel. 2004. "Bolivia: The Abandonment of the Land Reform in the High Valleys and Altiplano." *Land Reform, FAO* 2: 23–38.

———. 2006. "52 años de reforma y contrareforma agraria en Bolivia (1953–2005)." *Fundación Tierra*. Accessed November 3, 2012. http://www.ftierra.org/ft/index.php?option=com_content&view=article&id=770:rair&catid=130:ft&Itemid=188.

———. 2009. "¿Nuevo ciclo de reformas agrarias en América Latina?" *Fundación Tierra*, September 3. Accessed November 3, 2012. http://www.ftierra.org/ft/index.php?searchword=Urioste&ordering=&searchphrase=all&Itemid=151&option=com_search.

USAID (U.S. Agency for International Development). 2010. "Bolivia Land Tenure Profile." Accessed September 28, 2012. http://usaidlandtenure.net/sites/default/files/country-profiles/full-reports/USAID_Land_Tenure_Bolivia_Profile.pdf.

Vaca, Mery. 2008. "Bolivia: Estado de sitio en Pando." Accessed July 18, 2012. http://news.bbc.co.uk/hi/spanish/latin_america/newsid_7613000/7613726.stm.

Valdez, Carlos. 2010. "Bolivia Cuts Retirement Age, Nationalizes Pensions." Associated Press, December 3. Accessed April 15, 2012. http://www.businessweek.com/ap/financialnews/D9JSI7G00.htm.

———. 2011. "Policía desbarata mayor laboratorio de cocaína en Bolivia." Associated Press, October 21. Accessed March 12, 2012. http://es.noticias.yahoo.com/polic%C3%ADa-desbarata-laboratorio-coca%C3%ADna-bolivia-131149312.html.

———. 2012. "Bolivia's Textile Trade a Globalization Casualty." Associated Press, July 6. Accessed November 29, 2012. http://finance.yahoo.com/news/bolivias-textile-trade-globalization-casualty-191026142—finance.html.

Van Cott, Donna Lee. 2001. "Explaining Ethnic Autonomy Regimes in Latin America." *Studies in Comparative International Development (SCID)* 35 (4): 30–58.

———. 2003. "From Exclusion to Inclusion: Bolivia's 2002 Election." *Journal of Latin American Studies* 34 (4): 751–775.

van Dun, Mirella. 2009. "Cocaleros: Violence, Drugs and Social Mobilization in the Post-Conflict Upper Huallaga Valley, Peru." Accessed October 3, 2012. http://igitur-archive.library.uu.nl/dissertations/2009-0518-200359/dun.pdf.

Van Schaick, Alexander. 2008. "Landowners' Rebellion: Slavery and Saneamiento in Bolivia." *Upside Down World*, April 28. Accessed November 3, 2012. http://upsidedownworld.org/main/content/view/1254/1/.

Vásquez, Wálter. 2012a. "PGE aplicará medidas para mayor ejecución de recursos." *La Razón*, December 21, A12.

———. 2012b. "Trece proyectos petroleros están en duda por demandas indígenas." *La Razón*, January 22. Accessed March 24, 2013. http://www.la-razon.com/economia/Trece-proyectos-petroleros-demandas-indigenas_0_1546045399.html.

Venezolana de Televisión. 2013. "Evo Morales entrega infraestructura a Central Obrera Boliviana." June 24. Accessed July 20, 2012. http://www.vtv.gob.ve/articulos/2012/12/22/evo-morales-entrega-infraestructura-a-central-obrera-boliviana-9912.html.

Villaroel, Gratzia. 2011. "Bolivian Women Making the Revolution." *ReVista: Harvard Review of Latin America*, Fall. David Rockefeller Center for Latin American Studies, Harvard University. Accessed March 26, 2012. http://www.drclas.harvard.edu/publications/revistaonline/fall-2011/bolivian-women.

Walsh, Catherine. 2012. "Of Neo-Constitutionalisms, Lefts, and (De)Colonial Struggles: Thoughts from the Andes in Conversation with Breny Mendoza." *feminists@law* 2. Accessed October 25, 2012. journals.kent.ac.uk/index.php/feministsatlaw/article/download/.../10.

Wanderley, Fernanda. 2008. "Beyond Gas: Between the Narrow-Based and Broad-Based Economy." In *Unresolved Tensions Bolivia Past and Present*, ed. John Crabtree and Laurence Whitehead, 194–211. Pittsburgh, PA: University of Pittsburgh Press.

Webber, Jeffery R. 2010. "The Rebellion in Potosí: Uneven Development, Neoliberal Continuities, and a Revolt against Poverty in Bolivia." Accessed June 14, 2012. http://upsidedownworld.org/main/bolivia-archives-31/2643—the-rebellion-in-potosi-uneven-development-neoliberal-continuities-and-a-revolt-against-poverty-in-bolivia.

———. 2011. *From Rebellion to Reform in Bolivia: Class Struggle, Indigenous Liberation, and the Politics of Evo Morales*. Chicago: Haymarket.

Webber, Jeffery R., and Barry Carr. 2012. "Latin American Left in Theory and Practice." In *The New Latin American Left: Cracks in the Empire*, ed. Jeffery R. Webber and Barry Carr, 1–27. Lanham, MD: Rowman and Littlefield.

Webber, Jude. 2012. "FDI in LatAm: Good News and Bad News." *Financial Times*, May 4. Accessed November 2, 2012. http://blogs.ft.com/beyond-brics/2012/05/04/fdi-in-latam-good-news-and-bad-news/#axzz27E3InudE.

Weisbrot, Mark, and Luis Sandoval. 2006. "Bolivia's Challenges." Accessed June 15, 2013. http://www.cepr.net/documents/bolivia_challenges_2006_03.pdf.

———. 2007. "Bolivia's Economy—an Update." Accessed April 12, 2012. http://www.cepr.net/index.php/publications/reports/bolivias-economy-an-update.

Weisbrot, Mark, Rebecca Ray, and Jake Johnston. 2009. "Bolivia: The Economy during the Morales Administration." Center for Economic Policy Research, Washington, DC. Accessed February 11, 2011. www.cepr.net/documents/publications/bolivia-2009-12.pdf.

Weyland, Kurt. 2010. "The Performance of Leftist Governments in Latin America: Conceptual and Theoretical Issues." In *Leftist Governments in Latin America: Successes and Shortcomings*, ed. Kurt Weyland, Raúl Madrid, and Wendy Hunter, 1–28. Cambridge: Cambridge University Press.

Whitesell, Lily. 2009. "And Those Who Left: Portraits of Bolivian Exodus." In *Dignity and Defiance: Stories from Bolivia's Challenge to Globalization*, ed. Jim Schulz and Melissa Draper, 255–289. Berkeley: University of California Press.

Wiener Bravo, Elisa. 2011. "Resource: Study on the Concentration of Land Ownership in Latin America." *Traditional Knowledge Bulletin*, May 11. Accessed November 3, 2011. http://www.ibcperu.org/doc/isis/14520.pdf.

Wilpert, Gregory. 2006. "Corrupt Data: Taking on the Claim That Chávez Is on the Take." *Fair*, November/December. Accessed November 3, 2012. http://www.fair.org/index.php?page=3431.

World Bank. 2012a. "Country Data: Bolivia." Accessed November 18, 2013. data.worldbank.org/country/bolivia.

———. 2012b. "GNI per capita, Atlas Method (Current US$)." Accessed November 2, 2012. http://search.worldbank.org/data?qterm=GNI%20per%20capita&language=EN.

World Economic Forum. 2011. "The Global Gender Gap Report 2011." Accessed March 9, 2012. http://reports.weforum.org/global-gender-gap-2011/.

World Public Opinion. 2006. "Presidents of Bolivia, Argentina Get Highest Approval Ratings in Latin America." Accessed October 11, 2012. http://www.worldpublicopinion.org/pipa/articles/brlatinamericara/242.php?nid=&id=&pnt=242.

Wright, Laurence. 2010. "Lithium Dreams: Can Bolivia Become the Saudi Arabia of the Electric-Car Era?" *New Yorker*, March 22. Accessed October 13, 2011.

http://www.newyorker.com/reporting/2010/03/22/100322fa_fact_wright?cur
rentPage=all.

WWF (World Wildlife Fund). 2012. "Achievements." Accessed March 9, 2012. www
.panda.org/who_we_are/bolivia/our_work/forest_programs/achievements.

Zandivliet, Hans. 2010. "Evolución electoral del MAS en Bolivia en las eleccio-
nes y referéndums desde 2005 al 2009." Accessed February 14, 2012. http://de
mocracyctr.org/blog/Elecciones%20Bolivia%202005-2009.pdf.

Zegada, María Teresa, Claudia Arce, Gabriela Canedo, and Alber Quispe. 2011.
La democracia desde los márgenes: Transformaciones en el campo político boliviano.
La Paz: Muela del Diablo Editores/CLACSO.

Zegada, María Teresa, Yuri Torrez, and Gloria Cámara. 2008. *Movimientos sociales en tiempos de poder: Articulaciones y campo de conflicto en el gobierno del MAS.*
Cochabamba: Centro Cuarto Intermedio y Plural.

Zoido, Pablo. 2009. "Public Spending on Education in Latin America: Does It
Pay?" Policy Insights No. 80 OECD Development Centre. Accessed July 24,
2012. http://www.oecd.org/dataoecd/19/1/41561645.pdf.

Zuazo, Moira. 2009. *Como nació el MAS? La ruralización de la política en Bolivia.* La
Paz: Frederick Ebert Stiftung.

———. 2010. "¿Los movimientos sociales en el poder? El gobierno del MAS en
Bolivia." *Nueva Sociedad* 227: 121–135. http://www.nuso.org/upload/articulos
/3700_1.pdf.

Index

Note: The page reference "*insert*" refers to the photographic insert.

Vivir Bien (Living Well) concept, 99–100, 112, 149, 159–161
voter participation rates, 51

wages, 23, 67, 69, 148
War of the Pacific, 80
War on Drugs, 10, 130
water resources, 11, 36–37, 42, 74–76, 169n9. *See also* Cochabamba Water War
wealth inequality and redistribution, *33*, 42, 100–103, 112
Webber, Jeffery R., 148
western medicine, 109
wetlands, 20
Willke, Zárate, 16
Windsor Tea, 134
wiphala, 35, 48, 121, 168n1
women and gender issues: and coca cultivation, 130; and crime violence, 147–148; and decolonization, 58–59; and development policy, 93–96; and education policy, 104–105; and elections, 27; and income inequality, 23; and the informal economy, 29; and land tenure issues, 118, 121; and MAS governing style, 155; and rural poverty, 33; women's involvement in gov-

ernment, 77, 160; women's organizations, 9; women's rights, 66–67, 121–122
World Bank: demands on the Morales administration, 34; and dependency, 73; and education policy, 105; and globalization pressures, 28, 29; and inflation, 79; and poverty reduction measures, 103
World Health Organization (WHO), 109, 134
World People's Conference on Climate Change and the Rights of Mother Earth, 4
World Vision, 179–180n22

Yasukawa, Yoriko, 103
"Yes I can" campaign, 105
Yucarés, 53
Yungas, 129–135, 137–138, 143, 182–183n1, *insert*

Zamora, Jaime Paz, 64
Zapatista movement, 62
Zaveleta, René, 154
Zegada, María Teresa, 154
Zelaya, Manuel, 45
zinc, 81
Zurita, Leonilda, 66